NEW ACCENTS

General Editor: TERENCE HAWKES

Literature, Politics and Theory

Literature, Politics and Theory

Papers from the Essex Conference 1976–84

Edited by
FRANCIS BARKER
PETER HULME
MARGARET IVERSEN
DIANA LOXLEY

METHUEN
London and New York

First published in 1986 by
Methuen & Co. Ltd
11 New Fetter Lane, London EC4P 4EE

Published in the USA by
Methuen & Co.
in association with Methuen, Inc.
29 West 35th Street, New York NY 10001

The collection as a whole
© 1986 Methuen & Co. Ltd;
the individual contributions
© 1986 the contributors

Photoset by Rowland Phototypesetting Ltd
Bury St Edmunds, Suffolk
Printed in Great Britain by
Richard Clay Ltd,
Bungay, Suffolk

British Library Cataloguing in Publication Data

Literature, politics and theory: papers
from the Essex Conference 1976–84. –
(New accents)
1. politics and literature
I. Barker, Francis   II. Series
800   PN51

ISBN 0 416 90020 8
     0 416 90030 5 Pbk

Library of Congress Cataloging-in-Publication Data

Literature, politics, and theory.
(New accents)
A selection of papers
from the annual Essex Conference
on the Sociology of Literature, 1976–1984.
Bibliography: p.
Includes index.
1. Literature, Modern – History and criticism – Congresses
2. Literature and society – Congresses.
I. Barker, Francis, 1952–
II. Essex Conference on the Sociology of Literature.
III. Series: New accents (Methuen & Co.)
PN710.L58   1986   809'.03   86-16418

ISBN 0 416 90020 8
     0 416 90030 5 (pbk.)

Contents

General editor's preface

It is easy to see that we are living in a time of rapid and radical social change. It is much less easy to grasp the fact that such change will inevitably affect the nature of those academic disciplines that both reflect our society and help to shape it.

Yet this is nowhere more apparent than in the central field of what may, in general terms, be called literary studies. Here, among large numbers of students at all levels of education, the erosion of the assumptions and presuppositions that support the literary disciplines in their conventional form has proved fundamental. Modes and categories inherited from the past no longer seem to fit the reality experienced by a new generation.

New Accents is intended as a positive response to the initiative offered by such a situation. Each volume in the series will seek to encourage rather than resist the process of change, to stretch rather than reinforce the boundaries that currently define literature and its academic study.

Some important areas of interest immediately present themselves. In various parts of the world, new methods of analysis have been developed whose conclusions reveal the limitations of the Anglo-American outlook we inherit. New concepts of literary forms and modes have been proposed; new notions of the nature of literature itself, and of how it communicates, are current; new views of literature's role in relation to society flourish. *New Accents* will aim to expound and comment upon the most notable of these.

In the broad field of the study of human communication, more and more emphasis has been placed upon the nature and function of the new electronic media. *New Accents* will try to identify and discuss the challenge these offer to our traditional modes of critical response.

The same interest in communication suggests that the series should also concern itself with those wider anthropological and sociological areas of investigation which have begun to involve scrutiny of the nature of art itself and of its relation to our whole way of life. And this will ultimately require attention to be focused on some of those activities which in our society have hitherto been excluded from the prestigious realms of Culture. The disturbing realignment of values involved and the disconcerting nature of the pressures that work to bring it about both constitute areas that *New Accents* will seek to explore.

Finally, as its title suggests, one aspect of *New Accents* will be firmly located in contemporary approaches to language, and a continuing concern of the series will be to examine the extent to which relevant branches of linguistic studies can illuminate specific literary areas. The volumes with this particular interest will nevertheless presume no prior technical knowledge on the part of their readers, and will aim to rehearse the linguistics appropriate to the matter in hand, rather than to embark on general theoretical matters.

Each volume in the series will attempt an objective exposition of significant developments in its field up to the present as well as an account of its author's own views of the matter. Each will culminate in an informative bibliography as a guide to further study. And while each will be primarily concerned with matters relevant to its own specific interests, we can hope that a kind of conversation will be heard to develop between them: one whose accents may perhaps suggest the distinctive discourse of the future.

TERENCE HAWKES

Introduction

In the wake of the manifold political events of the late 1960s there followed a remarkable proliferation of activity and debate in the fields of cultural and literary theory. The connections between those political events and the evolution in radical theory which ensued were complex. Nevertheless it is important to emphasize at the outset the extent to which that global conjuncture which has come to be known as '1968' – the Vietnamese struggle against US imperialism, the Prague Spring, the Parisian *événements*, the anti-war and civil rights movements in the USA – gave shape to the project represented by the essays in this volume.

In a sense Czechoslovakia and France each disclose, symbolically, essential components of this context. The Soviet suppression of the Prague Spring crystallized for many on the left, within the Communist Parties and outside, the final necessity for a break with a 'classical' Marxism that was economistic and reductive in theory and Soviet-orientated in policy. The need was not merely for a 'de-Stalinization' of the tradition, but for a thorough re-evaluation of many of its fundamental themes and methodological procedures. The events in Paris also played a crucial part in precipitating this crisis in Marxism. The explosive combination of student protest and the emergence on to the streets of a wide range of newly active and vital political movements condensed into a revolutionary dynamic which, despite the overt hostility of the French Communist Party, came close to bringing down the government, if not the state itself.

May 1968 represents the decisive manifestation of novel political issues and forces which have informed the radical politics of the succeeding period in western Europe and, to a lesser extent, in North America. The work of metropolitan solidarity with movements of national liberation in the 'Third World', the proliferation and strengthening of Trotskyist and other 'far left' political parties, the growth of the women's movement, the spread of anti-psychiatry, of counter-cultural activity and community welfare action, all served to focus needs and problems which the extant theoretical tradition was profoundly ill equipped to explain, and in the face of which it was unable to serve as an effective guide to action. In particular, the absence in Marxism of adequate theories of ideology and gender were seen as disturbing omissions at a time when cultural–political activities were playing such an important part, and when the women's movement was determined to raise issues of sexual and gender politics on which the familar Marxism was simply silent when not actually hostile.

In Britain these pressures and developments took on a peculiar and local form. The youth culture of the 1960s and the radicalization brought about by the Vietnam War coalesced with the alienation from the vestigial socialism of the Labour Party felt by some sections of the left. In the academic sphere – and particularly in the new universities and polytechnics – work was already being done by the first years of the 1970s to engage the new issues that had been placed on the political agenda. However, the intellectual resources for this engagement needed in large measure to be imported. Despite the significance of the work undertaken during the 1960s by the group associated with the journal *New Left Review*, British socialism remained by and large ideologically heterogeneous and profoundly undertheorized. Writers such as Eric Hobsbawm, E.P. Thompson, Christopher Hill and Raymond Williams had already produced a detailed and extensive body of historical and cultural work which was – and indeed remains – a powerful counter to received bourgeois historiography. But this achievement proved vulnerable to the criticism that it was restricted in conceptual scope by its native empiricism. It was hardly possible at this stage to speak of a Marxist *theoretical* culture in Britain.

Correspondingly, the first phase of this importation took on a highly theoretical character. Louis Althusser's structural Marxism, itself a critique of the historicist, empiricist and humanist tendencies inherent in classical Marxism, provided key texts. Its conceptual complexity was seen as a positive move toward a scientific rigour lacking in previous left cultural work in Britain. The anti-reductionist drive of Althusser's concept of relative autonomy certainly furnished a more elaborate and nuanced account of the social formation than the economistic simplicities of an older Marxism had allowed for, and so provided a way of theorizing the new struggles and forces which did not fit the classical prescriptions. Equally, Althusser's theorization not only of the relative autonomy of the ideological instance of the social formation but also of its inner mechanisms supplied a set of powerful concepts and a framework for future work.

Thus, in this first phase, it was not precisely literary theory that was at stake, but rather the development of general theories of the social formation and of ideology. However, what might be described as a second phase recognized the need to construct, within the general framework, specifically literary and cultural theories. Continental work in these areas was certainly becoming better known in England by the early 1970s. The translation of Lukács's major books had begun as early as 1950; but increasingly it was his 'modernist' opponents, Brecht, Adorno and Benjamin, who were read and discussed. French literary theory had gained a new impetus through the rediscovery of Russian Formalism and the construction of various 'structuralisms' out of the linguistic theory of Saussure. The work of Lévi-Strauss, Barthes and Kristeva was crucial in this respect. But the structuralist project was in turn subject to the critique of the Althusserian philosopher Pierre Macherey, not translated into English until 1978 but earlier elaborated for an English-speaking audience by Terry Eagleton as part of his own attack on established forms of literary criticism. Prominent in the diffusion and discussion of these continental theorists were the cultural studies programmes of the Birmingham Centre and of Portsmouth Polytechnic, the Sociology of Literature MA course at Essex, the annual Communist University in London, and periodicals such as *New Left Review*, *Screen*, *Radical Philosophy* and the newly established interdisciplinary journal, *Literature and History*.[1]

It was in this immediate context, nearly a decade after the convulsion of '1968', that the series of Essex Conferences on the Sociology of Literature was founded, beginning with 'Literature, Society and the Sociology of Literature' in 1976, at which both Macherey and Eagleton were present. The conference opened with a paper by Stuart Hall, then of the Birmingham Centre, reviewing the theoretical development of the previous ten years (Hall 1977).

There were two basic ideas behind the establishment of the Essex Conferences: the provision of an annual national and international forum for left literary debate (a function as much to do with social and political solidarity as with intellectual exchange); and through the publication of its Proceedings the accumulation of a body of 'casework' which could provide a resource for teaching and a foundation for further research. It was decided to follow up the initial theoretical conference with a series of historically orientated meetings, each of which would focus on a moment of particular political significance and put the new theory to work in an 'applied' examination of the literary, cultural and ideological formations of these moments. This strategy aimed to counter the danger of 'theoreticism'. But also implicit in the 'historical turn' of the conferences was the abiding insistence that the new theoretical work, whatever its provenance, had to be brought into productive contact with the historical–materialist theses of Marxism.

The series developed through four historical conferences, each of which is represented in this volume. The conference on '1848' moved out from an examination of the cultural formation of the European revolutionary struggles of the 1840s and 1850s to occupy itself with some of the monuments of nineteenth-century bourgeois literary culture. '1936' investigated the period of the complex cultural politics that, for example, connected modernism and surrealism with the anti-fascism of the Popular Front. '1642' attended principally to the revolutionary struggles in England, but also to the discourses of European absolutism and colonialist expansion, themes carried through into '1789', where the French bourgeois revolution provided the initial focus, although a significant group of essays also addressed the high ground of English Romanticism. Five papers from these historical conferences are reprinted here. Each of them assumes a 'sociological' redefinition of 'text' away from the supposedly autonomous literary artefact. For Raymond Williams it is the full range of fictional forms at work in 1848 which marks out the field of study, while in Colin Mercer's essay it is his understanding of 'signifying practice' as an instance of 'historical inscription' that provides the ground for his reading of Baudelaire. Fredric Jameson reasserts the interpretative powers of historical materialism to read, at one and the same time, *Paradise Lost* and the 'English Revolution'; Catherine Belsey uses a conception of the unconscious critically and historically to disclose one of the constitutive moments of bourgeois subjectivity in the texts of 'Romanticism'; and David Musselwhite's paper offers an empirically detailed study of the nexus of discourses which constitute 'the trial of Warren Hastings'. The range of these papers also shows the ambition of the conference to move outside that traditional site of sociological criticism, the nineteenth-century novel. The new theories were put to work on texts, especially poetry, often considered resistant to such analysis, and at the same time they brought within their purview material once reserved for purely sociological or historical attention in a movement which effectively challenged the category of the 'literary' itself.

The period during which the historically orientated conferences were held also saw a considerable expansion in the range and variety of theoretical work published and translated. The common ground on which this diversity was based may best be suggested by once more recalling Althusser's contribution to the development of modern cultural theory on the left. In its French context Althusser's work was already in debate with classical Marxism, but also engaged with the problems of structure and representation which were, and continue to be, preoccupations of much contemporary theory. This conjunction of an anti-reductionist Marxist analysis of social practices and the understanding of meaning as the product of systems of difference led on immediately to a focus on problems of language and discourse as ideological, and indeed hegemonic; and to the elaboration of a method of decoding social practices as instances of such power-laden signification. But if the notion of signifying practice was, implicitly, at the heart of Althusser's theory of ideology, so too was the concept of the subject, the bearer of ideology constructed – through a process that Althusser designated 'interpellation' – by ideology itself. In the related areas of language, representation and subjectivity, psychoanalysis came to play a vital role while, at a later moment, Jacques Derrida's critique of the logocentrism of western culture and of 'the metaphysics of presence' provided a powerful critical tool. Developments within feminism also identified a need to investigate, along with the central problem of the social construction of gender, the questions of subjectivity and identity, where Jacques Lacan's rereading of Freud informed much important work. And, at yet another crucial nexus, Michel Foucault combined a theory of discourse with an historical analysis of the formation of the modern institutional modes of subjection.[2]

So in 1982 it was felt necessary to hold a further theoretical conference – 'The Politics of Theory' – whose purpose was to review these developments, to carry out some analytic discrimination between them and, above all, to re-emphasize the need to hold in sustained focus the relationship between politics and theory against the depoliticization evident particularly in some of the work which has come to be known as 'poststructuralism'. From that conference Graham Pechey's analysis of Bakhtin as a *sociologist* of discourse stands over and against the more formalist reception of Bakhtin's work common especially in the United States; and one of Renée Balibar's series of studies on the 'national language' in France represents that growing body of historical work carried out within an Althusserean framework, which has been an important influence on the direction of recent literary studies in England. The initiative of 'The Politics of Theory' was followed up in 1983 by 'Confronting the Crisis', which undertook to utilize the skills developed by the earlier conferences for an explicitly political analysis of the present conjuncture – a project exemplified here by Simon Barker's archaeology of the royalist and reactionary roots of the Thatcher government's 'resolute approach'.

The new theory had always understated, if not persistently denied, the issues of race and imperialism. Although these questions had been addressed within the context of previous conferences – notably in Homi Bhabha's 1982 paper on the discourse of colonialism, reprinted here – it was not until the last conference of the series, 'Europe and Its Others', that their full importance was properly acknowledged. Included here from that final conference are Edward Said's discussion of responses to his influential *Orientalism*, and Gordon Brotherston's paper which, exposing the ethnocentricity inherent in Lévi-Strauss's structuralism and Derrida's grammatology, realigns them to provide a framework for considering Native American texts.

It has become commonplace today to speak of a 'a crisis in English studies'. It remains debatable whether the development in literary theory over recent years is a response to this crisis, as it is usually said to be, or whether it did not itself provoke the crisis by its various challenges to the values and procedures of traditional academic study. The Essex Conference certainly had no simple or monovalent relationship to the partial break-up of that liberal humanist consensus. Its double articulation, not simply with the new critical practices but also with the crisis in Marxism, generated a peculiarly complex interaction of different intellectual perspectives. No strict intellectual coherence was aimed for. The conference brought together, as does the present volume, these different strands, which often overlapped, which were sometimes complementary with each other and sometimes contestatory, but which severally and together sought to explore and aggravate the 'crisis'. The conference, and its Proceedings, are thus located at the intersection of a variety of alternative practices, but the emphasis placed on their intersection avoids a merely pluralist repertoire of 'new' approaches to literary and cultural problems.

The present selection of papers, made from nearly two hundred published, represents in some measure the diversity of the work at the eight Essex Sociology of Literature Conferences. The volumes of Conference Proceedings are listed in the Bibliography under Barker *et al* (eds), and a full list of their contents is given at the back of this book (pp. 241–52). The papers have been lightly revised and in certain cases slightly shortened; some contributors have taken the opportunity to add an explanatory or contextualizing preamble.

THE EDITORS

Wivenhoe, March 1986

NOTES

1 Key works of continental theory were Brecht 1964, Adorno 1967 and Benjamin 1968. The important collection *Aesthetics and Politics: Debates between Bloch, Lukács, Brecht, Benjamin, Adorno* appeared in 1977 and was the subject of the main plenary session at the *1936* conference. Saussure's work had been translated in 1959 but was not widely studied in England until the late 1960s. Todorov's translation into French of the Russian Formalists appeared in 1965, the same year as the smaller collection produced by US slavists (Lemon and Reis 1965). The first major collection in English was Matejka and Pomorska 1971. Important post-Saussurean texts were Lévi-Strauss's *Structural Anthropology* (1958, trans. 1977), Barthes' *Mythologies* (1957 and 1970, trans. 1972) and Kristeva's *Le Texte du roman* (1971). Pierre Macherey's *A Theory of Literary Production* had appeared in 1966 (trans. 1978) and was a decisive influence on Eagleton's work (1976a and 1976b).

   The work of the University of Birmingham Centre for Contemporary Cultural Studies was well represented at Essex: for a more recent example of their work see *Rewriting English* (Batsleer *et al.* (1985). For an account of the Portsmouth project see Oakley *et al.* 1983. On *Screen* see Easthope 1983. On *Literature and History* see Eagleton 1985; a selection of essays is Humm *et al.* 1986.

2 Key works in this area were Althusser's essay on the ideological state apparatuses (in Althusser 1971), Derrida's *Of Grammatology* (1967, trans. 1976), Lacan's *Ecrits* (1966, partial trans. 1977), and Foucault's *Discipline and Punish* (1975, trans. 1977). For an account of the body of feminist work within this field see Toril Moi 1985 (prefigured in her paper at the 1982 Essex Conference, at which feminist theory played a particularly important part: see Moi, Lovell, Russo, Stone, Gallop, all 1983).

Notes on contributors and editors

Renée Balibar is formerly of the University of Tours. Her publications include *Les Français fictifs*, *Le Français national* and *L'Institution du français*.

Francis Barker teaches critical theory and Renaissance literature at the University of Essex. His principal publications include *Solzhenitsyn: Politics and Form* and *The Tremulous Private Body: Essays on Subjection*.

Simon Barker is a research student at University College Cardiff, currently teaching at the Welsh College of Music and Drama. His thesis is entitled 'War, theatre and the English Renaissance'.

Catherine Belsey is a lecturer in English at University College Cardiff. She is the author of *Critical Practice* and *The Subject of Tragedy*.

Homi Bhabha is a lecturer in English at the University of Sussex. He has published articles on aspects of colonial discourse, is commissioning and editing a book called *Nation and Narration*, and writing a book on E. M. Forster.

Gordon Brotherston is a professor of literature at the University of Essex. His principal publications include *The Emergence of the Latin American Novel* and *Image of the New World*. His *Book of the Fourth World* is in preparation.

Peter Hulme is a lecturer in literature at the University of Essex. He has published articles on Latin American and French fiction, and his book *Colonial Encounters: Europe and the Native Caribbean 1492–1797* will appear in 1986.

Margaret Iversen is a lecturer in art history and theory at the University of Essex. She is completing one book on Alois Riegl's historiography of art history and another on the semiotics of visual art.

Fredric Jameson is professor of French at the University of North Carolina. His books include *Marxism and Form, The Prison-House of Language* and *The Political Unconscious*.

Diana Loxley is a research student at the University of Essex, working on the discourse of colonialism. Her thesis deals with the topos of 'the island' in the literature of empire.

Colin Mercer lectures in cultural and media studies at Griffith University, Brisbane. He has edited and contributed to a number of books on popular culture and Marxist theory and is writing a book on entertainment as a cultural technology. He is an overseas editor of *Formations*.

David Musselwhite is a lecturer in literature at the University of Essex. He has recently completed a book on the nineteenth-century novel, and is engaged in a series of studies of colonial trials.

Graham Pechey is a lecturer in English at Hatfield Polytechnic. He has published articles on literary theory and 'romantic' writing, and is preparing a book on Mikhail Bakhtin. His current research interest is in colonial discourse and Third World (mainly African) writing.

Edward Said is Parr professor of comparative literature at Columbia University. His books include *Orientalism*, *The Question of Palestine* and *Covering Islam*.

Raymond Williams was until recently professor of drama at the University of Cambridge. His many works in the field include *Culture and Society*, *The Country and the City* and *Marxism and Literature*.

I

Forms of English fiction in 1848

RAYMOND WILLIAMS

There are many reasons for remembering 1848, and down among them the fact that the first bookstalls were opened on the new British railway system: one might say by a man called W. H. Smith, but in fact by a firm with a title that reminds us of one of the most famous novels published in that year – W.H. Smith *and Son*. This empirical reminder of W.H. Smith – and Son – in an analysis of the world historical year 1848 could well seem an impertinence. Indeed, it is an item of vulgar capitalist enterprise which can seem to stand between us and the more attractive uplands of high bourgeois ideology. Yet any historical analysis, when it centres on a date, has to begin by recognizing that though all dates are fixed all time is in movement. At any particular point there are complex relations between what can be called dominant, residual and emergent institutions and practices. Then the key to analysis is investigation and identification of the specific places occupied within an always dynamic field.

Thus, in terms of capitalist book-selling, Smith's bookstalls and the associated Parlour and Railway Libraries, cheap re-prints of popular novels, are emergent. In terms of *emergent production* we must look quite elsewhere. But between production and book-selling there are those other social relations indicated by what was actually, in majority, being read, and here W.H. Smith – and Son – are again relevant, since they recorded their 'top ten' authors. An interesting list: Bulwer Lytton, Captain Marryat, G.P.R. James, James Grant, Catherine Sinclair, the Canadian Thomas Haliburton, Mrs Frances Trollope, the Irishman Charles Lever, Mrs Elizabeth Gaskell and Jane Austen. I would imagine that most students and teachers of literature would be relieved when they came to the end of the list and found people they had been reading in the last two months. Again, if one looks at the titles, asking what 'they' were reading in 1848, we find that at the top of the list were *Agincourt, The Romance of War, The Last Days of Pompeii, Midshipman Easy, The Heiress of Bruges, Stories from Waterloo, Scalphunters, Rody the Rover, Pride and Prejudice* and *The Little Wife*.

A theoretical problem is then at once evident. In one now familiar mode we can move from the characterization of bourgeois society in that epoch to a characteristic bourgeois ideology and then its appropriate fictional form. I have indeed heard it said that 1848, that remarkable year for new major novels, is the moment of the initiation in fiction of a characteristic bourgeois realism. There are then two immediate problems. First, that what the bourgeoisie was reading was on the whole not bourgeois fiction, in any of its ordinary senses. Second, that the new major novels, from *Vanity Fair* to *Dombey and Son* and from *Mary Barton* to *Wuthering Heights*, can be characterized as bourgeois realism only by an extraordinary flattening, a mutual composition which in fact succeeds in hiding the actual and effective processes, the complex formation of the real forms.

In an alternative mode of historical as distinct from epochal analysis, the problems are still there but may be more specifically negotiable. For we have to begin by recognizing the very complex interlock in politics and culture of dominant and residual forms, and the even more complex process, in relation to that interlock, of specific and still-forming modes of emergence. In fiction especially this is clearly the true shape, the moving shape of the year 1848. Thus, in the titles that I cited, and in the majority of the authors, one can identify two popular 'forms' in the loose literary–historical sense of the term, as primarily determined by content but carrying its own formal consequences: the *historical romance*, which is virtually dominant, particularly when it is a historical romance associated with war; and the *consciously exotic*, itself often significantly associated with the new epoch of colonization. The historical romances, one should observe in passing, are different from the period of Scott, although that is how they tend to turn up in the textbooks. They have much less real historical content; the distinction we make between historical and costume novels or drama is appropriate to many of them. A place, a setting of a colourful kind, is there, but the historical movement, the historical tension within the period, is subordinate to the sense of historical spectacle. And of the exotic the same is true. It is not, needless to say, the story of the colonial wars: it is the adventure story extracted from that whole experience.

But these, I would argue, are in 1848 residual forms, in the sense that while they still command a majority readership among a given formed public, they are beginning to be written less. Through the 1840s there is a distinct decline in the production of both, and the beginning of other kinds. Nevertheless, the fact of this residual element is crucial because it is part of that interlock which is central to English culture in the 1840s: a complex interlock between what (in shorthand) are aristocratic and bourgeois views of life and value systems. The bourgeoisie, that is to say, is in these terms reading predominantly aristocratic fiction, with that kind of social universe assumed. And what is coming through in its own forms is at a lower level of development, in the first instance. The interlock between the residual and what in the course of the 1840s was becoming a dominant bourgeois culture is not negotiated through the residual forms, but through new kinds of consciously class-directed fiction. And here we must begin to make some distinctions within the dominant.

It is fairly easy, as a matter of fact, to find bourgeois fiction in the 1840s which corresponds quite directly to the explicit values and interests of the bourgeoisie. That is to say, you will find stories that are transferring their interest from birth to wealth, from inherited position to self-made position. As recently as the 1830s it had often been doubted whether the middle class were sufficiently interesting to have novels written about them – a doubt that has since occurred to others. But within the 1840s the aristocrat who had seemed the natural figure for a romance was beginning to be affected, in a certain category of fiction, by the new bourgeois ethic of self-making and self-help. Indeed, a strong emphasis on work as distinct from play carried with it, actually as one of the main incentives of this class of fiction, a clear diagnosis of poverty which it included as a fact directly related to lack of personal effort or indeed to some positive vice. Thus those explicit, conscious bourgeois values which are the formal social character of the class in that period got into fiction, but not, as a matter of fact, into any very important fiction: which is why the stereotyped terms 'bourgeois fiction', 'bourgeois realism' do not work as if they were simple formulas. You can find the straight ideology in a lot of the new magazine fiction, the family magazine serial fiction of the 1840s; you can find it in the tracts that were very widely written in fictional form and addressed to particular sectors of the working class with the aim either of religious conversion or conversion to temperance. These were put into fictional forms, with stories of how people could succeed by temperance and by effort, or could fail by drunkenness, weakness and vice, and with the moral directly attached, in spite of the fictional form, that you must not blame your poverty on others or expect others to relieve it; it is a matter of your own effort and your own sobriety.

Alongside that dominant, specifically *bourgeois* fiction – the association of self-making ways of wealth and virtue; poverty as a moral fault; emphasis on the sanctity of marriage; manipulation of plots to punish sexual offenders *quickly* – you find something which is not residual, except perhaps in one area, but is equally not emergent. There is a subordinate and there is a repressed culture, and each has its appropriate fictional forms within the specific interlock. The *subordinate* culture is, of course, that of the working class which, at the level of politics, at the level of social and industrial organizations, was already in the first phase of its maturity as a class, but which culturally was still in very marked ways subordinate. If there are elements of emergence – the discovery of new forms in which the experience of a different class can be expressed – they are right at the edges; often significantly near to the personal voice, in autobiography; or in certain kinds of poem. In fiction, and as a matter of fact in much of the popular verse of the time, there is an extraordinary reproduction, by working-class novelists and poets quite closely associated with the working-class political movement, of bourgeois forms though sometimes with the moral turned the other way. But much more often, in the complex interlock of the period, there is an identification of the *aristocracy*, of the land-lords specifically, as the class enemy. And this is crucial to understanding the period. That the working class was coming in part to perceive the industrial bourgeoisie as the class enemy was crucial to the politics. But within the culture – and this encouraged many quite powerful forms – the old aristocracy, the landlords, were much more commonly so perceived. If you look at what can be called the radical melodrama and the fiction associated with it through this period you will find some radicalism, but most of it is directed at the old class enemy – at the landowner. And this is after the period in which, in the real history, the landowning classes and the industrial bourgeoisie had begun to make their decisive social composition. And so much of the working-class fiction and poetry reproduces what are in fact dominant bourgeois forms. It does not do so entirely but when it moves into anything new it often moves towards something which overlaps with that other element which I referred to as the *repressed* culture.

The repressed culture is that consequence of the bourgeois failure to recognize even the facts of its own experience and, above all, its sexuality. A huge trade in pornography was a classic feature of book-selling from the late 1820s right through to the mid-Victorian period – actually not with much newly produced pornography, but mainly reprinting and adaptation of eighteenth-century work or translations. That area is there, and curiously there is an area of the subordinate fiction, very popular among working-class readers, which is not too far from it although it is not pornographic in a strict sense. But it is scandal: scandal about the court and about the aristocracy; not scandal about the bourgeoisie or about the working class them-selves. If you look at Reynolds' *Mysteries of the Court of London*, for example, directly imitating a French form in Sue, or if you look at Reed's *History of a Royal Rake*, you will find the sort of thing which had a distinct place in the social perspective of working-class readers because it told them that the highest people in society were, in fact, behaving scandalously. And the terms of this judgement were terms which that part of the working class shared with the newly self-organizing and consciously moral bourgeoisie. That Reynolds could move from speaking at a

Chartist meeting in Trafalgar Square to writing the *Mysteries of the Court of London* shows how, within the complex class inter-lock, opposition and the experience of subordination were being expressed at different levels which do not cohere. And while this was so, the emergence of anything which could be properly called a proletarian fiction is not really to be looked for. You get some adaptation of residual forms: the popular series of histori-cal novels about Wat Tyler or Jack Cade; versions of the Civil War written from the radical side, which fiction had not nor-mally done; romances of the radical melodrama kind in which a poor girl is seduced and abandoned (but here again the seducer is a fairly regular social figure, he is the aristocrat or the officer; he is not yet typically, as he would eventually be in this sort of literature, the manufacturer or the commercially rich man). So it is right, I think – with great respect to Samuel Bamford; to Ebenezer Elliot, who perhaps comes nearest to finding an authentic voice among those popular writers of the 1840s; to Thomas Cooper and to the many hundreds of others who tried – right to see it as a subordinate culture, though with significant links to what is actually crucial about the dominant culture in the long run, that it included this large repressed area where it could not admit what it was reading and could not admit experiences which it nevertheless craved.

It is in relation to the complex interlock of classes that you have to diagnose the problem of emergence. If you read what was then emerging backwards, either from your own historical or theoretical understanding of what should have been said – which is a natural temptation – or even from your calculation of the probabilities of what might have been said, you may be looking in the wrong place and you may yoke together things which were in fact emerging in significantly different ways – changes which we can better appreciate if we look at the matter in terms of the problem of form.

Let me say something in formal terms about seven novels written around this year: *Jane Eyre*, *The Tenant of Wildfell Hall*, *Wuthering Heights*, *Vanity Fair*, *Shirley*, *Mary Barton* and *Dombey and Son*. What we are often offered is a generalized diagnosis of the emergence of a conscious, incorporating bourgeois culture with its appropriate fictional form, which is realism; you know that diagnosis. One can fairly easily flatten these novels into that, at too early a level, though the real question is whether or not one can eventually significantly group them. Take first the easiest thing to say about *Jane Eyre*, *The Tenant of Wildfell Hall* and *Wuthering Heights*: that these introduce a new stress on the imperatives of intense personal experience, or indeed, as all the introductions put it, on passion. It is not that this isn't a perfectly reasonable general description, but when you look at it in terms of form there are immediately some interesting problems. *Jane Eyre* seems the simplest case because it is called an autobiography, edited, you remember, by Currer Bell – and with that characteristic distancing of the identity of the actual author in the pseudonym: 'an autobiography edited by . . .'. But this is at the level of the most external form of presentation, because the voice that takes over within the actual writing and which totally controls the narration and the observation is throughout a personal voice of a new kind, quite different from conventional personal-centred fiction. The difference is most obvious in the common problem of reading Charlotte Brontë aloud. There is a radical difference when you read her aloud and when you read her silently as a private reader, which is clearly what the voice is arranged for. For there are *secrets*, to put it at its plainest, that you and Charlotte Brontë are meant to share as if you were on your own; tones which are not so easily accessible if other people are listening. That very particular personal voice – the direct 'Reader, I married him' – is, with a necessary kind of intensity, making the direct invitation: 'Put yourself in my place, feel with *me*.'

That particular note is very distinct from, for an interesting reason, even *The Tenant of Wildfell Hall*, because if you look at that in terms of form what you find – well, you could say a *double* personal narrative. What you have is a male narrator enclosing the diary of a woman, and it is the diary which is the means of disclosure of the misunderstanding of the relationship which has troubled the narrator – who, actually, to provide a further complication, is supposed to be writing a very long letter to a friend: a misunderstanding which has troubled him in all the period up to the availability of the diary. Chapters I to XV are the very long formal letters to the friend, XVI to XXXXIV are the private diary, and XXXXV onwards resume in the male narrative. Now already this deliberate dispersal of points of view introduces a certain difference, a certain distinction, into what is otherwise flattened into the notion of an autobiographical subjective intensity. Indeed, it is much more significantly related to a more familiar form which is that of the misunderstood relationship – and here a word can be said which relates to a more general problem. The most familiar fictional device within the terms of bourgeois fiction for blocked intense sexual feeling was the discovery . . . Well, let me put it another way. Two people who, within the terms of this culture, cannot be in love and relate, find themselves doing so. What is in the way, normally, is not just the institution of marriage, but the actual existence of – usually – the wife, sometimes the husband. The characteristic device for escaping from this situation without breaking the morality is that the wife turns out to be insane, alcoholic or indeed deeply vicious. The tied partner displays extraordinary heroism in tending the alcoholism, the insanity or what may be, thus proving that self-sacrifice produces virtue. But there is a built-in moment at the end of this situation and at that point, having proved your virtue and, of course, waited, the relation can happen. Now this is not just something that happened in magazine fiction, for of course it happens in *Jane Eyre*. But aside from this fairly deliberate device for admitting relationships outside marriage without questioning marriage as such, *The Tenant of Wildfell Hall*, like some of the tracts and the magazine fiction, negotiates the man/woman relationship in terms of the ideality of brother/sister, ideal that is in that brother/sister could share everything that a man and woman could properly share, or needed to share. There is no hint, at least at any conscious level, of incest or anything of that kind. It is simply that they are good friends, helping and supporting each other.

What is seen as a guilty relationship (in terms of *The Tenant of Wildfell Hall*) turns out to be a brother/sister relationship, which can therefore be properly a substitute for a marriage relationship. Again, of course, there is a prolonged test of suffering, which in fact has occurred before the time of the narration, but which, within the time of the text, occurs in the middle, where the diary goes back over it. By the time you have reached that point the long suffering has happened. What has been perceived as a guilty relationship then becomes the ideal brother/sister relationship, and they can move on from it. This would not be possible without that specific form which modifies autobiography, in allowing the two points of view on a relationship which can be misunderstood.

In *Wuthering Heights*, too, there is again double narration, but significantly a double narration by persons who, both off-centre from the material of the narrative, have an attendant and in time differentiated relationship to the primary events. This has moved to a multicentred objective viewpoint, both in time and narration, on to a series of events through generations which can be *summarized* as an assertion of absolute primary intensity. And one can hardly read *Wuthering Heights* at all unless one recognizes *that* as the value at its centre. But it is very consciously placed within a structure which the most careful analysis discovers to be even more complex than had been initially noticed – a structure of time, of interrelation of modes of observation and stages of the primary relationship. If you look at the sequences through Lockwood and Nelly Dean, if you look at the constantly open relations between the modes of observation that Lockwood and Nelly Dean as narrators can command, and then the modes of experience that those they are observing are structurally involved with, directly and through the generations, you find something very much more complex in form and therefore in the whole structure of the experience than can possibly be represented by the singular expression of intense subjectivity. Indeed, we find both the subjectivity and a process of its displacement, and one must not take them, in my view, as constituting a value from either side. When Cathy has said 'If all else perished and he remained, I should still continue to be' she has made one of the classic assertions of a sense of identity and of a sense of relationship (identity in relationship), and this, I believe, is one of the most profound responses to the actual culture of the 1840s, although it is not at any overt level political or social: 'If all else perished and he remained, I should still continue to be.' And yet it is precisely in direct relationship to this that Nelly Dean can say: 'I was out of patience with her folly.' And at that point within a deliberate form, you have to consider the possibility of the truth of that observation; not that it is folly to believe it, but that it is folly to assume it, which is what Cathy at that point in the action is doing. She assumes that because she has a necessary relationship it is therefore a permanent relationship. Within a structure of this kind you are not asked, as in the ordinary account of bourgeois realist fiction you are supposed to be asked, to identify with a single point of view on the experience. The opportunities for very complex seeing, both within a given situation and within time, are absolutely built in to the form of the novel.

If you look at *Vanity Fair* you see at once how very distinct are these new forms that are emerging. *Vanity Fair*, powerful as it is, adopts in its narration an older, much more available stance. The prefatory notice is by the manager of the performance, and in an important sense this is a placing for the reader. The narrator/manager is able directly to intervene in a variable relationship with the reader. 'As we are to see a great deal of Amelia there's no harm in saying at the outset' he remarks, at once distancing the relationship to the reader. The writing moves in and out of scene, narrative and commentary towards that final placing of 'Come, children, let us shut up the box and the puppets, for our play is played out.' This is a conscious placing of what is actually a very remarkable social-critical perspective within the half-playful, half-managing tone of an older kind of fictional form. It interests me that the account that is usually given of nineteenth-century bourgeois realism is of a character who is engaged in a traverse through a range of society and who discovers at various points along that traverse certain unadmitted general facts about the society. This is held up to be the perspective of critical realism. The most obvious English novel corresponding to that model is *Vanity Fair*, although actually when you look into it you find that it is not really interpretable in terms of that model. The delineation of Becky is not primarily a delineation of a society but the delineation of a 'character', and that is a very much older fundamental form.

Just a few words about the others, because I want to move on to more general points. In *Shirley* Charlotte Brontë moves towards a more generally emergent social mode. 'If you think . . . that anything like a romance is preparing for you, reader, you never were more mistaken. Do you anticipate "this and this", do you expect "that and that"? Calm your expectations . . . something real, cool and solid lies before you.' Now the 'something real, cool and solid' – not that *Shirley* is very cool – is much nearer the amendment that presages bourgeois realism in a strict sense. Characteristically it is back-dated. 'The story is told. I think I now see the judicious reader putting on his spectacles to look for the moral. It would be an insult to his sagacity to offer directions.' This is a particular consciousness of a relationship to the reader: that the moral is there but it's not for me, the narrator, to draw; the narrator can assume other men of good sense and judgement. In this sense it is different from – earlier than – the realist novel, but it has that ambition.

It is *Mary Barton* that is usually taken as a classic example of the objective narrative which occludes the fact of narration. Obviously there are long periods in which this is so, and yet the location of the crucial stance at the beginning is more complex than that. At an important point when the narrator is describing the walk in the fields, she admits the partial knowledge of its reason; whether it is because they were on holiday or in effect, 'I don't know whether it was some other reason'. This close but limited information is actually the crucial formal relation of the narrative. There is a deliberately close but limited *access to* the writing that was actually being done by the class that Mrs Gaskell was writing about, as in her close reliance on Bamford, or in the inclusion of dialect in that deliberately associating, and yet at the same time outwardly explanatory, way. The first thing that struck me about *Mary Barton* was that as early as page 2 a piece of carefully reproduced dialect is footnoted and explained. It is at once, of course, the formal and the social relationship. She is determined not to misrepresent the lives, the speech of those she is writing about; she is not going to assimilate them to some other model; this is the crucial Gaskell emphasis. At the same time, in attempting this emphasis within a culture as deeply divided into classes, and especially on this issue of literacy and book-reading, as that one was, she knows that the readers will be in majority of another kind. Therefore she had to annotate the internally reproduced life. This paradox at a formal level can in turn be related to the well-known history of the transition from the initially conceived novel *John Barton* – an imaginative adherence – to the eventual *Mary Barton* – close but then profoundly qualified.

In *Dombey and Son* there is a general and even a commanding narrator. And yet the more I think about Dickens the less I think that 'narrative' in the ordinary sense is a good way of describing this mode. The word that insistently suggests itself is 'presentation'. For there is an unusual *mobility* in this narrator. He moves from place to place and from the point of view of one character to another, with much more diversity than any other novelist of his time. He moves from style to style with the same mobile assurance: that he can establish at a break a new mode. There is nothing of the uniformity of narrative of the classic realist text. And at the same time there is something else which I would like to consider because it introduces a crucial variable into the question of realist fiction and especially of its function in this year of 1848. One can say that much of the narrative mode of the novel-form that was emerging was predominantly *indicative*. It was, or offered to be, an account of what had happened and what was happening. If one takes *indicative* as that description then one can talk of an element of Dickens's writing which is *subjunctive*, which is clearly 'what if' or 'would that' or 'let us suppose that'. In other words, he introduces a perspective which is actually not socially or politically available. It is a hypothesis of a perspective, a feeling, a force, which he knows not to be in the existing balance of forces that was there to be observed. The notion of the subjunctive within the generally realist novel is one which we could think more about. The realist perspective is commonly held to exclude the possibility of an alteration of forces. The classic complaint against naturalism is that it simply reproduces the forces which are known to be operative and leaves us with greater knowledge but with no more capacity for action. The subjunctive mode within that kind of realist narrative, always difficult to extend and sustain, is often found in the ends of novels. There is a good example at the end of *Dombey*. It is present also in those characteristic interventions when Dickens invokes, beyond the terms of the realist text, the notion of a quite different but attainable perspective, in which we could see all the forces and relationships differently; in *Dombey* in the famous Chapter 47. The presence of that kind of subjunctive mode seems to me crucial; it is precisely the sense in which Dickens was connecting with things that lay far ahead of him.

I have so far been taking instances at the most simple formal

level of form as stance, or form as mode. There is a possibility
of considering whether there are not, below these differences,
deep forms which could be identified as deep ideological forms.
I have already mentioned one in passing. It is the classic
Lukácsian diagnosis of the nineteenth-century hero as the man
who wishes to live a fuller life but who discovers, in experience,
the limitations of his society: not only the blockages of his own
fullness but a general limit which is then capable of being an
alternative social perspective. He discovers, at the point where
he cannot fully realize his own life, the objective social limits
which prevent everyone fulfilling their own lives. But this is a
model derived primarily from French and from Russian fiction,
which are indeed full of examples of it. I think there are not
many examples in England which are properly that, and in any
case the question that needs to be put to it – it is a question that
bears evidently on *Jane Eyre*, on *Wuthering Heights*; it bears in a
way throughout Dickens – is that everything depends on something which that description of the deep form blurs. This is the
question of value at the point of the discovery of limits. To take
an example which happens to be theoretically much clearer,
though from just outside our period: one might assimilate *Felix
Holt* and *Jude the Obscure* to the Lukácsian formula of the
discovery of objective limits, that discovery being general. But
one would be very foolish to stop at that point because the
culmination of *Felix Holt* is precisely the discovery of limits in a
resigned mode, the discovery of certain 'true' limits, on the
human capacity to understand and act, whereas in *Jude the
Obscure* the discovery of limits – although much more destruc-
tive, there seems absolutely nothing left – is profoundly subversive of the limiting structure which has blocked the key figure.
This difference of weighting is structural. It is not simply what is
said at the end. It is something you can trace right back in the
whole organization.

Now if you think back in those terms to what can be called a
subjectivist intensity, which is undoubtedly a characteristic of
the new novels of 1848 in one of their groupings, you can move
quite quickly to discovering what the 'limits' are. We have seen
that there are structural limits in the established relationship,
which have to be circumvented before the intensity can be fully
expressed or realized. There is also, in a sense qualifying the

challenge of this new subjectivism, the possibility of subjectivism in quite another mode. The introduction by Charlotte Brontë of that effective mode in which it is very difficult to consider the feelings of any other character, or even the situation of any other character, except through the dominant terms of the feelings of the narrator, becomes in the end what I have called the fiction of special pleading. Indeed, at a certain point, subjectivism in that sense becomes a project of the elimination of other beings, except as they relate to the intensity of one's own (narrated) perceived needs. That limit often expresses itself in sentimentality and in certain kinds of evasion. One sees those limits, but they do not to me seem to be limits of the kind Lukács and others in that Marxist tradition are talking about. For although there are undoubtedly major factors in the social structure which are barring intense experience, which are certainly barring self-images of autonomy of being and feeling, as distinct from the social role and the social function, although such barriers are easily discoverable, the level of the most authentic protest seems separable from those local historical structures. They lie very deep within the whole cast of the civilization which is, for its own deepest reasons and often while denying that it is doing so, repressing intensely realized experiences of any kind.

It is then very difficult when you are looking at these works – this is the point which comes out with the other deep form – to distinguish between what is really the pressure of ideological limits and the widening area of actual social limits. Moreover, we have to distinguish between limits of these kinds and what is really an unfinished impulse towards something which, by definition, within those structures and forms, cannot be finished, but where *the move towards expressing it* is of major value.

Let me give another example of a deep form and how it both indicates and in a sense betrays some of this fiction. It is identifiable as a new fact of the fiction of the 1840s, and very marked in 1848 itself, that it admits class relations, including class conflict, as the conscious material of fiction. In this sense it is, although not unprecedented, very new in its emphasis. It has that direct relation to a period of intense, overt class-consciousness. Now the deep form that some have then perceived is that the conflict is admitted precisely so that it can be reconciled or evaded. This is becoming, I think, a popular analysis, to judge from the times I have heard it. And the example everyone goes to is *North and South*, on which I would say that it is not an inaccurate diagnosis; the conflict of *North and South* is set up to be reconciled. I mean, from the beginning it is so. The reconciliation is carried out in terms of one of the deep evasions of the nature of the conflict, characteristic of much of the fiction of that time; that when humanity and the necessity of profit collide, fiction moves to the fortunate legacy. There has to be a surplus of an external kind to finance the humanity within the terms of trade. This recourse to the legacy to solve the socially and economically impossible is, of course, widespread throughout the fiction around 1848; just as recourse to the empire as a source of fortunes or as a place to hide from the conflicts of the society is deeply characteristic. But it seems to me to be wrong to apply that back to *Mary Barton*, or to apply it to Dickens, in simple ideological ways. Of course, one sees that the notion of reconciliation is there, but one then has to distinguish very sharply between the types of reconciliation envisaged. There is the type of reconciliation which Dickens so often projects, of people having changed heart and realized their relations to each other in a different spirit. Or there is the kind of reconciliation which Disraeli projected, that the people and the aristocracy can unite against the industrial bourgeoisie and thus solve the class conflict by winning it; as when Sybil is not only the Chartist, but the dispossessed aristocrat, and marries an aristocrat. Their common union – 'Chartist marries aristocrat against the industrial bourgeoisie' – reconciles the class conflict by uniting against it and superseding it.

But then there is the type of reconciliation which, it seems to me, is deep in *Mary Barton*. This is intended to be the consequence of experiencing directly what you had only abstractly conceived: to experience the death of a son, to experience actual losses in the family. Certainly there is a sickliness in the Barton house, and a negotiation over the dead, but this does not seem at all the same kind as the *North and South* reconciliation or the Disraeli political fantasy. In other words the suggested deep form – that the conflict is introduced because it has to be and because it can then be evaded in false reconciliation – this I think is wrong. I would argue that there is a sense which is peculiarly inaccessible to a non-historical imagination, that in failing to distinguish between the *kinds* of subjective impulse and the *kinds* of reconciliation, the shallowest conventional forms are discovered to be the deep ideological forms, while works written within a tension between conventional forms, deep forms and serious attempts to move beyond both are simply degraded and collapsed.

The theoretical issues involved in this are central to the whole problem of production and reproduction. Clearly at a certain level the emergent fiction must be sharply distinguished – which is why I started with W. H. Smith and Son – from what the middle class were in majority producing and reading; the true reproduction of conscious bourgeois positions. And distinguished not only as a higher and more sophisticated form of the same thing. This is true even when we see that they have crucial features in common, so that it would be wrong not to consider the very large elements of simple reproduction in these new novels. But what, in my view, would be as wrong and much more damaging would be to fail to recognize the finitely significant openness of certain of the new impulses; of the inclusion of certain realities of the class situation and of class conflict; the pushing through to certain intensities however difficult they then were. For these, as new content, and as new forms of the content, are genuinely emergent elements: production, significant production, attempting to lift certain pressures, to push back certain limits; and at the same time, in a fully extended production, bearing the full weight of the pressure and limits, in ways which the simple forms, the simple contents, of mere ideological reproduction never achieve. Of course we now know more than these writers of 1848 about the pressures and limits – the deep and decisive social relations and conflicts – of what for us is now a period, a date. But to the extent that we know these substantially – not indifferently, not as mere 'knowing' – we have to recognize that a significant part of this understanding is that we know *them*; know what, in struggle and partially, then began to come through.

2

Baudelaire and the city: 1848 and the inscription of hegemony

COLIN MERCER

By the time this article appears, ten years will have elapsed since its original submission as an essay for the Sociology of Literature MA at the University of Essex. I must thank David Musselwhite for his encouragement and help at that time and for his suggestion that I submit it for a conference paper in the following year.

Ten years is, however, a long time in cultural politics, and had not the editors and publishers insisted on only minor amendments, there are some substantial revisions – and some toning down of the rather insistent and repetitive style – that I would like to have made. More work, for example, on the nature of the nineteenth-century 'public' and on the 'policing of populations' in the tradition of Richard Sennett and Michel Foucault would certainly have helped to theorize a little more what I now consider to be a rather vague relationship established between *flâneur* and crowd, between 'consciousness' and 'commodity', and so on. Also, had I known at the time, my analysis here would have benefited enormously from T. J. Clark's two works *The Absolute Bourgeois* (1973a) and *Image of the People* (1973b), in which it is precisely the 'occlusive presence of the public' as a discursive fissure which provides the terms of analysis for the work of some of Baudelaire's contemporaries: Millet, Daumier, Courbet and Delacroix.

Reformulated in these terms, my analysis would not need to rely, in the way it does at certain points, on the work of Lacan. It has now become clearer to me that rather than providing a way of explaining crucial aspects of Baudelaire's work, Lacan's own formulations are very much a part of the same tradition of French post-Baudelairean poetics. I offer no apology, however, for the 'Althusserean' tone of the piece. In spite of many recent disavowals of his work, not unconnected with the tragic circumstances in which he now finds himself, I remain convinced that the project which Althusser initiated within Marxism still remains enormously important and productive for contemporary critical theory. It is worth insisting on this as a final acknowledgement: that, as Michel Foucault remarked in an interview with the *New York Times* a few years back, 'Althusser is the key' for a whole body of contemporary critical theory of which this article forms a part.

*

Starting from Walter Benjamin's assertion that the decisive experience for Baudelaire was 'the jostle of the crowd', I will attempt here to locate his poetry as the scene of a crucial *displacement* of certain discourses and structured ways of seeing in the 1848 period. Baudelaire's signifying practice will be seen as a determinate *inscription* of a 'history' of 1848 rather than as a description, among other things, of history. Poetry, in other words, will be viewed not as the epiphenomenon of a superior historical reality but as precisely *another history*, and the poetic signifier, the 'word', not as a piece of opaque evidence or as a transparent lens but as the active practice in which the 'subject' is *subjected*. Central to this thesis is the 'dismantling' of the *subject* of lyric poetry, the definable lyric 'I' which came to its death/ dissemination in Baudelaire's poetry. The shift from the romantic hero to the ambiguous *flâneur* figure, from vital to urban metaphors, from definable narrator to barely recognizable narratee, will be examined and located in terms of the displacements of familiar terms of reference and discursive frameworks in this period, which is both revolutionary and also crucially formative for bourgeois hegemony.

What Baudelaire registers and inscribes in his poetry is the progressive societalization of human relations – the elaboration of pervasive hegemonic discourses in the face of an emerging and increasingly organized entity named concisely but ambiguously as 'the people' or 'the mob'. For if, in that earlier revolutionary scenario of 1789, the battle was clearly fought out on the barricades, eye to eye as it were, then the scene in the post-1848 period has crucially shifted and the glance of the earlier Bonapartist hero is now refracted disconcertingly through new and more complex relations.

It is, to be sure, tempting to pursue the 'matter in itself'. In the case of Baudelaire, it offers itself in profusion. The sources flow to one's heart's content, and there they converge to form the stream of tradition; this stream flows along as far as the eye can see between well laid-out slopes. Historical materialism is not diverted by this spectacle. It does not seek the reflection of the clouds in this stream, but it also does not turn away from this stream to drink 'from the source' and pursue 'the matter in itself' behind men's backs. Whose mills does this stream activate? Who is utilizing its power? Who dammed it? These are the questions which historical materialism asks, and it changes the picture of the landscape by naming the forces which are operating in it.

(Benjamin 1973, pp. 103–4)

It is with a fine critical irony that Walter Benjamin here runs the 'pastoral' metaphor into its industrial 'mills', for it is at least an analogous transition which marks and distinguishes the period with which we are concerned. But as it stands that statement is far too general: the terms of the metaphor have to be specifically located if we are to avoid a generalized and reductive location of the poet's work. As a poet Baudelaire is never concerned with the countryside in any meaningful sense. He is exclusively concerned with the city, with Paris, the capital *par excellence* of the nineteenth century. And even if we simply say that he is 'concerned' with the city as such, we have to be careful to specify that relation. It is crucial to understand that Baudelaire's work does not entirely depict or reflect the city as if he were a crudely transparent historical cipher; but neither is he a 'consciousness' and a 'presence' sufficient to himself and fully constructed 'in the face of' history in a simple relation of opposition or of congruence. What Baudelaire offers us in his poetry and critical essays is not the 'evidence' of a particular 'chunk' of history; it is precisely *another history*, the history of a specific signifying practice seized *within* and not *vis-à-vis* social relations.

We must agree, then, with Walter Benjamin that the decisive experience for Baudelaire was the 'jostle of the crowd' but we should exercise our powers of alignment very carefully, for Baudelaire and the crowd did not accompany each other on to the historical stage casting sideways suspicious glances at each other. The crowd as social phenomenon existed long before Baudelaire and is duly recorded in nineteenth-century French fiction by Hugo and Balzac among others. With Hugo's poetry, however, the crowd enters as the *object* of poetry, or to speak in more abstract terms, as the 'content'. The crowd in earlier Romantic fiction is the defined 'other' in opposition to the relatively secure or alienated lyric 'I'. The radical difference which marks Baudelaire's poetry is that the crowd cannot remain as an *object* of his writing in the simple descriptive sense but becomes *constitutive* of it. The crowd is for Baudelaire's poetry a *constitutive absence*; something which, while grasping a vanishing lyric persona he can attempt to signify in purely oppositional terms, but which denies that easy signification. This complex double articulation characterizes Baudelaire's poetry. It is to Baudelaire's credit that between the first generation of Romanticism and the doctrine of art for art's sake he attempted to come to terms with and to define the very meaning of modernism. He was to find that it was more than just abstract meanings and definitions at stake, for this was an attempt which shattered the persona of European lyric poetry in the form in which it had become dominant.

Characteristically, Baudelaire embraced his own destroyer, or rather he saw it embracing him – 'l'héroisme de *la vie moderne* nous entoure et nous presse' (Baudelaire 1968, pp. 223–4) – and his attempt to name, to signify, the new in an age when the quality of newness itself was coming to be negated by the mass production and standardization that novelty now entailed, was what drove him forward to his abîme/gouffre/néant. This is not to say that mass production directly 'affected' Baudelaire's poetry in any mechanically determinist way, but it does mean that the conception of newness involved a new narrative relation different from that of the earlier Romantic persona, a new 'narrative economy' involving new subject positions and new discursive practices (see Faye 1973). Baudelaire realized what Brecht was to stress seventy years or so later, that new social relations demand new artistic forms, but that the transition is neither immediate nor is it enabled by a simple frontal attack. In a process of shift and displacement it was Baudelaire more than any other poet who *writes* and *inscribes* this movement – the movement, as I will argue, towards a more pervasive and effective bourgeois hegemony than had previously been possible or, indeed, necessary.

In his attempt to signify – the woman, the crowd, the 'other' – Baudelaire's poetry strikes the implicit realization that there is no fixed relation between the word and the thing or concept; between signifier and signified. The constant grasping for new terms in his metaphors, his 'ragpicking' technique, his prose poems, are all testament to the fact that in this conjuncture of transition there is a massive determinate absence which simultaneously sets language in motion and denies it its power of adequate signification. In this context it seems to me to be an extremely important fact that Baudelaire 'accompanied' his poems in traditional form with poems in prose. Part of his project here was the attempt to 'fill in' newly emergent spaces in the life and environment of post-1848 Paris. The desire to define is made more explicit in the introduction to *Poèmes en prose*:

> Who among us has not dreamt, in ambitious moments, of the miracle of a poetic prose, musical without rhythm and without rhyme, supple and malleable enough to adapt to the lyrical movements of the soul, to the undulations of dream and the somersaults of consciousness?
>
> *It is above all from the frequentation of great cities, from the network of their innumerable relations that this obsessive ideal is born.*
>
> (Baudelaire 1968, p. 146; my emphasis)

At a general level the responses to that question are still resonating today. More immediately, Rimbaud and Lautréamont were to reply; Apollinaire, too, with his multiple personae in the very same streets which had so profoundly affected Baudelaire. Rimbaud's response – 'Je est un autre' – is perhaps most pertinent for our present concern. If the latter poet's lyric persona is abandoned to the famous 'Bateau ivre' then it was surely Baudelaire's work which provided the point of embarkation. The last stanza of *Les Sept vieillards*, where the persona's 'soul' is adrift on a monstrous and limitless sea as an old wreck with his reason trying in vain to grasp the helm, is an important prefiguration.

This poem occurs in the *Tableaux parisiens* section of *Les Fleurs du mal*, a crucial section for any study of Baudelaire's responses to the city, where there is a marked movement outwards from the poetic 'soul', from the interior into the streets. But this is not a once and for all movement since the poet attempts to take the interior with him. Benjamin has shown that the arcades, popular at this time, were an attempt to interiorize the exterior; and the unease felt in locating interiors and exteriors became a drama on the theme of where we should locate our 'glowing' centres or our 'souls', upon which solid and profoundly ideological foundation we may constitute ourselves as subjects. Baudelaire is not, however, describing this movement, he is *writing/inscribing* it in the materiality of language. The movement is written in the poem 'Rêve Parisien' dedicated, significantly enough, to Constantin Guys, the artist around whom Baudelaire developed his theory that the true artist should 'marry' the crowd (see the essay 'The painter of modern life'). The persona moves out to a dream landscape which is

> Babel d'escaliers et d'arcades
> C'était un palais infini,
> Plein de bassins et de cascades
> Tombant dans l'or mat ou bruni

and

> Nons d'arbres, mais de colonnades
> Les étangs dormants s'entouraient,
> Où de gigantesques naiades,
> Comme des femmes, se miraient;

and from this very distinctive *arcade*-ia he returns not to a comforting niche but to 'l'horreur de mon taudis'.

The dilemma of whether to stay inside or move outside to the streets and crowds is decisive not only for Baudelaire but also for

Edgar Allen Poe – just one of the artists *through* whom Baudelaire writes his own poetic. In the writings of both these men the
fear of claustration is matched only by the fear of *dissemination* by
the crowd. Mikhail Bakhtin has also located this scene of
activity in relation to the work of Dostoyevsky (Bakhtin 1973):
the movement from interior to exterior makes the threshold into
a pivotal point. If Baudelaire stepped beyond that threshold, he
went carrying his own 'intérieur' with him. To do this he had to
go as *flâneur*, attempting to leave the traces of his lyric footsteps
on the pavement in full knowledge of the fact that they would
immediately be smothered by the feet of the crowd. The spatial
metaphors tend to suggest a phenomenology, and consequently
a false dialectic of subject and object that is in fact merely a
mechanical, reciprocal relationship. This is always a danger
when spatial or optical metaphors are given theoretical precedence but the point is that though we may be dealing with
landscapes in 'dream', what is important and what constitutes
the real historical location of the text, is that it is *recounted* and
written in a language which is the history and the instrument of a
cultural hegemony. Bearing that in mind as a corrective we
should specify that the writing of this particular 'hero' is distinctive in that the *flâneur* is more than the traditional outsider of
Romantic fiction, more than a Quasimodo or a Childe Harold,
more than a King Kong or a Solzhenitsyn, he is a *failed* outsider.
Try as he may, he, unlike the romantic hero, cannot stay
outside. In the age of increasing repetition the poet can no
longer serenely contemplate. When he looks at the crowd the
return glance is no longer comforting, nor is it even the hostile
but definitive glance of the other – the enemy, society – against
whom the hero must do battle but in a combat where both
opponents retain their integrity.

Now the return glance profoundly changes what it looks at.
The meaning of the modification of the 'look' which is at the
same time structured as a process of signification can be more
precisely located if we remember what Marx has to say about
one particular – and dominant – ideological motif at this time.
Involved in the persona of the *flâneur* are residual notions of the
poet as outsider mixed with a peculiarly French brand of
bohemianism, but at another level this persona can be seen to
have a correlative in Louis Napoleon, or at least in the dominant

ways in which, given the residues and traces of previous eras, this persona was understood. Louis Napoleon was himself the pathetic repeat performance, in Marx's terms, of that earlier hero, Napoleon Bonaparte. It is possible, I think, to describe a narrative congruity between, on the one hand, Baudelaire's attempt in his critical essays to bring together, in a constant synthesis, image and discourse, the transient and the eternal, line and colour, harmony and melody, subject and object: 'What is pure art according to the modern conception? It is to create a suggestive magic containing at once the object and the subject, the world exterior to the artist and the artist himself' (Baudelaire 1968, p. 424); and, on the other, the attempt of Louis Napoleon to reproduce the discourse of the earlier hero. Baudelaire tries to form a unity over an absent centre, an attempt which, given the new conditions of existence, fails, but it is in his poetry rather than in his essays that that failure is realized and inscribed. The 'ideological project' is confounded by the 'conditions of existence' to use a terminology derived from Macherey. But we have to go beyond that useful though general formula and realize that this all takes place in language, the site of a primary discursive effect. And language is not of course only available to poets and novelists, though there it is most 'obvious' and artefactual. There are other narratives which are less obvious, though no less 'loaded' with ideological presuppositions. One such narrative was that of Louis Napoleon, who was by no means so aware of the fundamental dislocation and displacement which had taken place between the available ideological discourses and the conditions of existence. Louis Napoleon was, as Marx said, an *idée fixe*, and the *idées napoléoniennes* were the ideas of the undeveloped small-holding 'in the freshness of youth'. By the time Baudelaire was writing, by the time of Louis Napoleon, these ideas had become an absurdity. They were now signifiers without signifieds or, more correctly, the signifier in its 'floating relation' to the signified concept had become metaphoric. And this is not simply a question of abstract linguistics: Gramsci suggests that a primary ideological function of language is to maintain a *permanent reinscription* of certain subject positions and relations of dominance precisely through the 'naturalization' of metaphor, the fixing of hegemonic meanings (Buci-Glucksmann 1974, p. 416).

In this vital period of transition and rupture, the residues and traces of that earlier period of revolutionary activity in 1789 could no longer provide an adequate narrative. The heroic subject at the barricades in 1848 could not, as a result of the crucially changed historical situation, be constituted in the same way as that subject in 1789.

In 1851 Baudelaire published eleven poems in *Le Messager de l'Assemblée*, three of which were entitled 'Spleen'. Although all three of these were to appear in *Les Fleurs du mal*, only one of them was selected to appear with the title 'Spleen'. In the original the first line of this poem read:

> Pluviôse, irrité contre la *vie* entière

In the final version this became:

> Pluviôse, irrité contre la *ville* entière
> (my emphasis in both cases)

and that shift, that displacement of meaning, from 'life' to 'town', semantically radically different but phonemically similar, is crucial. It is crucial not just as a shift in an isolated and opaque word but as a determinate shift in utterance, in the structure of discourse. This movement marks the central period of Baudelaire's poetic production. Michel Butor has located a similar shift in Baudelaire's reading (and writing) of Poe (Butor 1969, pp. 23–98). In the eleven years which separate the essays *Notes nouvelles sur Edgar Poe* (1852) and *Le Peintre de la vie moderne* (1863), Baudelaire's interest in Poe's story *The Man of the Crowd* is displaced from a concern with external observation of the definable object of the story (*that* man in *that* crowd) to a concern with the status of the narrator himself. There is, in the second essay, an assimilation of the narratee into the narrator and vice versa. That necessary distance of *address* established in the first essay can no longer be maintained in the language of the second. The previous relation of signifier to signified has been crucially modified. The process of interpellation (the naming of individuals as subjects in discourse) has been challenged in its self-perpetuation. During these eleven years most of Baudelaire's major writings appeared. In those almost imperceptible slippages – from 'vie' to 'ville' – we can locate his most fundamental responses to the city and to the emergent social formation of which that city was symptomatic. Not just in what he depicts or describes – ragpickers, old men, old women, cats, sphinxes, etc. – but in their *inscription* is his response to emergent social relations, to a new but undefined audience, to a new relation of man to his objects (objects to their men and women) necessitated by the progressive and strategic articulation of human relations.

Voloshinov (1973) states that the reality of language is its generation and I think that we can fairly say that Baudelaire's *oeuvre* represents an overdetermined moment of such generation. Narrative declares action *and* produces it: it is not simply the epiphenomenon of a superior reality. To specify this is not a form of idealism; it is to emphasize the materiality of a pervasive component of cultural hegemony not just in terms of an 'acceptable' language but also in terms of a language which makes particular realities acceptable.[1] The generation – the engendering – of this *acceptability* is a primary function and effect of language, but if we talk, appropriately, of generation, we must specify historically the mode of generation (whose mills? whose dams?). We can turn to Marx for help here. In the foreword to 'The class struggles in France' he writes:

> What succumbed in these defeats was not the revolution. It was the pre-revolutionary traditional appendages, results of social relationships which had not yet come to the point of sharp class antagonisms – persons, illusions, conceptions, projects from which the revolutionary party before the February revolution was not yet free, from which it could be freed not *by the victory of February*, but only by a series of *defeats*.
>
> (Marx and Engels 1973, I, p. 205)

To the *bohème* to which Baudelaire partly belonged, without Marx's insight, and for whom revolution meant simply revolt, a defeat was a defeat. Baudelaire's bitter anti-democratic diatribes after the experience of 1848 were his explicit response to the situation. Historically, the defeats of June 1848 and June 1849 'cleared the stage' for the onset of decisive but fundamentally different forms of class struggle. In this overdetermined moment, characterized not so much by a clean break as by a varied dislocation of relations and the way of perceiving those relations, the traditional 'appendages' serve as a buffer against the emergent 'shocks' of the advent of the consolidation of industrial capitalism. Louis Napoleon, for example, becomes the figurehead over a struggle of sectional class interests from which, having been elected by the now economically subordinate peasantry, he was distinct. Or similarly, Baudelaire's attempt to create the aesthetic unity of subject and object at a moment when the terms in which those categories may be defined are in a state of transition. In periods of revolutionary transition and dislocation, such as the 1848 'moment', it is not just what is 'in front' of us that changes, but also our way of seeing, articulating or signifying it. It is not just that the objects change their appearance and thus appear false but also that the apparently solid and unified signifying subject is itself radically altered. The originating Cartesian *cogito* is radically challenged, although Baudelaire constantly strove to assert this *cogito* in a thrust towards what we might call *centralization*: holding back from the woman in a pre-ejaculatory fetishism in a poem like 'Les Bijoux' ('La très-chère était nue, et, connaissant mon coeur / Elle n'avait gardé que ses bijoux sonores'), or holding back from the crowd and the dissemination of his subjectivity in the persona of the *flâneur*, Baudelaire resists what Lacan has called 'the entry into difference'. He attempts to avoid the abandonment to difference, to other menacing significations. Centralization gives way to *vaporization*. The whole of the section *Tableaux parisiens* tends to work around this dialectic; the metaphors of mist and water and the 'harder' ones of crystal and steel constellate this struggle. The poet can no longer confirm his identity as subject: the return glance of the crowd or of the woman (as in 'A une passante') is no longer reassuring either as warmth or as hostility.

There are immense problems involved in introducing a terminology derived from psychoanalysis and applying it at the broad historical level, but I believe an historical poetics could do worse than to consider Lacan's assertion that 'the discourse of the unconscious is the discourse of the Other' and that the 'conscious' is therefore profoundly social and ideological, being constituted in the primary location of ideology and cultural hegemony – language. Tentatively, then, I would suggest that Baudelaire's signifying practice can be productively understood as the site of a particularly intense movement between the realm of the *Imaginary* – where subject and object maintain a comfortable pact of self-identity and plenitude (in fact this becomes *just* subjectivity since all else is an extension of that primary subject) – and the realm of the *Symbolic* – where the signifying subject is disrupted by the entry of the 'third term' of the 'Other', of 'Culture', of a language which is not simply a property to be spontaneously and creatively moulded to any shape we would like. The signifying subject is disrupted by his/her inability to fix the signifier to the signified because the signifier is constantly entering into relations of difference. In crises of cultural hegemony, where received discourses are no longer capable of sufficiently narrating the action, the entry into difference is overdetermined and particularly acute.

The erotic element of Baudelaire's poetry has been mentioned but it is important to stress that his poetic practice cannot be explained away as the 'evidence' of a lurking and constant 'id'. Against crude Freudianism, for which the sexual is *all*, we should stress in critical analysis that the sexual does not disappear, it remains a constitutive element of signifying practice, but *without any theoretical precedence*. Associated with giving precedence to the erotic is the danger of falling into a psychologism which accepts the mind as empirically given and as a founding disposition of the world. We should no more accept the *homo psychologicus*, which Freud did so much to dismantle, than we should accept the *homo oeconomicus* which Marx had shown some fifty years earlier, to be a profoundly ideological and historically specific category. But if we can now reject the primacy of those ideological subjects from a theoretical standpoint, we should acknowledge a debt at another level to Baudelaire, in whose poetry that process of dismantling was decisive. And that dismantling took place, of course, in literature, in poetry, in words, in the sign – the site of a primary ideological effect if we accept that ideology is not simply 'false consciousness' but structured in representations and miscognitions. But having rejected the theoretical primacy of the *subject* the psychoanalytic method developed by Lacan must also involve a more adequate conception of language than that suggested by the 'opaque' sign or signal. It should be considered not only in terms of its use value but also in terms of its exchange value, by which we mean that the sign – or more correctly the signifier – is neither a lens through which we can more or less clearly 'see' history nor is it a pointer indicating what is happening; it does not *depict* history, it is part of it. In poetry, where the sign is wrenched further away from its customary usage than in any other form of discourse, the complex articulation – the condensations, displacements and slippages – can tell us more about the historical matrix than any other theory which regards literature and poetry as mere epiphenomena of a superior historical reality.

In Voloshinov's terms, 'the organism and the outside world meet here in the sign.' To that we should add that the sign is not a 'raw material' available to the poet and created by him, but that it is 'always-already-given', loaded with the residues and traces of previous periods and conceptions. We have already noted that the *flâneur* contained a residual Romantic solipsism as well as the newly forming narrator/narratee of modernism. We can also see how, through the development of *Les Fleurs du mal*, Baudelaire's stance as persona/hero in his poems shifts from the crude solipsism of the earlier poems through to a major poem like 'Correspondances', in which the poet is back down among the 'forêts de symboles' where the glance of the persona, unlike that of the solipsist, is not returned either in hostility or in friendship: it is refracted via an unknown medium of half-suggested meanings mingled with confused sense impressions of perfumes, colours and sounds. Traces of past meanings and suggestions of future ones are held in a pervasive sense- and subject-distorting structure which, in the last (unusual) coupling of 'l'esprit et des sens' marks a crucial departure from earlier Romantic preoccupations with 'feelings' alone and carves out a narrative path for Arthur Rimbaud's desire for a 'systematic derangement of all the senses'.

I have already mentioned Baudelaire's attempt to forge an impossible unity in his critical essays – his assertive combination of the subjective and the objective in all art. This is consistent with his bringing together of the 'transient' and the 'eternal' in coming to terms with a modernism which must paradoxically involve, as Benjamin has written, a close relation with conceptions of antiquity: 'Modernity designates an epoch and it also denotes the energies which are at work in this epoch to bring it close to antiquity' (Benjamin 1973, p. 81). The function of antiquity and distance in the poetry is central: they are what Freud called (and Benjamin recalled) 'the other scene', to which traces found (read) in objects – the woman's hair, the perfume bottle, the rotting carcass – refer. And if, as Freud says, consciousness comes into being at the site of a memory trace, then Baudelaire's consciousness in his poetic practice is characterized by a constant shifting and displacement of meanings and images. Moving between desire and satisfaction (not just in personal terms but in a language which is eminently *social*), between presence and absence, between *Spleen* and *Idéal*, Baudelaire is constantly forced into a void which, in his most successful poems, is apparently the past of half-remembered experiences and impressions, topographically and temporally distinct, but which, in fact, *inscribe* in their distance and movement the future of new significations. Throughout *Les Fleurs du mal* the shifts in subject positions and the 'hierarchy of the hero'[2] are the testament to a real drama in language and narrative.

Ruptural crises in ideology produce in language, the site of its primary effect, a crisis of linearity. The paradigmatic, the associative, the metaphoric, become dominant over the syntagmatic, the denotative pole of language. This is not a question of one assuming absolute precedence over the other; but it tends, rather, to take the form of relations of dominance and of overdetermination. Word associations, whose realm of possibility and acceptability is structured by the processes of condensation and displacement operative in any ideological discourse, are no longer so clearly definable. If the signifier is no longer able to define what is 'out there' in front of it, if it can no longer 'point' at something, expecting the object to arrive where it is named but finding that the name enters into other relations, then it turns to other gestures such as the dance and the incantation. The major figures of post-Baudelairean aesthetics, Stéphane Mallarmé and Paul Valéry, were preoccupied with such gestures.

What we have to examine in the case of a poet like Baudelaire is not the isolated fact that his images are of distant isles, of the past, etc. We have to specify the simple fact that these images are *written*; that they are not just a matter of 'dream' but rather the 'dreamwork' – the *determinate recounting* in language of those images. The dreamwork is an eminently social act and the motifs and images which appear in Baudelaire's poetry are not important because they are 'adjacent' to certain historical facts – wine and the wine tax for example – but because they are *inscribed* in the constitutive discourses of the ideologies of the period. To talk of the isolated 'facts' with no concept of the way in which they are displaced, condensed, made acceptable and so on, is at best an abstract procedure, at worst pure reductionism. Any recounting by the individual in society and in language is overdetermined by residues and traces already in the language which structure the discursive realm of possibility. Our proper concern should be therefore with *this* recounting and with *these* memory traces and with the primary fact that this whole process operates within language which in its process of generation is not characterized either by a mechanical evolution or by a direct and repressive structure of dominance, but by an over- and underdetermined discursive hegemony.

We can begin to understand, then, what Baudelaire means in 'Correspondances' when he writes 'Ayant l'expansion des choses infinies', and indeed what that expansion of 'things' and their meanings meant in terms of the '1848' period. This period marks the transition from a predominantly rural economy and the beginning of the process of consolidation of large-scale industrial capitalism. There is a marked shift from the artisanal mode of production where, in broad terms, man accompanies his made object to the market place and there exchanges it for something he needs, to a mode of production where man not only does not accompany his object but frequently enough does not even see it. It would be reductive to say that this simple physical fact altered consciousness; it is, rather, symptomatic of a whole ensemble of changes necessitated by the period-changes which can be *read* discursively. One of these changes was in the make-up of the crowd. We have already stated, in order to avoid historicism, that Baudelaire and the crowd did not accompany each other on to the historical stage. We should now add that the crowd had changed its social complexion during the 1848 period, for if in the revolutions between 1789 and 1848 there was a distinctive mixture of peasant, petit-bourgeois, bourgeois republican, Jacobin and workshop-master, the revolution of 1848 had strange new elements. The beginnings of modern industry and the necessary emergence of a proletariat to serve that industry, plus the erratic emergence of socialist ideas, gave *this* crowd a decidedly new and menacing aspect. The crowd, though still to a large extent dominated by bourgeois or pre-industrial ideology, now had autonomous workers' organizations with their own banners in its midst. And if it was largely the same occupational groups in the 1848 revolution as in the previous ones, then we should note that now the agitation no longer came from the workshop-masters, but from the workers themselves. And if the centres of revolutionary activity were previously those faubourgs where the artisanal mode of production was dominant (Rudé 1964), then we should now add the contribution of the railway workers and engineers from the north of Paris. Both Marx and de Tocqueville were quick to realize that this meant the emergence of the scenario for a decisive class struggle, and if at first the state was to insist on using overt and heavy-handed methods of coercion and repression against the workers' movement, it was gradually becoming clearer that such overt actions were less and less necessary as encroaching bourgeois hegemony began to be established at all levels and in all apparatuses, including the literary, and as it began in complex and pervasive ways to *subject* its subjects.

When talking of the progressive societalization of human relations in this era Adorno comes very close to what could be described as a concept of hegemony and the 'subjective moment' within it. He writes that this gradual process did not:

> simply confront the mind from without; it immigrated into its immanent consistency. It imposes itself as relentlessly on the autonomous mind as heteronomous orders were formerly imposed on the mind which was bound. Not only does the mind mould itself for the sake of its marketability and thus reproduce the socially prevalent categories. It also grows to resemble ever more closely the status quo even where it subjectively refrains from making a commodity of itself.
>
> (Adorno 1967, p. 21)

With reservations about some of the idealist 'traces' in that language, I think it is useful to accept the central tenet that the individual consciousness has less room for evasion under the hegemony required by industrial capitalism than it had under the more directly coercive state prior to the 1848 period.

Baudelaire stands at the primary stages of this increasing hegemonization. His attempt to grasp a receding concreteness in a poem like 'Harmonie du soir', which vibrates in a strongly associative paradigmatic structure of emphatic rhyme, assonance and repetition, is a significant response to this undefinable encroachment:

> Voici venir le temps où vibrant sur sa tige
> Chaque fleur s'évapore ainsi qu'un encensoir;
> Les sons et les parfums tournent dans l'air du soir;
> Valse mélancolique et langoureux vertige!
>
> Chaque fleur s'évapore ainsi qu'un encensoir;
> Le violon frémit comme un coeur qu'on afflige;
> Valse mélancolique et langoureux vertige!
> Le ciel est triste et beau comme un grand reposoir.

This gestural incantation prefigures Mallarmé's 'presque disparition vibratoire' in its 'vaporization' and turning away from a world in which the syntagmatic action of pointing at 'reality' is undermined by the disintegration of a discursive framework within which the pointing subject constituted him/herself.

In the dialectical images *written* by Baudelaire – images which are not a 'content' of a generalized consciousness of the time but rather a 'constellation' of it, we can read the momentary presence of what Althusser has called the 'informed gaze' – the moment of presence of a determinate absence that subverts the subtle and pervasive structures of a censorship which is hegemonic in its narrative. Baudelaire's poetic practice denies the flow of the 'stream' between the 'well laid-out slopes' and enables us to read the 'landscape' of 1848 not in easy relation of sign to referent, but in a *signifying practice* whose thrust and recoil *inscribe* the 'moment' of transition.

If I have stressed the materiality and centrality of *writing* in this paper, it is because, by repetition, I wanted to give some theoretical precedence to this practice in language and to stress that any materialist analysis of literary production must acknowledge this precedence in place of the spatial and optical metaphors which can lead to phenomenological and positivistic reductions of literature either as subjective products or historical epiphenomena. To concentrate on the writing and the language of a poet like Baudelaire can help us avoid such reductionism but, more importantly, it can suggest to us that those 'peripheral' aspects of class struggles may be more important than we imagined. We may, as Adorno reminds us, have been looking for too long at what we understood to be the 'centre' of that dialectic at the expense of those 'obvious' practices like language and writing which have been made theoretically marginal. If the concept of hegemony is to mean anything more than a simple class dominance, then we need to look at all those subtle, pervasive, spontaneous and 'obvious' practices which we have not normally associated with the 'real' class struggle. The *mis-cognition* of such primary obviousnesses is the function of any ideology. I believe that we can go some way to correcting this if we remember, with Gramsci, the very simple fact that 'Language also means culture and philosophy' (Gramsci 1973, p. 349; and cf. Gramsci 1985).

Notes

1 For the theory behind this argument see Faye 1972 and 1973; and for the connections with Gramsci see Mercer 1979, and Lo Piparo 1979.
2 This concept is taken from an essay by Voloshinov entitled 'Discourse in life and discourse in art (concerning sociological poetics)' (Voloshinov 1976).

3
Religion and ideology: a political reading of *Paradise Lost*

FREDRIC JAMESON

Nothing is more appropriate, in the second year of the Iranian Revolution and the first of the Islamic Republic, than a return to 1642 and a meditation on the work of the greatest English political poet. The renewed vitality of a religious politics – and in particular the will to abolish the split between the public and the private, between state and church – can be expected to impose new ways of reading Milton; while the theological coding of the first great bourgeois revolution in the west – an experience which may be called a properly English cultural revolution – ought to place the Iranian situation in a more comprehensible, or at least less alien, light. It should at any rate be clear that Marxists can no longer afford the luxury of assigning the problem of religion to the ashcan of history. An impulse that turned out the largest urban demonstrations ever recorded in the history of the human race (Halliday 1979, p. 90), and that overturned a regime that was the model and showcase for high technological repression in the Third World, certainly has something to teach us about how theory 'grips the masses'. Nor should the vital role played by radical religion in the American anti-war movement of the 1960s be forgotten, nor the crucial and strategic one currently being played by the theology of liberation in revolutionary struggles in Central and South America.

I would not want to be understood as claiming that religion is not also often reactionary: indeed, I am afraid that at a certain moment in the revolutionary process it must always become that, and Milton will be no exception, as we shall see. Nor am I suggesting even a primary role for religion in the initiation of revolutions: indeed, it would be the worst kind of historical error, and an affront to the dead, to attribute to the Iranian mullahs a revolution which was in fact begun by armed left guerrillas in winter 1971, and in which the left played a major role (Abrahamian 1980, p. 3).

What I would like to do in the following remarks is twofold: to make at least a beginning in the historically actual and indispensable task of understanding the relations between religion and politics; and to do this by way of a more specifically literary or interpretive problem, namely that of proposing a political reading of *Paradise Lost*, or better still, of deconcealing the political content of *Paradise Lost*. The difficulties of this second project should not be underestimated: not merely must such an interpretation impose itself as unavoidable, so that anti-political readers and interpreters are forced to waste precious energies in conjuring it away; it must also open up a perspective on something like a line-by-line or paragraph-by-paragraph rereading or rewriting of the poem.

This means that the political focus generally proposed for Milton is insufficient: to be sure, in a general way, there is no great problem in understanding the relationship between the global impulse of *Paradise Lost* and the political situation itself: the moment of the failure of revolution, the dissipation of the revolutionary ethos, the reappearance of the old institutions and business as usual (or in other words, in the language of the time, of sin). And one can well imagine that the disintegration of a successful revolution, its ignominious bottoming out in restoration, is a more bitterly disillusioning experience than the triumph of counter-revolution in bloody repression, as in June 1848 or in Chile. Arguably, the English Revolution also knew its June 1848: Christopher Hill fixes it in the Battle of Burford in May 1649, when the Levellers in the army are definitively crushed (Hill 1975, pp. 345, 360). Still, the stronger analogy would probably be the sense of frustration and bitterness, the self-criticisms and guilty introspection, the fatigue and depoliticization, that followed May 1968. This inward turn – a displacement from politics to psychology and ethics – is marked not merely by the revival of the Calvinist meditation on original sin and the Fall, but very explicitly by the emphasis on personal, private salvation and the repudiation of millenarianism in *Paradise Regained* and the last two books of *Paradise Lost*.

All this strikes me as self-evident, as I have said, but at best it offers us a perspective in which we are tempted to substitute those old slogans of optimism or pessimism for some concrete reading of the text. In that sense, one cannot even propose an analysis of *Paradise Lost* in the tradition of the repentant ex- or post-revolutionary narrative, such as Mary Shelley's *Frankenstein*, which explicitly frames an allegory of Jacobin hybris and the dangers of summoning up that very Adamic and Miltonic monster, the mob or the people. The political allegory of *Frankenstein*, however, is constructed within the now individualistic categories of the essentially expressive literature of the new bourgeois subject: it may well be possible to read *Samson Agonistes* in this fashion, but *Paradise Lost* is not yet a narrative of that later type, as we shall see, and is unavailable or inaccessible to this kind of expressive or allegorical reading.

I propose that we retrace our steps, and begin again with the seemingly more abstract problem of religion. But first an initial qualification: if you believe in the theory of modes of production, that is, if you are committed to the idea that capitalism is a qualitatively and structurally distinct type of social formation from the various other kinds that have preceded it upon the earth, then you will want to make room for the possibility that religion in its strong form in pre-capitalist societies is functionally and substantively distinct from what it is today, which is to say a mere private hobby and one ideological subcode among many others. In a pre-secular and pre-scientific world, one in which commerce is itself a limited and interstitial phenomenon, religion is the cultural dominant; it is the mastercode in which issues are conceived and debated; it is then – religion, the sacred, the centred body of the despot, the centred space of the Forbidden City and the four cardinal points – the form taken by ideology in pre-capitalist societies, except that since ideology is a modern term and a modern phenomenon, there is something anachronistic and misleading about putting it this way.

But perhaps this point should also be made in existential terms. We are accustomed, whatever our positions on the matter, to think of religion in terms of belief. But belief is a very privatized and subjective phenomenon. Rodney Needham once wrote an interesting little book (1972) to show that the category of belief, as used by anthropologists in relationship to so-called primitive or culturally alien societies, was itself a category of Otherness: belief is always what somebody else 'believes', it is that peculiar and superstitious, quite incomprehensible thing that takes place inside an alien head. In our own society it seems clear that belief in this privatized sense is an accompaniment of social fragmentation and atomization, of *anomie*, of the construction of equivalent monads within the market system, each one of which is endowed with freedom to sell its labour power. Belief in that sense is thus a by-product of that very dissolution and destruction of the older organic social groups of which religion, in the older strong sense, was precisely the organizing ideology and the cement. So we will find ourselves pursuing a mirage if we conceive of an earlier religious position, an object of theological debate, such as Milton's Arianism, in terms of a belief, a ghost in the machine, with which you could expect to empathize, much as you feel your way back into Proust's notion of temporality from the inside, or come at least to a suspension of disbelief about Yeats's 'vision'.

To conceive of a social formation for which subjectivity in this modern sense does not exist means, however, to attempt to grasp religion not as a private language or a unique incommunicable form of consciousness, but rather as the sign of group praxis and group membership, as a badge of collective adherence, as something like a set of pseudo-concepts whose concrete function is to organize this or that form of communal relationship and structure. I am sorry to say so, but I am afraid that here we still must come to terms with Durkheim's fundamental insight (in *The Elementary Forms of Religious Life*) into religion as the privileged mode in which a pre-capitalist collectivity comes to consciousness of itself and affirms its unity as a group. What follows, however, is a consequence that Durkheim did not draw, namely that religious and theological debate is the form, in pre-capitalist societies, in which groups become aware of their political differences and fight them out.

So we must learn to read theological discourse and discursive productions related to it, such as Milton's Christian epic, in terms of class struggle. But now I want to go further than this, and to draw another, perhaps more scandalous or at least paradoxical consequence from this view of religion: namely that if it is the master-code of pre-capitalist society, we ought to be able to read its major themes as mystified or distorted anticipations of secular and even scientific preoccupations which are ours today. Indeed, I want to see whether one can make a case for reading the terms and conceptual categories of Calvinism and heroic, militant protestantism and distorted anticipations of the dialectic itself.

Such a thesis would be the reverse of Norman Cohn's notorious conclusion to *The Pursuit of the Millenium* when, speaking of the radical movements of the 1960s, he observes, 'The old religious idiom has been replaced by a secular one, and this tends to obscure what otherwise would be obvious. For it is the simple truth that, stripped of their original supernatural sanction, revolutionary millenarianism and mystical anarchism are still with us' (Cohn 1970, p. 286). Cohn's operation here is to reduce the struggles and values of living people to so many forms of that culturally and psychologically pathological impulse his book purports to document: his strategy is thus ultimately of a piece with the old argument – generally produced as the final nail in the coffin – that Marxism is essentially just a religion.

But this is a two-edged sword, whose thrust it is important to reverse. To disclose the materialist and political kernel within the mystified forms of a protestant theology is surely to affirm our solidarity with the heroic and militant struggles of the past. These dead belong to us, as Ernst Bloch taught us about Thomas Münzer, as Christopher Hill and others have shown us about the Diggers and the Ranters. Indeed, if Bloch sought to convey one thing throughout his long career, it was that socialism and political action today will be a poor and impoverished thing if it is unwilling to affirm its deeper kinship with millenarianism, with radical Utopianism, with what Norman Cohn describes contemptuously as those 'fantasies of a final, exterminatory struggle against "the great ones" and of a perfect world from which self-seeking would be forever banished' (Cohn 1970, p. 286).

On the other hand, let us remember that we have spoken of *distorted* anticipations of historical materialism; and I stress this now to distance the approach I have in mind from the rather facile way in which a Lucien Goldmann found traces and anticipations of the dialectic in all the great writers and thinkers in history. Religion is not a cognitive but a figural mode, and any attempt to reappropriate it must include a meditation on the nature of figuration itself. 'Through a glass darkly', allegory, types, figures, iconoclasm, the letter rather than the spirit – all these expressions alert us to the essential ambiguity of a plane of expression that risks fixing the mind in external trappings, thereby generating the institutional necessity of a priesthood, of the guardians of interpretation, with their monopoly of meaning and exegesis, who alone have the right to tell us what a given figure really means. That radical protestantism, however, was only too keenly aware of the dialectic of figuration it is perhaps superfluous to observe.

Figuration – the ambiguous situation in which a figural *expression* of a cognitive truth is still little more than a picture-thought or hieroglyphic degradation of that same truth – is thus the source of the limits and distortions which the religious or theological master-code imposes on its political content. Yet we must add that the political strength of religion is also intimately related to this very ambiguity. Max Weber thought of the charismatic and militant moment of heroic protestantism as something like a vanishing mediator between the older tra-ditional societies in the process of ruthless disintegration, and the newer secular or desacralized world of capitalism and the market system. This mediatory role is enabled by figuration, on the one hand, in which an unstable suppression of the gap between base and superstructure becomes possible, as well as by the diachronic situation of the moment of radical religion, in which an older hegemonic theological code can provisionally be appropriated for an expression of far-reaching new social possi-bilities, like new wine poured in old bottles. The instability of this moment of religious activism is, of course, over and over dramatized by its cooling off into the apolitical quietism of movements like that of Quakerism. Yet this is the price paid for the momentary and transitional power of a religious figural politics to 'grip the masses' and to produce a vision in which praxis and social analysis, the possible future and the structure of the present conjuncture, lived experience and the class structure, are not yet disjoined.

But we have not yet specified the essential, namely how the religious categories of Calvinism can be said to overlap in any way with those of Marxism. Providence – as the absolute foreknowledge of history – is the most obvious place to begin, with its twin certainties of the secret justification of the most senseless events (generally those involving wanton or gratuitous human suffering) and of teleology. We are today, I think, much more keenly aware of everything that is unsatisfactory in the religious or providential attempt to justify the ways of God to men, than we are of what we must still share in this general view of history, and tend to be surprised when the more aggressive Christians continue to claim history as their own particular invention. We are, for one thing, deeply marked by the existential view of suffering, which Dostoyevsky dramatized in his cry that an eternity of bliss could never redeem an instant of suffering and pain inflicted on a small child. Nor does anyone today feel very comfortable with the old idea that suffering ennobles and is ultimately good for you. Yet the theologians were themselves keenly aware of such contradictions, which were registered virtually from the beginnings of Christian theory in the problem of whether God himself can be said to have willed evil.

Milton seems to have solved this problem to his own intellectual satisfaction in a disarming way: by separating God's will from God's foreknowledge. Knowing how a thing is going to turn out is quite a different matter from wanting it to turn out that way; God knows in advance what Adam will decide, what Eve will do, but that does not mean he likes it, nor does it mean that they were not free to do otherwise. Three observations need to be made about this solution, and the first has to do with the relations between freedom, temporal perspective and explanation. We do not seem to have any great difficulty in reconciling the two temporal perspectives on an act: the freedom of choice that precedes it, and the possibility of explanation that now weighs the completed act (including the reasons and the freedom of choice that went into its execution). Yet perhaps that is only because we do not pose the problem sharply enough, to the point where it becomes revealed as an antimony, as an unthinkable paradox or aporia. Consider, for instance, Gide's little fable, *Lafcadio's Adventures*, which is about a man exasperated by the humiliation of having his acts judged and explained, most immediately by the behaviourists and the positivists, who see everything you do as being determined, but more generally in any kind of character judgement, in which other people say, Well of course he would have done that: he's that kind of person (spiteful, generous, indecisive, etc. – all judgements which reify you by making your character into a kind of determinism in its own right). So Lafcadio, in order to evade this reifying judgement and to remain free, invents a new kind of ethics, that of the famous gratuitous act or *acte gratuit*, the act that absolutely evades all *ex post facto* explanation. In the final irony of the novel, a stray button provides evidence that the murder which Lafcadio designed to embody this absolute gratuitousness is on the contrary susceptible of the most banal explanation and motivation possible, namely that of simple jealousy. Meanwhile, in the later Sartrean versions of this dilemma, the screw is given yet another turn by a final reifying judgement by other people: if such and such does this gratuitous and absolutely unmotivated thing, then the reason is obvious: it is to keep us guessing; in fact, it is quite in character and quite motivated, since the person in question is very precisely defined as *capricious*. These ethical fables serve to suggest that there may be something absolutely incommensurable between the temporal perspective of action, the choice and the project; and that of explanation, of meaning, of inevitability.

My other two observations will be briefer: on the one hand, it is clear that even Milton's category of foreknowledge still presupposes the organizational framework of an individual subject. We will return to this point in a moment. And the other point is related to this one, but is too complex for me to develop here at any length: it is this, that the ethical categories, the ethical binaries of good and evil, to which the Providential vision is irredeemably shackled, are to my mind the ultimate form of ideological closure, far more damaging and influential in the long run than either metaphysics or idealism, which have traditionally been the ways in which ideological false consciousness has been characterized. Nietzsche taught us, however, not merely that ethics is absolutely a projection of the positioning of the individual subject (what's good is what's related to my self, to the centre; what's evil is what is other, eccentric, marginalized), but also that all genuine historical and political thought must somehow do the impossible and invent an intellectual space for itself 'beyond good and evil', that is to say, beyond the categories of ethics.

Now I will say that, with these qualifications, the idea of Providence is the distorted anticipation, within the religious and figural master-code, of the idea of historical necessity in historical materialism. Yet this idea is fully as widely misconstrued and misunderstood as the other, and demands some explanation in its own right. The doctrine of historical inevitability is not, as Popper thought, a 'belief' of any kind, and certainly not a belief in the predictability of future events: to put it another way, it is not a teleology and has nothing to do with an eschatological certainty about the end of history. The function of this concept is a far more disappointingly modest and descriptive one, which we may characterize by saying the notion of historical inevitability or historical necessity is simply the enabling presupposition of the historian herself, and governs the form with which historiography endows the events of the past, the things that have already happened once and for all. The concept of historical necessity is simply the assumption that things happened the way they did because they had to happen that way and no other, and that the business of the historian is to show why they had to happen that way. If you like, then, this is a pseudo-idea: it could have real meaning only if you were able somehow to repeat the past or replay the tape under controlled experimental or laboratory conditions. But of course the latter are themselves a fiction – the enabling presupposition of the natural sciences – and even this counter-factual alternative is therefore incoherent and rigorously meaningless. It may thus be preferable to describe the pseudo-idea of historical necessity or inevitability as something like a meaning-effect, as the neo-Aristotelians might say, produced by great historiography, the generic satisfaction achieved by historical discourse as a form when it restructures the empirical randomness and chronicle-like sequence of apparently atomic facts, learned by rote out of history manuals, into a sequence that suddenly strikes us as being rigorous and inevitable. But those words are merely synonyms for meaningful; and vice versa: when we talk about meaning in history, we mean little more than inevitability and necessity.

But of course the problem with this secular version of historical necessity is the same problem – that of action – that arises with its religious variant: namely, what happens to human activity when people come to 'believe in' ideas like Providence or historical necessity. This is for one thing the dilemma of predestination: if God knows from all eternity that I am one of the elect, does that mean I can do anything I want to, no matter how unimaginably sinful? This is for another the dilemma of the antithesis between voluntarism and fatalism: if history is inevitable, if revolution depends on the ripening of objective conditions, then my own political praxis or lack of it would not seem to have much bearing on things.

But the Calvinist and the Leninist solutions to these dilemmas are perfectly sensible, provided you understand how profoundly Hegelian both of them are. For Hegel's is the only consequent way of formulating the problem, and for better or for worse we have got no further than his slogan: the owl of Minerva flies at dusk, historical necessity is visible only after the fact, the historical understanding – what Hegel calls Absolute Spirit – is only called into play on the Sunday of life, after action and praxis are over, when history for however brief a moment has come to a stop. Hegel's 'solution' is thus a thoroughgoing double standard, in which the past is necessary and its chain of events as inevitable as in any Providential scheme, but where this understanding of necessity has nothing whatsoever to do with the possibilities of action in the present. The Kairos is then Lenin in April: you cannot know whether a thing was possible until it is tried; only after the fact does it transpire that what finally happened had to happen that way and no other.

All of which – these anticipatory relationships between Marxism's notion of historical inevitability and providential religion – may be taken as a gloss and commentary on Walter

Benjamin's enigmatic opening image, in the *Theses on the Philosophy of History*, of the chess-playing automaton with the dwarf hidden inside it to guide its moves: 'The puppet called "historical materialism" is to win all the time. It can easily be a match for anyone if it enlists the services of theology, which today, as we know, is wizened and has to keep out of sight' (Benjamin 1968, p. 253). The paradox here evidently turns on the sense of the expression 'to win'. Meanwhile, the Hegelian and retrospective character of historical knowledge is underscored in another image from this same text, perhaps the most famous of all, on Klee's Angelus Novus:

> His face is turned toward the past. Where we perceive a chain of events, he sees one single catastrophe which keeps piling wreckage upon wreckage and hurls it in front of his feet. The angel would like to say, awaken the dead, and make whole what has been smashed. But a storm is blowing from Paradise; it has caught in his wings with such violence that the angel can no longer close them. This storm irresistibly propels him into the future to which his back is turned, while the pile of debris before him grows skyward. This storm is what we call progress.
>
> (Benjamin 1968, pp. 257–8)

Such an image may serve to demonstrate a final proposition about the Hegelian/Marxist notion of historical inevitability which is perhaps less widely understood than anything else; namely that it is not a teleology (unless one could conceive of a teleology after the fact). Nobody today surely believes that anything is inevitable in that teleological sense, certainly not socialism or world revolution. This angel, or Absolute Spirit, cannot look over its shoulder into the future.

It is perhaps fitting to dramatize the paradoxes and the antinomies of such historical concepts by way of Benjamin's images: for this process brings us back to the second feature of our discussion of religion, namely the figural character of the theological master-code and the relationship between the latter's structural limits and cognitive distortions and the process of figuration itself, a term I happen to prefer to the current one of representation which is, I suppose, a general synonym for it. We have begun to suggest that it is in the precognitive aspects of the theological code, and the requirement for its contents to be expressed in essentially narrative categories, that the ultimate structural limits and distortions of the political consciousness of a religious and precapitalist period are to be sought. When we turn to the artistic and cultural expressions of such religious impulses, however, we confront the figural mode again, as it were to the second power. Is it possible that this second-degree process of figural articulation – the process of cultural production generally – may do more than simply replicate the first; indeed, that it may in some central way serve to foreground and to bring out the contradictions and structural limits of its primary theological raw material?

This is at least the theory proposed by Louis Althusser in his *Letter on Art* and methodologically developed by Pierre Macherey in *A Theory of Literary Production*: which it will now be useful to test against the case of Milton. The idea is that the act of figuration or representation does not merely illustrate, exemplify or replicate its ideological – we may even say its ideational – content; rather, it decisively transforms the latter, so that what looked initially like an idea or a concept when taken in its purely ideological form (Macherey's central example is Jules Verne's 'idea' of progress) is unmasked as ideology when the artist attempts to give it full representation. The ideological, all the while claiming to project a coherent vision, is always contradictory, always structurally incoherent and ultimately unsusceptible of formal intelligibility. Thus, when ideology is taken at its word and endowed with the beginnings of a visionary, figural or representational form, the impossibility of that representation and the essential incoherence of the ideology itself becomes foregrounded and visible in its own right. This is indeed the very vocation of culture itself for Althusser and Macherey: not to transmit ideology, but rather to make ideology visible as an object, to demystify the ideological, not through conceptual analysis, but through the process of its production as figure and representation. Whatever the absolute value of this theory as a transhistorical description of culture generally, it would certainly seem to have some relevance for a text which explicitly sets out to celebrate, dramatize and justify a preexisting ideology, namely that of Providence.

We should add, however, for those who may be uneasy about

the projection of such sophisticated post-contemporary methods into the pre-capitalist past, that something analogous is surely known to the text itself; for the militant protestants and radical reformers, indeed, representation is fully as suspect a process as it is for the *Tel quel* group or the Judaic and Islamic traditions. Still, the demands of representation and the epic require Milton to render God anthropomorphically as a character; or, in other words, in our previous terminology, to articulate Providence and the whole theme of foreknowledge of the historical totality within the confines of the individual subject, thus turning history back into a representation offered to that supreme individual consciousness, God; much as, quite against the spirit of his own system, the demands of Hegelian representation end up forcing the latter towards that weaker anthropomorphic personification which is Absolute Spirit.

Parts of *De Doctrina* document Milton's sense of the way in which anthropomorphic representation distorts and reifies the theologial content of the notions of God and Providence, which we have identified with history; but his Arianism will let us make this point in a more tangible way, and in the process illustrate what was meant earlier by the proposition that such theological issues are not matters of personal 'belief' but rather something quite different. In this case, I will suggest that Milton's Arianism – the repudiation of the Trinity and the emphasis on the created, secondary nature of Christ – is less a matter of opinion, heretical or not, but rather first and foremost a result of the requirements and dialectic of figuration. Milton senses that in endowing the place of historical necessity with something like an individual subjectivity, an anthropomorphic appearance, some fundamental ideological incoherence is betrayed: thus, the radical dissociation of the figure of Christ from God, the insistence on Christ's proper status as an *actant*, a narrative character – as distinct from this other seeming 'character' who is really not one at all, or should not be one – becomes an attempt to recontain the contradiction, to limit the ravages of demystification released by the representation process.

This reading now allows us to reformulate the positions of William Empson's splendid and passionate book, *Milton's God*, in a more theoretically adequate way. Leaving aside Empson's admirable eighteenth-century Enlightenment hatred of religion and superstition – which, as I observed initially, is probably not the most productive position for people on the left to take today – what is unsatisfactory about *Milton's God* is the retention of a framework in which the organizing perspective remains the biographical Milton, as author and individual subject, with his opinions, flaws, weaknesses and strengths, and the like. Surely Empson's detailed account of the tricks and strategems whereby Milton's God arranges both for Satan and for his human creations to fall, in order to fulfil his original plan; as well as his characterization of the human and sacrificial bloodthirstiness of the deity – these things are quite unanswerable: only we would now prefer to take them, less as testimony about Milton's theological beliefs, than as a demonstration of the way in which the requirement to give anthropomorphic figuration to the ideology of Providence ends up denouncing itself, and undermining the very ideology it set out to embody. Yet this is an objective and impersonal, what today would be called a textual, process: by a kind of ruse of reason, Milton's symbolic act is alienated from itself, turns against itself, ends up producing the opposite of what it originally intended. But if this is an accurate description of what happens to ideology in the text, then it may well be a source of embarrassment to the older strategies for political interpretation, whose aim was to enlist the great writer on your side as an individual subject, and to stress the progressive or humanistic characteristics of Shakespeare, Balzac, and most recently of Milton himself, in Christopher Hill's great biography.

On the other hand, it must be admitted that the comments we have made so far on Milton's ideology are not yet terribly political either. Perhaps turning our attention from God to Satan will help us make some further progress along these lines. On the face of it, indeed, it would seem *a priori* quite unavoidable, in the revolutionary situation in which Milton wrote, for Satan's rebellion against God not to give off at least faint overtones of the great Rebellion itself, of the militant revolt against a king by divine right; and this, even if we exclude that other predictable psychological reaction which would involve collective guilt and trauma at that historically unique act which is the public execution of a monarch.

Oddly enough, none of this seems to be present in the text, and the current view of Satan as a great feudal baron seems to stand up well to careful reading: the revolt of a peer has in fact little enough in common with the dynamics of middle-class revolution but a great deal with the convulsions of medieval feudalism or with that anachronistic contemporary event, the Fronde. Thus, the War in Heaven, the prehistory of the Creation before Eden, oddly inscribes a peculiar and anachronistic diachrony within the first great monument of bourgeois literature – a reminiscence of the distant feudal past that would seem to have little enough relevance to the war aims of the New Model Army or the visions of the radical reformation.

Still, I think we can locate the place in which the contemporary reference is repressed: and its structural absence, the irritatingly protestant self-righteousness and complacency of that repression, is not unrelated to the figure of Satan, yet in a rather different way than we might have expected. Milton's party need feel no guilt about the revolt against the king for a simple reason, that he is not really a king at all, but something quite different, namely a tyrant: and the latter is defined as himself being a rebel against God's law. Thus, not the regicides, but the king himself is the rebel, occupies the place of Satan: the thrust of the accusation is structurally reversed – I banish you! you are the only guilty party here!

But note that the structural displacement achieved by the political unconscious at this crucial point succeeds in eliding something significant: there is henceforth, in this particular narrative apparatus, no longer any place for the army of the saints themselves, for that particular emergent subject of history which is the very protagonist of the bourgeois revolution. There are now two separate strategies for overcoming the tyrant, for triumphing over Satan-Charles, but neither makes a place for a collective actor, and only the first is properly political at all. That is of course secured by God himself before the creation of humankind: and the fall of Satan-Charles – the end of the feudal age – with that archaic reminiscence of feudal warfare on which we have already commented – thus comes before us less as class praxis than as what we might today call a systemic transformation, a break between two modes of production, a virtually structural *coupure*: one should perhaps summon up a little of E. P. Thompson's indignation with Althusserean structural history in order to deplore this elision of collective praxis and action from the Miltonic narrative.

As for the second method of routing Satan – of exorcizing what Winstanley will call 'kingly power', the sinfulness on which tyranny breeds – that belongs of course to the quietistic and anti-political turn of the post-revolutionary period, to the business of a merely personal and private salvation. 'Dream not of their fight / As of a duel' (XII, 386–7) Michael warns Adam about the struggle between Christ and Satan in the course of purely earthly history: millenarianism is over and bankrupt; after the end of ideology and the end of Utopia, all political, properly revolutionary aims are suspect – and the last two books of *Paradise Lost* open up that privatized and post-political world, to whose disillusionments the mediocrity of *Paradise Regained* is immediately attributable, with its characteristic failure of hope following upon the failure of revolution, as most recently in the aftermath of May 1968.

Still, in between these two moments we have the Garden, and here, if anywhere surely, the political content of *Paradise Lost* is to be sought. It is no secret, if still mildly paradoxical and unaccountable in a Puritan writer, that Milton is the great poet of sex of the English language. We may today reread with a certain piety, if not contempt, T.S. Eliot's once influential remarks about the Miltonic 'Garden of Eden, where I for one can get pleasure from the verse only by the deliberate effort not to visualize Adam and Eve in their surroundings' (Eliot 1966, p. 16): an effort, one would have thought, a good deal more Puritanical than anything in Milton himself. Still, the ideological signal emitted by this prelapsarian Eden is structurally and strategically ambiguous. That great estrangement effect, which by the unimaginable fiction of emergence

> As new awaked from soundest sleep
> Soft on the flowery herb I found me laid
> In balmy sweat
>
> (VIII, 253–5)

causes us to perceive the now fallen world again as for the first time, transfigured – this estrangement effect will also serve to reinforce the very opposite of a revolutionary and millenarian materialism, and will at one and the same time be evoked to document the classic anti-millenarian position that goes back to Saint Augustine, where it is very precisely the fact of the Garden and the fact of the Fall that preclude the re-establishment on Earth of paradise in anything but an internal, allegorical sense. The vision of the Garden of Eden thus in one of the classic semiotic functions of ideology emits two distinct and contradictory messages all at once: that a carnal heaven on earth is imaginable and thus to be sought for here and now by means which in Milton's time have become irredeemably political ones (the Hussites, the Anabaptists, the Diggers), but also that it is impossible in this life and that only renunciation, personal repentance and self-discipline remain for us.

Yet there is another aspect of the representation of Adam that has, if not political, then at least historical resonance in another sense and that deserves brief attention. We have shown how the moment of feudalism is inscribed in this text; but we have not yet determined whether the latter is open enough to history in some way to register the momentous systematic transformation with which Milton's own society is convulsed; and if so, how and in what fashion this diachronic Novum is seismographically recorded. For myself, I cannot help feeling that nothing in *Paradise Lost* is quite so electrifying as that instant in which Satan, struggling laboriously against the downdrafts of Chaos, suddenly glimpses a modification in the order of Creation as he knew it before his fall, a minute yet perceptible shift in the very spatial relations of that older universe he took to be eternal. 'Strange alteration!' Meanwhile, the very impact of the new itself and the inhabitual has been prepared and underscored in this passage by an otherwise gratuitous foreshadowing of yet another miraculous emergence, which will not find its official representation until Book X: the construction by Sin and Death of their great causeway from hell gate. Why anticipate that here, except to link the force of these two instants in which, *ex nihilo*, something quite inconceivable in the previous system suddenly springs into being, modifying the latter beyond all recognition and creating a wholly unforeseeable system of new relationships that never existed before?

> But now at last the sacred influence
> Of light appears, and from the walls of Heaven
> Shoots far into the bosom of dim Night
> A glimmering dawn; here Nature first begins
> Her farthest verge, and Chaos to retire
> As from her outmost works a broken foe,
> With tumult less and with less hostile din,
> That Satan with less toil, and now with ease
> Wafts on the calmer wave by dubious light,
> And like a weather-beaten vessel holds
> Gladly the port, though shrouds and tackle torn;
> Or in the emptier waste, resembling air,
> Weighs his spread wings, at leisure to behold
> Far off the empyreal Heaven, extended wide
> In circuit, undetermined square or round,
> With opal towers, and battlements adorned
> Of living sapphire, once his native seat;
> And fast by hanging in a golden chain
> This pendent world, in bigness as a star
> Of smallest magnitude close by the moon.
> Thither, full fraught with mischievous revenge,
> Accurst, and in a cursed hour, he hies.
>
> (II, 1034–55)

Alongside the feudal world of God and his court, of Satan and his host, Adam is clearly of another species – the commoner, the first bourgeois, that extraordinary mutation which is middle-class man, destined as we know today to be fruitful and multiply, and to inherit the earth. In that case, that unexpectedly new space of our 'pendent world' and Eden itself, resembling heaven, yet unique and utterly unlike anything that has hitherto existed, springing up 'in the interstices' of that older Creation 'like the Gods of Epicurus in the intermundia or the Jews in the pores of Polish society', marks out the structural place for that equally unforeseen historical emergence which is the market system and capitalism itself. (And if we had time, we might gloss the dual perspective on Nature – before/after, fallen/unfallen – as a reflection of the way in which each closed system, each new mode of production, comes into being complete with its own spurious temporality, its own nostalgic projection of an idyllic past proper to it.)

The result is that – thus registering the diachronic event of this great transformation, or transition from one mode of production to another – Milton's poem is historical, even though as we have just seen it fails to be political: let us see if by way of concluding we can find anything to account for this uneven development in the poem's levels. It seems appropriate to approach the problem by way of Milton's own theory of levels or instances, as he outlines it in the *Second Defence of the English People*: 'I perceived that there are three main kinds of liberty essential to a satisfying mode of life: religious, domestic or private, and civil' (Milton 1957, pp. 830–1). Social life is then here mapped as a concentricity of the three instances of the political or state power; the religious or church organization; and the domestic or the family. We must first observe that in the secular world in which we live today, we recognize only two of these levels: the public and the private, the political and the personal, the objective and the subjective – the great and incommensurable fissure that cuts across everything in our experience and maims the lives of modern people. It is appropriate, then, to observe that this experiential double standard in modern life presupposes the eclipse of precisely that 'vanishing mediator' which is the religious instance; and this may well lead us to some final thoughts on the relationship between religion and politics. For Milton's formula shows that in his society the religious community serves as a concrete mediation between the public and the private and as a space in which problems of institutions and power meet problems of personal relationships and ethics or private life.

Indeed, we have omitted something from our evocation of the kinship between Marxism and religion which must be rectified at this point: it is the way in which all the issues that turn around church organization and the community of the faithful constitute a point-by-point anticipation of all the most vital problems of political organization in our own time: problems of the party, of class solidarity, of the soviets, of communes, of democratic centralism, of council communism, of small group politics, of the relations of intellectuals to the people, of discipline, of bureaucracy – all these crucial issues which are still so very much with us are those most centrally at stake in the great debates of the Reformation and of the English cultural revolution. The problem of community – bound for us, for better or for worse, to its concrete expression in the institution of the political party – was for them linked to its concrete or allegorical expression in the notion of a church or congregation or community of the faithful; and the excitement and actuality of the English cultural revolution as it unfolds from 1642 to 1660 is surely at one with this burning preoccupation with the nature of collective life.

So what is astonishing about *Paradise Lost* is the utter silence and absence of all these great themes of church and collectivity. The narrative moves at once from the family – with its great evocation of married love and sexuality – to the fallen privatized world of individual belief and individual salvation; nor are the other collectives glimpsed in its course – Satan's host or God's – 'gathered' communities of this type, but rather, as we've said, feudal castes. Milton's text thus anticipates the social impoverishment of the modern world, and as a narrative confronts the formal dilemma of relating the henceforth sundered and distant levels of the political and the domestic.

These meet on the occasion of the fall and of the temptation: only we know that for Milton the content of the occasion is absolutely insignificant – the tree itself, the apple, are little more than pretexts about which Satan himself will make a contemptuous joke. The real issue as we know is obedience itself, the other face of hierarchy, the only theme which permits a homology to be established between Satan's fall and that of Adam and Eve. Indeed, our historical reading suggested that from the perspective of modes of production, these two narratives – the one a feudal revolt, the other the privatization and monadization inherent in the development of a capitalist market system – are quite heterogeneous and unrelated. It therefore becomes interesting and strategic to examine the motif of disobedience, and, following our earlier method, to see what the process of figuration or representation foregrounds about this particular component of the ideology of social hierarchy.

As far as Eve's disobedience is concerned, the poem is formal, and her motivation has nothing in common with that feminine vanity which C.S. Lewis complacently attributed to Adam's 'lesser half':

> so to add what wants
> In female sex, the more to draw his love,
> And render me more equal, and perhaps,
> A thing not undesirable, sometime
> Superior: for inferior who is free?
> (IX, 821–5)

This final touch – the 'sometime superior' – is surely the classic inscription of Milton's own sexual anxiety: the devouring woman, Mary Powell, the Delilah from whom all masculine miseries spring. But when one recalls the more amusing features of the narrative sexism – and in particular the bourgeois interior scene of Books V–VIII where Eve, having served the men, Adam and the angel Raphael, leaves them alone to pursue their scientific discussion,

> not as not with such discourse
> Delighted, or not capable her ear
> Of what was high: such pleasures she reserved,
> Adam relating, she sole auditress –
> (VIII, 48–51)

the amphetamine-type stimulation of the apple suggests a chance for Eve to speak and to converse with Adam as an equal. At any rate, the marks of Milton's sexism here and throughout are too obvious and too embarrassing ('for well I understand in the prime end / Of Nature her the inferior', VIII, 540–1) to document at any great length. Meanwhile the poet's courageous defence of divorce has often been celebrated as a progressive position and a contribution to the struggle for social freedom. Is it ungrateful to suggest something Islamic in this conception of a democratic community of males who are free to repudiate their wives? In any case, the limits of Milton's politics – that protestant conservatism and commitment to hierarchy and elite authority which cuts him off from the greater radical- ism of his time – is surely profoundly at one with his sexual politics and his belief in the inequality of the sexes. I would only want to resist establishing causal priorities between these two dimensions of the personal and the political, and reconfirming their separation by encouraging the temptation to show that class attitudes condition Milton's sexual politics, or on the other hand that patriarchal values end up programming his public positions in the political field.

Yet, as I argued earlier, these personal biases and ideological opinions of the biographical individual John Milton are not really what is at stake here; the point was rather to show that the poem itself inscribes this insight, and faithfully demystifies its own initial raw material (among the latter Milton's private attitudes), designating the latter as ideology and reversing its messages. The official ideological message, the conscious intent of the poem was the defence and justification of the position that sin, the fallen world, the failure of revolutionary politics, all result ultimately from disobedience, from lack of discipline, from insufficient respect for hierarchy. Yet in the second-degree constructivist reading we have proposed this sequence is reversed, and the poetic narrative rather offers testimony of the constitutive relationship between this image of sin and of the fall and the failure to imagine genuine human equality. Eve has to fall, not because she is sinful or disobedient, but because Milton cannot find it in himself to imagine and to give figuration to an equality between the sexes that would open up into a concrete vision of the community of free people. The poem thus illustrates and documents, not a proposition about human nature, not a type of philosophical or theological content, but rather the operation of ideological closure: in this way, a poem in which, as we have said, the political is repressed none the less ends up producing a political reading of itself.

4

The Romantic construction of the unconscious

CATHERINE BELSEY

I

'What is the status of psychoanalysis?' The question is not a new one: it is implicit in a good many of the current debates on the left, explicit in the *Screen* debate of the late 1970s, and central in Foucault's *History of Sexuality* (1979, I). The question is not, to my mind, as it once was, an epistemological one ('is it true?', 'how do we know?'). Post-Saussurean linguistic theory, a theory of language as a system of differences with no positive terms, closes off questions about how accurately language represents the world. It opens up, at the same time, the political questions identified in Foucault's work ('what are the power relations inscribed in specific knowledges?'). In asking 'what is the status of psychoanalysis?', I want to pose a political question: 'what challenge to the existing order is inscribed in the discourse of psychoanalysis?'; 'what is its radical potential?'

The immediate answer, I think, is 'not much' – not much, that is, in the universal, transhistorical and transcultural psychosexual drama of the subject confronting and submitting to the possibility (or, in the case of women, the fact) of its own castration, and in the image of Freud, heroic adventurer, *discovering* and colonizing the virgin territory of the unconscious, an unknown continent awaiting exploration, replete with teeming jungles. The forms of power are not transcultural but historically specific, and the mapping of the jungles has been the prelude to a more thorough conquest by psychiatric practice on behalf of a more effective control of possible areas of resistance. A modern Pierre Rivière would almost certainly have been referred to a psychiatrist as soon as they caught him slicing the heads off the cabbages. But a second possible answer is that psychoanalysis as 'the science of the unconscious' (Lacan 1979, p. 203) offers a model of subjectivity which radically undermines the central theoretical justification of liberal humanism, the concept of consciousness as the origin and determinant of meaning and of history; and that in doing so it offers a mode of enquiry which challenges the procedures of bourgeois criticism, in so far as this depends, in the last analysis, on the concept of the author or reader as the origin and determinant of the meaning of the text. This second position is to varying degrees the assumption of most post-structuralist criticism. What is disturbing, however, is that in this criticism which repudiates the possibility of a metalanguage, psychoanalysis tends to be introduced precisely as if it were such a metalanguage, a 'discovery' which enables us to define the essential structures of subjectivity across history.[1]

I want to suggest that subjectivity has a history of its own, that psychoanalysis is itself a part of that history and that, understood in that way, psychoanalysis can contribute to our understanding of the historical specificity of the present. I want to propose that the history of subjectivity is a discursive history, a textual history – that is, a history of textual and discursive forms, not authors – and that in some of the texts of the late eighteenth and early nineteenth centuries we can identify one of the founding monuments of the bourgeois subject, in that it is in these texts that the unconscious is *for the first time* produced in discourse.

II

I want to begin by urging that for us now the radical element in Freud's theory is not sexuality but the identification of the unconscious as a site of meaning.[2] It is this hypothesis which offers a fundamental challenge to the impoverished concept of democracy – electoral and consumer choice – which more and more explicitly underwrites the capitalist mode of production. The capitalist valorization of consumer freedom depends on the notion of a unitary and autonomous subject, ultimate origin of its own choices. The existence of the unconscious puts this notion in question. Freud himself defined the effect of his work as a wounding blow to 'human megalomania', since it demonstrated to the ego 'that it is not even master in its own house, but must content itself with scanty information of what is going on unconsciously in its mind' (Freud 1953–73, XVI, p. 285). For precisely this reason, psychoanalysis has been in flight from the implications of its own research ever since Freud's early work. According to *The Interpretation of Dreams*, part of the dreamwork (which distorts the dream-thoughts to the point where they are fit to be admitted into consciousness) is displacement, the process of stripping highly charged thoughts of their psychical intensity and transferring this to elements of lesser importance. Freud attributes the activity of displacement to 'the censorship of endopsychic defence' (Freud 1953–73, IV, p. 308). Psychoanalysis escapes the censorship of the bourgeois ideology of its own practitioners by an increasing displacement, an increasing metonymy, which locates sexuality as the core of our being and so leads to a concept of the psychoanalytic process as a quest for a hidden truth, the secret of our sexuality which will make us whole. In this way psychoanalysis evades the ideological scandal of its own finding – the split subject, no longer master in its own house.

That sexuality was the essence of the repressed was plausible in 1900. The transgression, the subversion, the radical nature of psychoanalysis was that it spoke the unspeakable: it talked about sex. But this hypothesis is no longer plausible. Foucault's *History of Sexuality* (1979) shows how sex has been at the centre of an explosion of discourse, a proliferation of speech, however surreptitious, from the eighteenth century onwards. Incited to speak in the confessional, in literature, and finally in psychoanalysis itself, sexuality becomes a basis for the affirmation and constant surveillance of the subject of liberal humanism. Here is Foucault in *Herculine Barbin* on sex and psychoanalysis as oppression:

And then, we also admit that it is in the area of sex that we must search for the most secret and profound truths about the individual, that it is there that we can best discover what he is and what determines him. And if it was believed for centuries that it was necessary to hide sexual matters because they were shameful, we now know that it is sex itself which hides the most secret parts of the individual: the structure of his fantasies, the roots of his ego, the forms of his relationship to reality. At the bottom of sex there is truth.

It is at the junction of these two ideas – that we must not deceive ourselves concerning our sex, and that our sex harbors what is most true in ourselves – that psychoanalysis has rooted its cultural vigor. It promises us at the same time our sex, our true sex, and that whole truth about ourselves which secretly keeps vigil in it.

(Foucault 1980b, pp. x–xi and see also Foucault 1980a, p. 61)

Foucault is right, I believe, to see psychoanalysis as a mode of surveillance – but he is right only in so far as psychoanalysis is perceived as the science of sexual difference and as the source of timeless truths. Lacan's reading of Freud makes possible a return to what is radical for us in psychoanalysis. Or rather, a *reading* of Lacan's reading of Freud, because Lacan's own work participates to some extent in the flight from the scandal of the split subject in its concept of the phallus as the primary signifier. The phallus in Lacan's theory becomes the anchoring point which fixes meaning, arresting the incessant sliding of the signified under the signifier (see Forrester in MacCabe 1981, pp. 45–69, 56, 58). And in this attempt to reinstate a centre, a point of origin, the concept of anatomical difference makes a reappearance, however tentatively (Heath 1978, p. 64). Even if the phallus is not to be identified with the penis, none the less men and women have an eternally different relationship to it. But the post-Saussurean linguistics which Lacan appropriates do not need a centre and have no place for a point of origin, a primary signifier. Saussure's system of differences is a network of relationships, perpetually in process, where an alteration in one part of the system implies a shift in the whole. The sliding of the signified, the play of meaning, cannot be arrested. Sexuality and sexual difference are part of the polyphony of the unconscious, not its origin.

The dangers of Lacanian phallocentrism have not always been evident in the very place where they should have seemed most threatening, that is, in the discourse of feminism. There is no liberation for women in an anatomical psychoanalysis, a discourse which finds the origin of all difference, its single, central cause, in sexual difference. The social oppression of patriarchy should not lead us to a romanticism of the sexual specificity of the body, an essence outside the social and socially alienated from its true being. If the slash of castration is logically prior to the oblique stroke of difference, women, always already castrated, can never enter fully into the symbolic order, have inevitably a shaky purchase on meaning, and remain forever at the mercy of the phallic power which is patriarchy. Defined in terms of an anatomical absence, relegated to a place on the threshold of language, the heroine of a certain sub-Lacanian radical feminism (which in my view is neither radical nor feminist) is confined to rhythmic bursts of incantatory gibber- ish, while passively encircling the secret crevices of her own body. Such a psychoanalysis is an ideological psychoanalysis, reproducing the structures of the primal patriarchal scene: Adam, knowing difference, naming the animals, and Eve, fissured and defenceless against the penetration of the serpent. Sexuality is always social, and sexual pleasure is not knowable outside or anterior to signification. Foucault, in whose earlier work another kind of romanticism of the body perhaps plays a part, has recently put the body itself in question in publishing the story of *Herculine Barbin*, where the protagonist, who can live only as a woman and love only as a man, is anatomically neither (Foucault 1980b). The body has no 'natural' being which precedes culture: it too is socialized, held in the signifying chain from the moment of birth.

But in spite of the discourses which have stemmed from Lacanian phallocentrism, it is Lacan, none the less, who emphasizes, in his insistence on the structure of the analytic discourse rather than the meanings that can be derived from it, the division which constitutes the radical challenge to the subject of bourgeois ideology, and it is Lacan who thereby puts in question once again 'the mirage that renders modern man so sure of being himself' (Lacan 1977, p. 165). It is Lacan who, by concentrating on the model defined in Freud's earlier texts, extricates from his work the concept of an unconscious which is not an origin, which has nothing to do with the primal and the instinctive, but which is produced in the same moment as the subject, with the entry into language or, more properly, the symbolic order. 'The unconscious is neither primordial nor instinctual; what it knows about the elementary is no more than the elements of the signifier' (Lacan 1977, p. 170). The unconscious speaks – in dreams, in parapraxes, in symptoms which signify in and across the body. And this speech is a site of meaning which collides with the speaker's conscious thoughts: 'The unconscious is that chapter of my history that is marked by a blank or occupied by a falsehood: it is the censored chapter' (Lacan 1977, p. 50). As a site of meaning, a chapter, the unconscious is discursive, but it is 'that part of conscious discourse, in so far as it is transindividual, that is not at the disposal of the subject in re-establishing the continuity of his conscious discourse' (Lacan 1977, p. 49). It is another discourse, underlying the conscious one, interrupting it, impeding the subject's identification with the unitary self of imaginary misrecognition. Produced, like the subject itself, in the domain of the symbolic, which is always external and anterior to the subject, the unconscious is the discourse of the Other (Lacan 1977, p. 172). It is the condition of conscious meaning – the difference, the absence, the possibility of death – which necessarily escapes the subject in the moment of production of meaning and of subjectivity. 'The process of loss which enables us to gain language produces for us a place and an identity (a name and its substitution rules) within language, but this place is produced by the necessary absence of the differences that constitute it' (MacCabe 1978, p. 7). The gap between the subject of the utterance, the subject as speaker, source of meaning, and the subject of the utterance, the subject as signifier, held in place in its own speech, is the site of desire, which also speaks, but from another position and with another meaning. This other discourse offers the possibility of other positions for the subject and thus demonstrates the nature of subjectivity as an effect of language, the system of differences which always precedes it.

III

The *Analysis of a Phobia in a Five-Year-Old Boy* ('Little Hans') (Freud 1953–73, X) must be the most disarming of Freud's case histories. In Freud's account this is a story of the Oedipus complex resolved by the resolution of the castration complex. But within this psychosexual reading it is possible to detect another – psychodiscursive -- meaning for the story of Little Hans, whose entry into the symbolic order, the order of language and culture, beginning when he is nearly 3, involves the mastery of a system of differences – between, for instance, black and yellow; faeces and urine; babies and faeces; and faeces, liver and meat croquettes. This increasing mastery is accompanied by fantasies in which difference is repudiated (Freud 1953–73, X, pp. 63, 68, 84–6) and by an anxiety which stems initially from the possibility of the absence of his mother but which cannot be allayed by her presence (Freud 1953–73, X, pp. 23–6). The anxiety takes the form of a fear of horses, which is overcome only when Hans is able to find a subject position with which he can identify. The polyphonic horses are his father, whose death he wants and dreads, his mother who draws babies about in boxes, and Hans himself, proud and exultant like an untired young horse. His fear disappears only when Hans decides to allocate his 'children' to his mother and become their father, to marry his father off to his father's mother (thus granting him 'the same happiness that he desired himself' (p. 97)), and subsequently to defer fatherhood until he grows up to be like his father.

Little Hans's repressed wishes are mutually contradictory, and they also collide with what he consciously knows:

I: 'Was the horse dead when it fell down?'
Hans: 'Yes!'
I: 'How do you know that?'
Hans: 'Because I saw it.' (He laughed.) 'No, it wasn't a bit dead.'
I: 'Perhaps you thought it was dead?'
Hans: 'No. Certainly not. I only said it as a joke.' (His expression at the moment, however, had been serious.)

(p. 50)

The contradictory discourses place Hans in contradictory subject positions. When Freud calls his fear of horses 'nonsense', Hans willingly accepts the designation, and thereafter refers to the phobia as his nonsense which the Professor will cure (pp. 28ff.). At the same time, however, Freud's text is careful to repudiate the notion that Hans's fears are without meaning: 'a neurosis never says foolish things, any more than a dream' (p. 27). The discourse of the unconscious, which intrudes upon the meanings acceptable to consciousness, is always a signifying nonsense, which cannot rest, but reappears, Freud says, 'like an unlaid ghost', until it has made itself understood (p. 122). In the case of little Hans, it is the abandonment of his nonsense for the sense offered within the symbolic order which effects a cure. On the basis of *The Psychopathology of Everyday Life*, however, we may conjecture that even for the untroubled Hans of the postscript, further nonsense must have made itself evident in parapraxes, bearing witness to the 'indestructibility of unconscious desire' (Lacan 1977, p. 167).

It is the insistence of a corresponding nonsense in some of the literary texts of the Romantic period that I want to point to as evidence for the Romantic construction of the unconscious. I should, perhaps, stress at this point that I do so not in order to treat authors as patients, or to rewrite novels and poems as case histories, but to suggest that certain texts are intelligible as demonstrations of the dialectic of jubilation and loss which defines the speaking subject as it finds meaning by encountering difference, and that these texts also invite a similarly dialectical reading process. Withholding a unitary position 'outside language' from which they would be intelligible, the texts in question are addressed to the split subject who, as an effect of language, cannot finally master meaning from a place outside it. What they have in common is the supernatural or the uncanny, but I do not want to seem to reiterate the familiar popularization that the unconscious is full of demons, 'the locus of the divinities of night' (Lacan 1979, p. 24). The distinguishing feature of these texts is that they are composed of irreconcilable discourses, constructed of signifying nonsense which intrudes substantially on sense and remains unmastered by it.

Not all Romantic texts, of course, are of this kind. I want to begin by making a distinction between what is mastered – acknowledged as fantasy – and what is not. The fantasies of Little Hans, cheerfully acknowledged as untrue, keep at bay only temporarily the world of difference which confers meaning but in doing so denies imaginary plenitude. In one instance his father explains to him

> that chickens lay eggs, and that out of the eggs there come other chickens.
> Hans laughed.
> *I*:   'Why do you laugh?'
> *He*:   'Because I like what you've told me.'
> He said that he had seen it happen already.
> *I*:   'Where?'
> *Hans*: 'You did it.'
> *I*:   'Where did I lay an egg?'
> *Hans*: 'At Gmunden; you laid an egg in the grass, and all at once a chicken came hopping out. You laid an egg once; I know you did, I know it for certain. Because Mummy said so.'
> *I*:   'I'll ask Mummy if that's true.'
> *Hans*: 'It isn't true a bit. But *I* once laid an egg and a chicken came hopping out.'
> *I*:   'Where?'
> *Hans*: 'At Gmunden I lay down on the grass – no, I knelt down – and all at once the children didn't look on at me, and all at once in the morning I said: "Look for it, children; I laid an egg yesterday." And all at once they looked, and all at once they saw an egg, and out of it there came a Little Hans. Well, what are you laughing for?'
>
> (Freud 1953–73, X, p. 85)

Little Hans willingly abandons a series of bids for plenitude as fantasy. So do the earliest Gothic novels. *The Castle of Otranto*, the first of them, published in 1764, is a textual fantasy which refuses the differences – the exclusions – imposed by the constraints of the emerging novel form. In the Preface to the second edition, Walpole explains that it is an attempt to bring back 'imagination and improbability' to the modern novel, in which 'the great resources of fancy have been dammed up, by a strict adherence to common life' (Walpole 1964, p. 7). The strategies of the novel are here conflated with elements of fairy tale and Arthurian legend, Shakespeare and eighteenth-century etiquette books, to produce a narrative which is a blend of high adventure and high comedy. Its success was immediate and overwhelming: *The Castle of Otranto* ran to twenty-one editions before the end of the eighteenth century. The fantasy is acknowledged and distanced, firmly enclosed in inverted commas by the Preface, which proclaims the story to have been printed in Naples in 1529, and written much earlier, probably between 1095 and 1243. This solemn antiquarianism is all part of the joke. *The Castle of Otranto* offers no challenge at all to the subjectivity of the reader. It was, of course, a challenge to eighteenth-century common sense, and when Clara Reeve's *Old English Baron* was published in 1778 it was explicitly an attempt to write in the spirit of *Otranto* but at the same time to keep 'within the utmost verge of probability' (Reeve 1967, p. 4). The result is a text which is no more probable, but which does remain strictly within the bounds of classic realism in that all that is enigmatic is finally explained, and subjective impression is finally distinguished from objective reality. We eventually know what is 'true' within the fiction. The supernatural, part of this 'truth', is brought under the control of Providence, and is employed to reunite the hero with his proper inheritance, terrorizing only the wicked. (Providence is seen to endorse the most rigid social stratification and the careful and rightful distribution of property.)

Probability – or supernatural content – is not, then, what is at stake in my argument. When M.G. Lewis's *The Monk* appeared in 1796, it represented something quite new, not because of its implausibility, or even because of its explicit treatment of sexuality, but in that it withholds from the reader the security of a single position from which the narrative as a whole is retrospectively intelligible. Little Hans willingly abandons a world where everyone lays eggs, but his terror of horses is not dissipated when he calls it his nonsense. In a similar way *The Monk* itself repudiates as nonsense precisely those elements of which it is substantially composed, which render it intelligible, and which therefore cannot simply be dissipated by being defined as nonsense. The text is a product of two distinct discourses which are never reconciled. Since neither masters the other, the reader is unable to take up a position of extra-discursive knowingness shared with the author, but is constantly offered the opportunity to see meaning as an effect of discourse itself.

The opening of the novel reproduces the discourse of romantic comedy: two gallants encounter a beautiful girl and a hideous old duenna. There is much comic misunderstanding, to the point where one of the gallants finds himself the suitor of the duenna. Required to kiss her hand, he performs the deed manfully and then recoils in horror, protesting that he now smells of garlic, and will be taken by the fashionable world for a 'walking Omelet, or some large Onion running to seed' (Lewis 1973, p. 24). The setting is a monastic church in Madrid in the days of the Inquisition. All at once the church is empty. The other gallant falls asleep and dreams of marrying the beautiful girl. Suddenly, as the bride appears

> before He had time to receive her, an Unknown rushed between them. His form was gigantic; His complexion was swarthy, His eyes fierce and terrible; His mouth breathed out volumes of fire . . .
>
> Antonia shrieked. The Monster clasped her in his arms, and springing with her upon the Altar, tortured her with his odious caresses.
>
> (p. 28)

The dream is, of course, prophetic – of the kind of episode (and discourse) which is to constitute the substance of the text. But the sophisticated eighteenth-century comedy reappears at intervals as a norm of sense against which to measure the gothic extravagance.

The constant theme of this 'sense' is the repudiation of superstition and the absurdity of belief in the supernatural. The gross superstition of Agnes's parents is the cause of one of the novel's two main plots, and in the other a similar weakness in the character of Ambrosio (the monk of the title) leads him to a life of sin which culminates in incest and parricide (pp. 130, 192, 238). It is because Agnes rejects the supernatural that she survives against all odds. But her sceptical mock-heroic account of the spectral Bleeding Nun is followed by the apparition of the ghostly Nun herself, and this proves so nearly fatal to Agnes's lover that his malady can be cured only by the magical ministrations of the Wandering Jew.

The supernatural nonsense offers, however, at least to a psychoanalytic (psychodiscursive) reading, its own kind of sense. Ambrosio, the monk, refuses the restraints of his vocation, and then all human restraints, and finally makes a pact with the devil which seems to offer absolute freedom and the fulfilment of every desire. He ends helpless, his body broken and dislocated, the prey of other living things. His refusal of all order in a quest for the imaginary plenitude of unconstrained subjectivity reduces him to the powerlessness of the fragmented human animal which precedes subjectivity, itself the product of a pact sustained by and within the signifying chain.

IV

The contradictory planes of meaning in *The Monk*, the collisions between the supernatural plot and the thematic repudiation of the supernatural, are never united in any kind of closure. In Ann Radcliffe's *The Italian* (1797), written in direct response to *The Monk*, the gap glimpsed here is hastily closed in a narrative which perfectly fulfils all the requirements of classic realism. What might have seemed supernatural turns out to have been perfectly naturally motivated, and subjective experience is finally differentiated from objective reality. But the problem of the distinction between subject and object, the difference which gives meaning to subjectivity, called into question in *The Monk*, goes on to haunt Romantic writing. The absolute freedom of the subject which Ambrosio claims for himself has analogues in Wordsworth's 'egotistical sublime' and in Coleridge's Imagination.

René Wellek has defined European Romanticism as an attempt to reconcile subject and object, to heal the split between them and assert 'the one Life within us and abroad' (Wellek 1968, pp. 129, 132). It is the heroic impossibility of this task which produces Romantic exultation and despair. The obliteration of the object in a subjectivity which expands to incorporate it ('In our life alone does nature live') is the negation of desire, because desire depends on the existence of an object that can be desired precisely in so far as it is outside the subject, radically other. The negation of desire, imaginary plenitude, presents a world whose existence and meaning depends on the presence of the subject, a world of absolute subjectivity. But the obliteration of the object implies the fading of the subject, because it is also the negation of difference. Subjectivity has meaning only to the extent that it is differentiated from something. But a world of difference is a world of lack, of absence, of desire. The reinstatement of the subject is the reinstatement of a world independent of the subject, a world of loss. This dialectic of plenitude and difference, pleasure and desire, is the condition of speech. 'As speaking subjects we constantly oscillate between the symbolic and the imaginary – constantly imagining ourselves granting some full meaning to the words we speak, and constantly being surprised to find them determined by relations outside our control' (MacCabe 1976, p. 14).

The impossible project of Wordsworth's poetry is to hold desire at bay, simultaneously to preserve and eliminate the distinction between subject and object. 'Tintern Abbey', for instance, defines a subject present to itself, differentiated from *and* interfused with the objects which it *both* perceives and half creates (lines 106–7), and guaranteed by a 'presence' 'far *more* deeply interfused' (lines 94–6, my emphasis), which inhabits both nature and the mind, and which drives both subjects and objects, impels

> All thinking things, all objects of all thought
> And rolls through all things.
> (Wordsworth 1952, pp. 259–63, lines 100–2)

This 'presence', the Absolute Subject, both sustains and transcends difference. *The Prelude* is a more detailed interrogation of subjectivity, a more precise confrontation with the same contradiction, and here in the famous narratives of childhood we find a constant dialectic of jubilation and loss, of imaginary plenitude and that which is radically other. Danger mastered in the birds-nesting episode evokes the 'strange utterance' of the wind; the exultation of skating leads up to 'an alien sound of melancholy' (I, p. 338; lines 470–1).[3] At the same time the discursive organization of the text presents an oscillation of sense and nonsense as each episode is contained by passages of 'philosophy' which constantly strive to master its meaning. Poetry, of course, is conveniently allowed to be nonsense – at least since Arnold's comment that in Wordsworth the poetry was the reality and the philosophy an illusion (Arnold 1973, 9, p. 48).

Probably the most familiar piece of signifying nonsense in *The*

Prelude is the narrative of the stolen boat in Book I. Here the child is seen to appropriate the boat in the field of the Other, just as the text attempts to appropriate meaning for itself, to be the source of its own significance. The act, a transgression of the symbolic order, is one of 'troubled pleasure', of mastery and loss. At first the subject is the triumphant source of action:

> lustily
> I dipp'd my oars into the silent Lake,
> And, as I rose upon the stroke, my Boat
> Went heaving through the water, like a Swan.
> (lines 401–4)

But the independence of the object, which gives meaning to subjectivity and inaugurates desire, asserts itself as the cliff rears up, 'as if with voluntary power instinct' (line 407), and strides after the guilty child. He turns, 'with trembling hands' (line 412), replacing the boat with an act of submission to the symbolic order. But the recognition that such submission implies the determination of action outside the control of the subject precipitates a crisis which obliterates for a time all difference and all meaning, all subjectivity and all objects:

> and after I had seen
> That spectacle, for many days, my brain
> Work'd with a dim and undetermin'd sense
> Of unknown modes of being; in my thoughts
> There was a darkness, call it solitude,
> Or blank desertion, no familiar shapes
> Of hourly objects, images of trees,
> Of sea or sky, no colours of green fields;
> But huge and mighty Forms that do not live
> Like living men mov'd slowly through my mind
> By day and were the trouble of my dreams.
> (lines 417–27)

The triumphant nominative 'I' progressively gives way to 'my brain', 'my thoughts', 'my mind', and finally 'my dreams'. And as the 'I' recedes, confidence in language diminishes: 'a darkness, call it solitude/Or blank desertion'. The 'unknown modes of being' are plural, unnameable, like living, not living. If there is no subject-as-origin in the symbolic order, there is no subject at all outside it.

The account of the purifying ministry of nature which frames this episode neither explains nor dissipates what is disturbing for the child and for the reader in this passage. Quite simply, the two bear little relation to each other. *The Prelude* is composed of two distinct discourses which coexist uneasily, frustrating the reader's impulse to reduce the text to a single, coherent meaning, and thus withholding from the reader the mastery which is also denied to the child. The process culminates in the 'spots of time' passage which is offered as the thematic centre of the text, an attempt to define the succession of indelible moments which *The Prelude* sets out to recount and theorize (XI, lines 258–343). The gap between these dramas of subjectivity and the explanatory discourse which so signally fails to explain is here most gaping, and what returns to threaten the plenitude of the subject is precisely the repressed condition of its own being: absence, difference, death.

The passage opens in the unmistakable accents of the Cartesian *cogito* at its most confident – polysyllabic, generalized, abstract and assured, as the plural pronouns imply:

> There are in our existence spots of time
> Which with distinct pre-eminence retain
> A vivifying Virtue
>
> (lines 258–60)

Lines 271–3 seem to define an overbalance of idealism, which is presumably punished by Nature in the episode which follows. In any case, it seems that the narrative is offered as an instance of these 'spots of time' by which 'our minds/Are nourished and invisibly repair'd' (lines 264–5). The episode follows the pattern of jubilation and loss displayed in the previous narratives of childhood. The 'proud hopes' give way to anxiety and isolation, to an encounter with the Other which destroys plenitude and engenders desire:

> We had not travell'd long, ere some mischance
> Disjoin'd me from my Comrade, and, through fear
> Dismounting, down the rough and stony Moor
> I led my Horse, and stumbling on, at length
> Came to a bottom, where in former times
> A Murderer had been hung in iron chains.

> The Gibbet-mast was moulder'd down, the bones
> And iron case were gone; but on the turf,
> Hard by, soon after that fell deed was wrought
> Some unknown hand had carved the Murderer's name.
> The monumental writing was engraven
> In times long past, and still, from year to year,
> By superstition of the neighbourhood,
> The grass is clear'd away; and to this hour
> The letters are all fresh and visible.
>
> (lines 285–99)

Absence, death and writing. In these monumental letters, of ancient and unknown origin, but still miraculously fresh and visible, the subject encounters the radical otherness of the symbolic order, always external and anterior to its own being, the signifying cause of its existence, and the condition of mastery which inevitably gives way to loss. The child's terror at confronting the letters is more sharply defined in the 1850 version of the text:

> A casual glance had shown them, and I fled,
> Faltering and faint, and ignorant of the road.
>   (XII, lines 246–7)

The lack which appears in the division between the subject and language which always precedes it is literally unspeakable:

> I should need
> Colours and words that are unknown to man
> To paint the visionary dreariness
>   (1805, XI, lines 309–11)

The curious banality of what follows displays the inability of the Cartesian discourse to provide a coherent explanation of the importance of this encounter. But among the reassertions of imaginary plenitude ('from thyself it is that thou must give,/ Else never canst receive', lines 333–4), there appears a glimpse of another way of conceiving of the subject, an approach to the recognition of its dual being, in quest of another scene, which flickers and forever eludes it, because it is the work of consciousness to shut it off:

> the hiding places of my power
> Seem open; I approach, and then they close.
>   (lines 336–7)

V

The project of *The Prelude* is both to sustain and finally to eliminate difference, and by doing so to contain desire, to define a reciprocity between subject and object which 'consecrates' the mind till it breaks free of its objects, 'In beauty exalted, as it is itself/Of substance and of fabric more divine' than they are (XIII, lines 451–2). What *The Prelude* achieves is the constant demonstration of difference in episodes which dramatize the experience of the subject as alternately source and effect of meaning. Its subversive potential lies precisely in its inability to achieve its own project, and in its consequent refusal of a single position of intelligibility for the reader. Offering to theorize the 'interfusing' of subject and object to the point where the subject becomes transcendent, it finds itself trembling on the brink of a recognition which Lacan was to formulate 150 years later:

> The signifier, producing itself in the field of the Other, makes manifest the subject of its signification. But it functions as a signifier only to reduce the subject in question to being no more than a signifier, to petrify the subject in the same moment in which it calls the subject to function, to speak, as subject.
>
>   (Lacan 1979, p. 207)

The position could not be theorized at the time. Coleridge's attempt to produce a theory of subjectivity in the *Biographia Literaria* fails spectacularly. Chapter 12 begins to announce the imminence of the proposed theory of the Imagination, and spends several pages explaining that the higher reaches of transcendental philosophy are not available to everyone. There then begins a preliminary quest for a postulate which will guarantee the truth of what is to follow, and this is located in an absolute truth which is self-consciousness, the identity of the knowing subject and the object known in the I AM, self-grounded, unconditional, resembling the 'presence' of 'Tintern Abbey'. This is followed in Chapter 13 by an account of intelligence as the result of two contrary forces, but suddenly the text breaks off, and a (totally fictitious) letter from a friend encourages Coleridge to defer publication of the 100 pages which were to follow. In consequence of this 'judicious' advice, the *Biographia* confines its account of the Imagination to a single cryptic paragraph in which all that is clear is that perception is an act of creation which is a repetition of the eternal act of creation in the I AM. Subjectivity expands to fill the universe which it itself creates and which is then the object of its own knowledge.

In the Venn diagram in which Lacan defines the choice of the subject (which is not, of course, a real choice) between meaning and being, the choice of being forces the subject to disappear, to fall into non-meaning, to take up a place outside and beyond the symbolic order, which is no place at all (Lacan 1979, p. 211). When Ambrosio chooses absolute freedom of being he is left to die, broken and dislocated on the mountainside. Coleridge's text shares something of Ambrosio's fate. Broken, full of gaps and fissures, the definition of subjectivity falls into non-meaning in the moment of its utterance. Unspeakable and unspoken, the analysis is to be found in the unwritten 100 pages, in the *Logosophia* to be announced at the end of the *Biographia* (it was not announced) and in the essay prefixed to 'The Ancient Mariner' (which was never written). These silences speak across the text's effort to transcend difference, absence, desire (a condition which is so amply dramatized in 'Kubla Khan', 'The Ancient Mariner' and 'Dejection', each easily worth another essay). Coleridge's idealism, parallel to but more thoroughgoing than Wordsworth's, more thoroughly negates desire – in so far as negation, as Freud points out, is a way of 'taking cognizance of what is repressed' (Freud 1953–73, XIX, p. 235).

VI

Nearly a century later Freud 'successfully' theorized the split in the subject which Romantic writing demonstrates and denies. In so many ways a man of his time, Freud shared the bourgeois conviction that the subject produced in bourgeois ideology is natural and eternal. There is no reason to suppose that this is the case. Indeed, Lacan himself sporadically implies as much in his isolation of the Cartesian *cogito* as the mirage that renders *modern* man so sure of being himself, and in his identification of the early seventeenth century as the 'inaugural moment of the emergence of the subject' (Lacan 1979, p. 223). Elsewhere he attributes to Erasmus an 'alteration in the relations between man and the signifier' which changed the course of history 'by modifying the moorings that anchor his being' (Lacan 1977, p. 174).

One of the things that changes the course of history significantly is an alteration of the relation between human beings and the first person pronoun. Although the word 'I' always designates the speaker of a specific utterance, it does not always follow that 'I' always means the fixed, unitary subject of bourgeois ideology. In the middle ages, too, 'I' designates the speaker, but what it *means* is a temporary alliance of body and soul, localized site of a cosmic struggle between powers which have an existence external and anterior to it. The medieval subject is explicitly dispersed across a range of forces, representatives of cosmic good and evil. To this extent it makes no sense to talk of a medieval unconscious. Desire is permanently present and it is explicit, seen as the longing of the soul for heaven and of the body for the world. Each prevents the full satisfaction of the other.

In a paper offered at the 1980 Essex Conference I attempted to trace in plays of the sixteenth and seventeenth centuries some of the contradictions which are the consequence of a discontinuity between the fragmented subject of the middle ages and the fixed, unitary subject of bourgeois ideology.[4] The instability of this unity is evident in the efforts of British empiricist philosophy of the seventeenth and eighteenth centuries to define the relations between subject and object. But the crises of the 1790s (economic, political and ideological simultaneously) are contemporary with an interrogation of subjectivity in a mode of writing (fiction/poetry) which permits glimpses of that other discourse which constitutes – and disperses – the bourgeois subject.

If so, psychoanalysis is not the discovery of a timeless truth of human nature, but a theory of subjectivity that radically undermines specifically the sovereignty of the subject of bourgeois ideology, source of meaning and of history, and guarantee of the 'freedom' inscribed in the capitalist relations of production. The challenge of psychoanalysis to the existing order lies in the possibility it offers of locating – precisely within the assertion of the most grandiose claims on behalf of the bourgeois subject – the signifying nonsense, intrusive and insistent, which exposes the hollowness of those claims. This assertion, I have suggested, begins in Romantic writing, but it has not yet ended. Subversion is plural, of course; psychoanalysis has no exclusive radical potential. Nor does it offer a key to all mythologies, as its adherents often seem to claim. Contests for power are local, historical and specific. Foucault gives us the possibility of a subject unconsciously dispersed across a range of conscious discourses – and despises psychoanalysis.[5] But only psychoanalysis theorizes the signifying nonsense which is worth appropriating now in the contest for the meaning of subjectivity.

Notes

1 For a reiteration of the concept of Freud's work as a 'discovery' see e.g. MacCabe 1981, pp. xi, xii. Paul Willemen goes further, claiming for psychoanalysis a final knowledge: 'What is sexuality? What is desire? . . . are questions only psychoanalysis can deal with adequately (and, I would argue, *has done so*)' (1980, p. 53; my emphasis).

2 Cf. Heath 1978, p. 61.

3 Wordsworth 1959. References are to the 1805 version unless otherwise specified.

4 Belsey 1981, pp. 166–86; see also Belsey 1985.

5 Though on this point see the brief and inconclusive debate with Jacques-Alain Miller in 'The confession of the flesh' (Foucault 1980a, pp. 194–228, pp. 213ff.). These observations, which I discovered after writing this paper, seem to me to concede something to the (selectively) Lacanian position I have tried to define.

5
The trial of Warren Hastings

DAVID MUSSELWHITE

The trial of Warren Hastings is intended to be the first of a series of studies dedicated to a project which I have called 'trials of empire' of which a later paper, given at the Cross-Cultural Studies Conference at Essex in 1985, on the trial of the Egyptian leader Arabi, is a second example. In choosing to focus on a series of trials I hoped to explore a very specific milieu where 'discourse' and 'power' are most immediately entwined. The 'trials of empire' theme also seemed to me to offer a way of negotiating my own slight shift of interest from what I felt was the increasingly narrow, even provincial, concerns of the 'sociology of literature' to a broader concern with 'cross-cultural studies'. The 'trials' theme offered a rich body of archival material for basic empirical research which I believe to be all the more necessary in the face of the somewhat excessive fetishization of 'theory' in recent years. Finally, what particularly fascinates me – though it does not come out strongly in the Hastings piece – is the way in which such trials often show the confrontation of systems of thought and cultural codings and expectations which are completely impenetrable to each other and which encourage us, therefore, to try to imagine what it would be like to think the 'unthinkable'.

*

On 13 February 1788 Warren Hastings was impeached before the House of Lords on twenty charges of 'High Crimes and

Misdemeanours', all alleged to have been committed during his term of office as Governor-General of India from 1773 to 1784. The prosecution was brought, on behalf of the House of Commons and the People of India, by a group of 'Managers' appointed by the Lower House and which included, among others, four of the most brilliant speakers of the period: Edmund Burke, Charles James Fox, Richard Brinsley Sheridan and Charles Grey. On the first day there were also present in Westminster Hall the historian, Edward Gibbon, the painter, Joshua Reynolds, the diarist Fanny Burney, the actress, Sarah Siddons, as well as many other figures distinguished in aristocratic, political or fashionable circles. Moreover, as the trial dragged on through seven long years to 1795, the ripples of connection and influence spread until at some point or other they touched upon practically every major figure of the period. It was not just that the impeachment of Hastings was 'the greatest public sensation of the seventeen-eighties' (Plumb 1950, p. 171) but, rather, that it absorbed and engrossed a massive quantum of political, juridical and general social energy.[1]

In many ways the trial was an immensely complex affair and while, in the event, Hastings was acquitted, scholars and historians to this day will argue over the correctness of the verdict, the conduct of the proceedings, the validity of the evidence, the facts of the history and the merits of the protagonists. In what follows I have refused to be drawn into any such debates – partly because I doubt whether I would have the competence to understand their complexity, but also because I would like to consider some of the general features and implications of the trial. Such, for example, as the function the trial might have had in the contexts of Indian and English political history, or the reasons for its inordinate length and repetitiveness, or the grounds of its virulence, confusions and misunderstandings. Above all I shall be concerned with its institutional and discursive location: why the cumbersome and already slightly anachronistic device of impeachment? What is the connection between the trial and the explosion of the popular press in the 1770s and 1780s? How is India 'represented'? How is the shift from colonialism to empire negotiated in thought? What are the languages of the trial?

The major development during the latter half of the eighteenth century was the change in the status of the East India Company from being a purely commercial concern to being an organ of imperial power. The process begins with Clive's putting down of the rebellion led by Siraj-al-daula in 1756 and replacing him on the throne of Bengal by Mir Jaffar. This was the first use of British power to establish compliant rulers over Indian territories, and it was followed by a period of plunder and exploitation by the Company officials and other adventurers which was to bring the province to bankruptcy. In 1760 Mir Jaffar was replaced by Mir Kasim – who had paid £200,000 for the privilege – but, the latter proving hostile to British rule, he in turn was deposed in 1764 and Mir Jaffar was returned to the throne. This time, however, the administrative machinery was vested in a 'diwan', or government official, named Nandakumar, appointed by the Company. This was the beginning of a system of 'dual control' which was to last up to the administrative reforms of Hastings. In 1765 Mir Jaffar died and power passed, during the minority of the new Nawab, Mubarak-ud-daula, to two of his widows, Munni Begum and Babbu Begum, while Nandakumar was replaced by another appointee, Muhammed Reza Khan. This arrangement lasted until 1771 when, because of the chaotic nature of the state's revenues, the Directors of the East India Company ordered their Council in India to 'stand forth as *diwan*', that is, to dispense with the Indian intermediary, Muhammed Reza Khan, and assume direct responsibility for the collection of the revenues. Muhammed Reza was deposed and, it is alleged, thanks to a bribe, Munni Begum was confirmed as the legal authority in Bengal with Guru Das, Nandakumar's son, to help her. Thus, by 1772, the Company had moved from being a mere trading organization to being, after the confusing period of 'dual control', the effective sovereign power in Bengal.

Meanwhile, a threatened insurrection in 1765 by the Moghul Emperor, Shah Alam and the Wazir of Oudh, Shuja-ud-daula, had allowed Clive and the Company to intervene in the affairs of Oudh too. In that year Clive managed to arrange a treaty of alliance with Shuja-ud-daula in the face of the long-standing threat to both Oudh and Bengal from the Maratha federation to the south, and he also bought off the Emperor by giving him the provinces of Allahabad and Cora. In 1773 Hastings renegotiated the treaty with Shuja-ud-daula: among its terms it was stipulated that the Wazir would subsidize the maintenance of Company troops in Oudh and that he could expect the support of such troops against the Rohillas to the north whom he suspected of aggressive designs on Oudh – the Rohillas being a remnant of the Afghan forces that had invaded the north of India in 1756. In 1774 the Rohillas were attacked and defeated by a body of British troops and their leader, Hafiz Khan, was killed. In the aftermath of the battle the soldiers of Shuja-ud-daula are alleged to have butchered the Rohilla survivors in their lust for revenge and booty. It was this incident, and Hastings' complicity, that formed the basis of accusations of genocide later levelled in the Commons.

In 1775 Shuja-ud-daula died and was succeeded by his son, Asaf-ad-daula, but Shuja-ud-daula's wealth was allowed to pass to his widow and his mother, the Begums of Oudh. Hastings, at the time, offered to guarantee this transfer of power – alien to the Muslim legal code – but in 1781, on the grounds that the Begums had been involved in the insurrection of Cheit Sing, the Raja of Benares (see below), and because he needed money to support the various wars he was fighting throughout India at the time, he reneged on this guarantee and through the Resident, Middleton, encouraged the Wazir to reassume the Begums' treasures and *jagirs* (revenue districts). It was this treatment of the Begums and of their principal servants that provided the substance of the charges brought, in a most sensationalist manner, by Sheridan against Hastings before the Lords.

Benares had formerly been a tributary province of Oudh though, by this period, its *zemindars* (revenue collectors – one of the great difficulties throughout this whole period of change and transition was to define what a *zemindar* was), first Bulwant Sing and later his son, Cheit Sing, had more or less established their independence of the Wazir. Even so, technically, they were still tributaries of the Wazir and, in 1773, as part of the treaty with Hastings, Shuja-ud-daula had handed over the revenue due on Benares to the Company. To begin with Hastings seems to have been satisfied with the regular tribute but, in 1778, due to the bankruptcy of the Company and the exigencies of military campaigns in the south of Madras and the west at Bombay, he called on Cheit Sing for additional contributions of both money and troops. Hastings was also to argue that he had grounds for suspecting Cheit Sing's loyalty. Be that as it may, Hastings's demands became more and more exorbitant and in 1781 Cheit Sing rebelled. British officers and a number of *sepoys* were massacred at Benares but Cheit Sing could not expect to defeat the British troops and he fled into exile, his place being taken by the Raja Mahipnarain.

What we are witnessing, then, whether we consider Bengal, Oudh or Benares, is the increasing involvement of the East India Company in Indian affairs, first by strategies of 'dual control', then by treaties of alliance, then by control of the revenue supplies and finally by the exercise of direct authority. The whole process was, of course, also being watched from England with a mixture of envy and concern at the huge fortunes of the returning 'nabobs' and of humanitarian outrage as stories filtered back of brutal conquests and atrocities. The two major attempts to reorganize the Company's administration in India and to make it more responsible to the authorities at home were the Regulating Act of 1773 and the India Act of 1784. The first set up a Supreme Council in Bengal under a Governor-General. Hastings was appointed as the Governor-General and the Council consisted of himself and another Company employee, Richard Barwell, and three other members appointed by the crown and parliament, General Clavering, Colonel Monson – both king's men – and the man who was to become the bitterest opponents of Hastings, Philip Francis.

Francis is the most difficult character to place: his hatred of Hastings was almost pathological and his letters home, often written in a frenzied code, abound with vituperation and abuse. It was Francis, as much as, if not more than Burke, who was the main force behind the campaign to impeach Hastings. On the whole, history has tended to treat him as little more than the spiteful and vengeful rival of Hastings. But this is not to do him justice. There are at least two things to be noted about Francis that are of particular importance for the present study. The first, hardly connected with Indian matters, is that it is now generally accepted that he was the author of the 'Junius' letters which from 1768 to 1771 rocked the political world in England.

Again, as with the trial itself, I am not so concerned with the substantive themes of the letters as with their status as an *institutional phenomenon*. According to the historian of *The Times*:

> From the time of 'Junius' London daily journalism enters upon a new phase. . . . The importance of the 'Letters of Junius' was both political and journalistic. For the first time in English journalism the influence of an independent writer was exerted upon discriminating readers, and the regularity of the articles, as much as their ability, was responsible for developing the factor in political society now known as 'public opinion'.
>
> (*The History of the Times* 1935, p. 21)

It was the intervention of the 'Junius' letters which played a major part in the struggle for the freedom of reporting which was to come to a head in the Wilkes's Case. When, in 1771, journalists won the right to report parliamentary debates, a right which in turn directly stimulated the growth of daily journalism in the 1770s and 1780s, much of the credit for the initial impetus of the movement must be given to 'Junius', to Philip Francis.

The second thing to note about Francis is that his opposition to Hastings over the matter of revenue was at least coherent, principled and theoretically consistent. Hastings was a pragmatist, and while the revenue system he had inherited on assuming power in 1772 had many shortcomings it was Hastings's intention to make it work as efficiently as possible. The Collector system that he established was basically a crude form of revenue farming and the system clearly lent itself to innumerable abuses. Francis hated this system and in 1776 produced an alternative revenue scheme based on physiocratic principles and the experience of agricultural capitalism in England and Scotland (cf. Guha 1963). His plan was to regard the *zemindars* not simply as fiscal functionaries but as potential improving landlords on the English pattern, and to offer them a permanent tenure in their lands. Hastings, much more informed about the complexities of the Moghul system, realized, better than Francis, that it was impossible to compare the *zemindars* to bona fide English squires. What is significant about this difference of opinion is it shares no common ground: on the one hand Francis is imposing Enlightenment and European principles of political economy on India while, on the other, Hastings is concerned to manipulate as best he can the residual machinery of the Moghul Empire. It is the kind of radical difference of approach to the complexities of India that was to make the trial of Hastings such a protracted affair.

The other institution which the Regulating Act set up in Bengal was a Supreme Court under Sir Elijah Impey: it was intended as a means of extending British law both to the Indians and to the Company employees. Neither Hastings nor, for that matter, Burke later, were in favour of this procedure. For Hastings the Supreme Court was a mistake on at least two counts: in the first place he felt it was profoundly wrong to attempt to subject Indians, with their own Islamic and Hindu systems of law, to British principles of justice; in the second place he regarded the Supreme Court as a possible threat to his own freedom of movement and a rival to the Company's own internal system of policing. It was partly to counteract the first that Hastings was to encourage the study and translation of Hindu and Islamic codes of law. Thus it has been argued that British Oriental scholarship originated in the need to counterbalance the effects of the introduction into India of British judicial processes (Edwardes 1976, p. 74). The second threat, to the Company's autonomy, Hastings removed in 1780 by offering to Impey the position of head of the Company's internal system and in so doing virtually amalgamating the two systems. It was a typically pragmatic move on Hastings's part, but it was later to furnish further grounds for impeachment, it being argued that Hastings had 'bribed' Impey into submission. Perhaps the most notorious illustration of the collusion alleged to have taken place between Hastings and Impey is the trial and execution of Nandakumar. In 1775 Nandakumar had threatened to bring evidence of bribery against Hastings. It was then found that Nandakumar had himself earlier been guilty of a forgery: he was brought to trial, judged according to British justice and hanged. Not even Hastings' defenders have felt easy about this act for, apart from anything else, in trying Nandakumar in a British court Hastings was clearly in violation of his own principle that Indians should be ruled by Indian law – but it is symptomatic of the very confused status of the institutions of power at this period and of Hastings's ruthlessness.

Pitt's India Act of 1784 submitted Indian affairs to further governmental control. Henceforward the Governor-General was to be a political rather than a Company appointee, and as Governor-General he was to be given total executive authority – unlike Hastings who had been subject to the decisions of the Council in Bengal. Furthermore, the Governor-General was to be responsible to a Board of Control at home under a ministerial president. Thus what the two acts of 1773 and 1784 indicate is the gradual erosion of the Company's autonomy: first its subjection to a tussle between crown and parliament and then to a purely parliamentary control. The struggles in India, then, closely reflect the intense constitutional struggles going on at the time in England.

George III's attempts to reassert the rights of the crown had provoked, by the 1780s, an acute and embittered constitutional crisis. The East India Company was an important pawn in the game. On the one hand, it offered an immense field of patronage and whoever managed to gain control of it would have a tremendous political lever. On the other hand, returning Company 'nabobs' were using part of their wealth to buy parliamentary seats. This meant that it represented a direct threat to the landed and aristocratic interests, Whig and Tory alike, by an execrated new 'monied interest'. It is clearly easy to see that much of what was at stake in the Hastings trial derived from this struggle between the Tory-Whigism represented by Burke and the emerging monied interest represented by Hastings – that Hastings was popular with the crown is only symptomatic of the complexity of the political alignments at the time.

With the loss of the American colonies in 1781, the crisis came to a head. In 1782 the North administration fell and was succeeded by the first Rockingham ministry, and then by the highly unstable Shelbourne/Pitt compact. This in turn was defeated by the hastily assembled Fox/North administration, an opportunistic alliance of discredited Whigs and Tories. In the search for sources of patronage Fox proposed his India Bill of 1783 which was to become the basis of Pitt's Act the following year. It passed the Commons but, on strong direction from the crown, it was defeated in the Lords and the government fell. In

1784, at twenty-four years of age, Pitt became Prime Minister for the first time. It was the year of Hastings's return from India, and the beginning of the proceedings in the Commons that were to lead to the impeachment before the Lords in 1788.

C.B. Cone argues, in his authoritative study of Burke's life and work, that the 'passage of the motion (of impeachment) was a personal triumph, a vindication of years of effort, and perhaps Burke's greatest specific parliamentary victory' (Cone 1964, p. 199). Be that as it may, the direction of the impeachment in the Lords was to impose on Burke a terrible burden which was to weigh upon him for the rest of his parliamentary life, and which at times seems to have driven him very nearly to the edge of madness. The Managers' efforts were severely handicapped from the start. To begin with they were denied the opportunity to bring before the Lords two of their most compelling and winnable charges. In 1787 Sir Elijah Impey had been charged on the Nandakumar 'murder' but, through the deployment of a highly skilled defence, he had been acquitted. This meant that the Nandakumar case could hardly be used against Hastings, even though most modern commentators are agreed that Impey's conduct of the trial of Nandakumar was highly questionable if not downright censurable. The other blow to the prosecution's case was that the Commons, influenced by Pitt and through him by the crown, refused to appoint Philip Francis as one of the Managers – ostensibly on the grounds that his personal hostility towards Hastings might prove prejudicial to the Managers' position. It was a staggering setback to Burke for, of all the prospective Managers, Francis alone had any immediate knowledge of India and his detailed study of the revenue system, with its critique of Hastings's 'farming' methods, provided the strongest ground of all for impeachment. Thus even before the case was transferred to the Lords, the prosecution had been deprived of both their most dramatic and their most comprehensively documented briefs.

The Managers were to face two more serious setbacks early in the proceedings. The first was a ruling by the Law Lords that the prosecution should present all its evidence on all the charges before Hastings should be called upon to make any defence. What the prosecution had hoped to do was to present each charge separately, as they had done in the Commons and, while the evidence was fresh before the judges, to have the verdict at once. They probably felt also that they had a better chance of gaining a conviction if the verdict could be brought in while the court was still under the more powerful emotional impact of the Managers' highly charged rhetoric. In winning the ruling of the Lords the defence more or less ensured that the prosecution would talk itself out, that its fervour would become wearied as it strained to maintain moral outrage on charge after charge, year after year. In the event this is what happened.

The second setback, again a technical one but which was to have a determinate effect, was the ruling by the Lords that the trial should be conducted according to the rules prevailing in the lower courts. Burke had tried to argue that the House of Lords, and the device of impeachment itself, was not constrained by the normal procedures of justice and rules of evidence, that parliament, as Supreme Court, must stand aloof and unhampered. In fact the strict application of the rules of evidence was to reduce the trial, at times, to something very close to farce. In the first place not one of the Managers was legally trained, and even the Articles of Charge were loosely, not to say sloppily, drafted. Much of the Managers' case, moreover, rested on evidence that was circumstantial and characterological – guilt to be established by association, self-incrimination and intention – little of which could be admitted as substantive by the rules of the court. More particularly, when the Managers found that witnesses who had spoken out against Hastings in the Commons now, before the Lords, retracted or changed their positions it was ruled that the Managers were not allowed to 'brow beat' such witnesses into recalling their previous testimony. One of the greatest difficulties faced by the Managers was the tendency of important witnesses, including Hastings himself, to 'forget' significant events and details. The most notorious example of this was Nathaniel Middleton, who had been Hastings's appointee at the court at Oudh and deeply involved in the Begums issue; he became popularly known as 'Memory' Middleton – an ironic reference to the famous parliamentary reporter of the period, 'Memory' Woodfall – such was his inability to remember anything when cross-examined by Sheridan. Sir Elijah Impey could not recall whether the affidavits he had collected as to the complicity of the Begums in the Benares rebellion had been authenticated by an interpreter or not, or even, indeed, whether he, Impey, had read them or not (*The History of the Trial of Warren Hastings*, 1, 1796, p. 44).

Completely outmanoeuvred by the technical expertise of the defence and that generally backed by the overall inclination of the Lords, especially the Chancellor, Thurlow, towards Hastings, the prosecution must have had little hope from the beginning of obtaining a verdict of guilty. At times, as the trial dragged on and the sense of frustration intensified – aggravated by the splits between the Managers themselves over the French Revolution – the prosecution increasingly threw legal and even simple logical decorum to the winds and argument turned to rhetoric and rhetoric in turn seemed more and more like bluster. Burke's plight was perhaps the most tragic; personally separated from his colleagues after the publication of his *Reflections on the Revolution in France* in 1790, caricatured in the press as some demented Quixote tilting at windmills, goaded almost to frenzy by the massive propaganda campaign conducted by Hastings's supporters, his language lost all constraint and seemed at times, one commentator thought, to have come direct from Bedlam. Such was the notoriety of Burke's abuse of Hastings that the editor of *The History of the Trial of Warren Hastings* compiled a small appendix of the choicest pieces:

> 1789 – He gorged his ravenous maw with an allowance of 200l a day. He is not satisfied without sucking the blood of 1400 nobles. He is never corrupt without he is cruel. He never dines without creating a famine. He feeds on the indigent, the decaying, the ruined, and them he depresses together; not like the generous eagle, who preys on a living, reluctant, equal prey: No; he is like the ravenous vulture, who feeds on the dead and the enfeebled. . . . Mr Hastings feeds in the dark alone; like a wild beast he groans in a corner over the dead and dying; and like the tiger of that country, he wishes to withdraw into a cavern, to indulge with unobserved employment in all the wanton caprices of his appetite.

> 1794 – This swindling Maecenas – swindling of glory, and obtaining honour under false pretences – a bad scribbler of absurd papers, who could never put two sentences of sense together. . . . A fraudulent bullock-contractor. . . . A man

whose origin was low, obscure and vulgar, and bred in vulgar and ignoble habits. . . . Such are the damned and damnable proceedings of a judge in hell, and such a judge was Warren Hastings. . . . Sir Walter Raleigh was called a spider of hell. This was foolish, indecent, in Lord Coke. He had been a Manager on this trial, he would have been guilty of a neglect of duty, had he not called the prisoner a spider of hell.

(*The History of the Trial*, 6, 1796, pp. 151–5)

While Burke sought to impugn Hastings through sheer weight of invective, Sheridan strove to move the Lords and the audience by means of a powerful theatrical performance. Even before taking the case to the Lords, Sheridan's speech on the Begums charge, already made before the Commons, was something of a celebrated act. In 1788 he works up towards his peroration:

FILIAL PIETY!

It is the primal bond of society – It is that instinctive principle, which, panting for its proper good, soothes, unbidden, each sense and sensibility of man! – It now quivers on every lip! – it now beams from every eye! – It is that gratitude, which softening under sense of recollected good, is eager to own the vast countless debt it ne'er can pay – for so many long years of unceasing solicitudes, honourable self-denials, life preserving cares! – It is that part of our practice, where duty drops its awe! – where reverence refines to love! – It asks no aid of memory! – It needs not the deductions of reason! – Pre-existing, paramount over all, whether law or human rule – few arguments can increase and none can diminish it! – It is the sacrament of our nature – not only the duty but the indulgence of man – It is his first great privilege – It is amongst his last most endearing delights when the bosom glows with the idea of reverberated joy.

(*The History of the Trial*, 1, 1796, p. 99)

In 1794, six years later, it is the same ploy, with variations:

'Woman', exclaimed the Manager, 'is by nature, perhaps, a *passionate animal*'. [A loud approbation.] '*I* do *not* say that it is a *moral obligation* to be a SCOLD'. [An approbation louder still.] 'But less condemned than MEN to accident and violence, she must be less apt to cope with it, when it comes, either with the patience that can be perfect only through suffering, or with that active fortitude which, strengthening while it struggles, sometimes learns at last to check assailing fortune, to encounter, to overcome it! While with WOMAN all is passive as to her powers and resources! Her weapons are words – her assaults are her sorrows! She eludes sometimes, by shrinking, calamity not otherwise to be escaped! But when all fails, when bruised and broken in spite of bending before the storm, she is not to be bereft of the last sad consolation, the cry of nature, the tears that overflow from anguish, the groans and exclamations which lighten the overloaded heart! – It was *not* an OPEN ENEMY that had done me this dishonour; for then I can have borne it! – Neither was it MINE ADVERSARY that did magnify himself against me; for then, peradventure, I would have hid myself from him. BUT – it was even THOU, my companion, my guide, mine own familiar friend – we took sweet counsel together'.

(*The History of the Trial*, 7, 1796, p. 113)

It was powerful stuff, with both Burke and Sheridan managing at times to collapse at critical moments and with the ladies in the audience fainting in their places.

In complete contrast came Hastings's defence – first against the Benares charge:

My Lords, I scarcely need tell you, that whatever our various resolutions or opinions might be, individually or collectively, they could not affect the right or title of Cheit Sing to the Zemindary, nor the tenure by which he held it. He was neither more nor less than a Zemindar. His Sunnud and Pottah were made out, not from a copy of stipulations and agreements between him and the Company, but from common formulae of such instruments granted to Zemindars in the Company's original provinces. The Rajah never pretended any right to stipulate or command: he was content with what the Company was pleased to allow him. My Lords, I do again insist upon it, that no arguments, votes, or resolutions, of our Board, could confer any right or title upon

Cheit Sing, which he did not possess from his Pottah and Sunnud: therefore the whole of the evidence, which the Managers have brought respecting our various opinions on the rights of Cheit Sing, is null and void; and he must be considered the same as any other Zemindar of the British Government, with the exception of certain privileges conferred upon him, which were accurately defined in the Sunnud and Pottah.

(*The History of the Trial*, 4, 1796, p. 87)

and then against the Begums charge:

Had my accusers thought fit to have taken the other side of the question, they could with as much ease, and with much more justice, have influenced the minds of their hearers against the mother for her unnatural conduct to her son, then they did influence them against the son for ill conduct to his mother. – I say with much more justice, because the son had a right by the laws of his country, which his mother had not. If the latter was deprived of the treasure, she was only deprived of that some years later, of which she could make no use, and which she ought voluntarily to have given up some years sooner. My Lords, I speak this on the equity of the case; for though it may be contended that the Begum had a right to the treasure, by the Nabob's concession and our guarantee, she never had, nor could have, an *equitable* right to retain it.

(*The History of the Trial*, 4, 1796, p. 89)

Compared to the invective of Burke and the emotional appeal of Sheridan, Hastings's language is restrained, informed, almost disdainful – it was this tone that infuriated Burke. While Sheridan and Burke base their prosecution on universal sentiment and moral outrage, Hastings quietly marshalls scrupulous distinctions and precise details. Sheridan's theatricality and Burke's escatology just look cumbersome and inept as Hastings's patient but telling exposition of the Islamic systems of land tenure – zemindar, pottah, sunnud – and inheritance drains the wind out of them.

By the time Hastings rose to make the final speech of his defence, there is a sense that a storm had blown itself out and the vessel that it had threatened remained intact, under control and calmly defiant:

> To the Commons of England, in whose name I am arraigned for desolating the provinces of their dominion in India, I dare to reply, that they are, and their representatives persist in telling them so, the most flourishing of all the States of India – it was I who made them so. The valour of others acquired, I enlarged and gave shape and consistency to the dominion which you hold there; I preserved it: I sent forth its armies with an effectual, but an economical hand, through unknown and hostile regions, to the support of your other possessions; to the retrieval of one from degradation and dishonour; and of the other, from utter loss and subjection. I maintained the wars which were of your formation, or that of others, *not of mine*. I won one member of the great Indian Confederacy from it by an act of seasonable restitution; with another I maintained a secret intercourse, and converted him into a friend; a third I drew off by diversion and negotiation, and employed him as an instrument of peace. – When you cried out for peace, and your cries were heard by those who were the object of it, I resisted this, and every other species of counteraction, by rising in my demands; and I at least afforded the efficient means by which a peace, if not so durable, more seasonable at least, was accomplished with another. I gave *you all*, and you have awarded me with *confiscation, disgrace, and a life of impeachment*.
>
> (*The History of the Trial*, 4, 1796, pp. 101–3)

On 23 April 1795 Hastings was acquitted on all charges. He had won.

But had he? In 1795 Hastings was 63 years old and heavily in debt. The trial alone had cost him some £70,000 and though the Company granted him an annuity of £4000 and a further interest free loan of £50,000 he was to remain in financial difficulties for the rest of his life. Nor was this all: though he had been acquitted his reputation and career were in ruins. Hastings is the only Governor-General of India never to have been offered a title and there is something rather pathetic in the way in which he treasured the minor marks of recognition that were to come to him only many years later. The problem for

Hastings was that though he had been vindicated by the House of Lords he had at the same time been tried and condemned before a new and much more redoubtable tribunal: the daily press and popular opinion.

The growth of the daily press is possibly the most important phenomenon of this period. From the time of 'Junius' in 1769 and Wilkes in 1771, and the opening up of parliamentary reporting in that year, the number and influence of the daily journals increased dramatically. *The Morning Chronicle* was founded in 1769; *The Morning Post* in 1772; *The General Advertiser* in 1778; *The Morning Herald* in 1778; *The Daily Universal Register* was founded in 1785 and became *The Times* in 1788; its great rival, *The World and Fashionable Advertiser*, was founded in 1787; *The Observer* began in 1791 and 1792 saw the birth of both *True Briton* and *The Sun*. Already Walpole had found it expedient to employ hirelings in the press, but after 1770 the diversion of Treasury funds towards the payment of compliant journalists began to develop on a systematic basis. The brief-lived Shelbourne government paid out over £1000 for press support, and by 1788 the Pitt government was earmarking over £5000 a year for retainers to journalists.

From the beginning both Hastings and the Managers realized that the real trial was going to be in, as we would say today, the 'media' as much as in the House of Lords. In the course of the trial Major Scott, Hastings's principal supporter and director of propaganda, spent nearly £6500 on articles, letters, commentaries and cartoons in the press. *The Letters of Simpkin the Second*, supportive of Hastings, were touted from *The Morning Herald* to *The Morning Post* and were finally placed in *The World*. Nor was it simply that the press 'lived off' the trial: at one stage, when it was going through one of its many boring stages, it was the letters of Simpkin that maintained public interest in the trial: the point is that the trial and the press can be seen to be working together in the establishment of public interest and public opinion. The importance of the Hastings trial at this formative moment in the evolution of the press and of public opinion may be further evidenced by the fact that, in the elections of 1788, Pitt could use the Warren Hastings trial, together with the scandal surrounding Mrs Fitzherbert, as issues on which to attack the opposition.

Francis and Burke were never in any doubt that the important forum for their attack on Hastings and all that he represented was not the Lords but the press and public opinion. Francis, as we have seen, knew the power of the press better than anyone, thanks to his experience as 'Junius', while for Burke 'the ultimate judges under God for all our actions' were the 'public' (quoted in Marshall 1965, p. 84) and there can be no doubt but that he directed his speeches far beyond the immediate auditors of the court. To this extent that decision by the court to take all the charges at once rather than separately may have militated against a legal verdict of guilt, but it very much helped Burke in his principal design of building up a picture of Hastings's essential malignity by means of the accumulation of a vast amount of circumstantial and even trivial evidence. It is this, also, that accounts for the avowed 'mobbishness' of Burke's speeches – a typical example of his adopting a jacobinical device (O'Brien 1968, p. 54). The most outrageous example of such tactics is Burke's account of the atrocities committed by one of Hastings's revenue collectors, Debi Sing:

And here, my Lords, began such a scene of cruelties and tortures as I believe no history has ever presented to the indignation of the world. . . . My Lords, they began by winding cords round the fingers of the unhappy free-holders of those provinces until they clung to and were almost incorporated with one another; and then they hammered wedges of iron between them, until, regardless of the cries of the sufferers, they had bruised to pieces and forever crippled those poor honest, innocent, laborious hands . . . (they) were tied two and two by the legs together; and their tormentors, throwing them with their heads downwards, over a bar, beat them on the soles of their feet with rattans, until the nails fell from the toes; and then attacking them at their heads, as they hung downwards, as before at their feet, they beat them with sticks and other instruments of blind fury, until the blood gushed out of their eyes, mouths, and noses. . . . Wives were torn from the arms of their husbands, and suffered the same flagitious wrongs, which were indeed hid in the bottoms of the dungeons in which their honour and their liberty were buried together. Often they were taken out of the refuse of this consoling gloom, stripped naked, and thus exposed to the world, and then cruelly scourged; and in order that cruelty might riot in all the circumstances that melt into tenderness the fiercest natures, the nipples of their breasts were put between the sharp and elastic sides of cleft bamboos.

(Burke n.d., p. 84)

Apart from the irrelevance of such material – Burke was trying to prove Hastings evil because he had employed an evil man, a very tenuous line of argument – and from his own suspicions as to its reliability, this was just the sort of material that Burke felt he could best exploit:

Oh what an affair, I am clear that I must dilate upon that; for it has stuff in it, that will if any thing work upon the popular sense.

(quoted by Marshall 1965, p. 84)

And this is the way in which the Managers proceeded to conduct the prosecution: by implication, innuendo, exaggeration, caricature, distortion. The goading of Cheit Sing, the harrassment of the Begums, the bribery of Munni Begum, the machinations of Nandakumar, the atrocities by Debi Sing all become so many occasions for lurid colours and bravura effects, a whole series of magic lantern slides to pass from a public hungry for sensation and whose attention can be held only by seeking for greater stridency and ever more exotic outrage.

Of course what was at issue in the Hastings trial was not simply confined to domestic matters – the emergence of public opinion as opposed to the rule of law as a hegemonic force, the status of the Commons *vis-à-vis* the Executive and the Judiciary, the development of daily journalism – but concerned as well the emergence of that other major institution, the British Empire itself. Perhaps the most fascinating aspect of the trial as a whole was the way in which it illustrates the elaboration of two quite distinct and almost diametrically opposed kinds of imperial discourse.

Edward Said has spoken of two kinds of 'Orientalism':

Orientalism is the discipline by which the Orient was (and is) approached systematically, as a topic of learning, discovery and practice. But in addition I have been using the word to designate that collection of dreams, images, and vocabularies available to anyone who has tried to talk about what lies east of the dividing line.

(Said 1978, p. 73)

Elsewhere Said characterizes the differences between the two kinds of Orientalism as that between 'imaginative geography and history and positive geography and history' (p. 55), or as between 'lexicography' and the 'imagination' (p. 149). In the Hastings trial we have a truly dramatic illustration of the ways in which these two Orientalisms were constituted and set to work.

Burke's 'India' was a magnificent imaginative achievement. No one has more glowingly appreciated it than Macaulay:

India and its inhabitants were not to [Burke], as to most Englishmen, mere names and abstractions, but a real country and a real people. The burning sun, the strange vegetation of the palm and cocoa tree, the rice field, the tank, the huge trees, older than the Moghul empire, under which the village crowds assemble, the thatched roof of the peasant's hut, the rich tracery of the mosque where the imaum prays with his face to Mecca, the drums and banners, and gaudy idols, the devotee swinging in the air, the graceful maiden, with the pitcher on her head, descending the steps to the river side, the black faces, the long beards, the yellow robes, the spears and the silver maces, the elephants with their canopies of state, the gorgeous palanquin of the prince and the close litter of the noble lady, all those things were to him as the objects amidst which his own life has been passed, as the objects which lay on the road between Beaconsfield and St James' Street. All India was present to his eye, from the halls where suitors laid gold and perfumes at the feet of sovereigns to the wild moor where the gipsy camp was pitched, from the bazaars, humming like beehives with the crowd of buyers and sellers, to the jungle where the lonely courier shakes his bunch of iron rings to scare away the hyaenas. He had just as lively an idea of the insurrection at Benares as of Lord George Gordon's riots, and of the execution of Nuncomar as of the execution of Dr Dodd. Oppression in Bengal was to him the same thing as oppression in the streets of London.

(Macaulay 1850, p. 316)

Macaulay knew India, of course, and we might take the fore-going as his testimony to the veracity of Burke's image of India, but what it is more important to realize is that here Macaulay's India is precisely that romantic and exotic India that Burke had done so much to construct.

There are many instances in the trial of this construction of a romantic, edenic, sensual, threatening India. A common motif is that of the innocence of India: writing to Lord Clive, Francis announces a theme that is to thread its way through the trial and into the doxology of imperialism:

> In a few words, when your Lordship came here in 1765, this country was in a state of Innocence and Purity! It was Paradise before the fall, compared to the condition in which we found it!
>
> (Weitzman 1929, p. 222)

And speaking to the Benares charge Grey has the Rajah break forth:

> 'My fields', says the Rajah, 'are cultivated, my towns and villages are full of inhabitants, my country is a garden, and my ryots are happy. The principal merchants of India, from the security of my government, resort to my capital, and make it their residence. . . . The traveller and the stranger, from one end of my country to the other, lay down their burdens and sleep in security.'
>
> (*The History of the Trial*, 1, 1796, p. 20)

Around the Rohillas, too, a gossamer web of poetic association was woven – originating in part in the confusion of their leader's name, Hafiz Khan, with that of the Persian poet. Perhaps the most saturated version of this idyll of a chivalric Rohilcund is to be found later in Macaulay:

> The Rohillas were distinguished from other inhabitants of India by a peculiarly fair complexion. They were more honourably distinguished by courage in war, and by skill in the arts of peace. While anarchy raged from Lahore to Cape Comorin, their territory enjoyed the blessings of repose under the guardianship of valour. Agriculture and commerce flourished among them; nor were they negligent of the arts of

rhetoric and poetry. Many persons now living have heard aged men talk with regret of the golden days when the Afghan princes ruled in the vale of Rohilcund.

(Macaulay 1850, p. 240)

It is all very lovely but the loveliness is that of myth.

And that is precisely the point. Myth is functional: what it establishes is a kind of instrumental space, a horizon within which values can be established and operative decisions made and legitimized. To this extent myth is essentially manichaean. What the idyll allows to be constructed and thought is its obverse: the Orient as threat, seduction, decadence. Burke describes Debi Sing as the organizer of a 'legal brothel':

A moving seraglio of these ladies always attended his progress, and were always brought to the splendid and multiplied entertainments with which he regaled his Council. In these festivities, while his guests were engaged in the seductions of beauty, the intoxications of the most delicious wines of France, and the voluptuous vapour of perfumed Indian smoke, uniting the vivid satisfactions of Europe with the torpid blandishments of Asia, the great magician himself, sober and the centre of debauch, vigilant in the lap of negligence and oblivion, attended with an eagle's eye the moment for thrusting in business, and at such times was able to carry without difficulty points of shameful enormity, which at other hours he would not so much as have dared to mention to his employers, young men rather careless and inexperienced than intellectually corrupt. Not satisfied with being pander to their pleasures, he anticipated and was purveyor to their wants, and supplied them with a constant command of money; and by these means he reigned with an uncontrolled dominion over the province and over its governors.

(Burke n.d., pp. 72–3)

A whole interpretative grid is being established here: the intoxication of delicious wine versus the voluptuous vapour of opium; the vivid satisfactions of Europe versus the torpid blandishments of Asia; sobriety versus debauchery; vigilance versus negligence and oblivion; inexperienced youth versus the corruption of the great magician. True, the simple polarities are here troubled by Debi Sing's assumption of power – it is the fear that must haunt any such specular topos – but what is important is the set of symmetrical opposites that allow of us and them, west and east, Europe and India.

The effect of all these strategies is to render India radically 'different' while at the same time making it readily imaginable. The Orient has to be, as Said puts it, 'Orientalized'. It is this, for example, that makes some of Burke's evidence read like extracts from the Arabian Nights (see his account of the conspiracy of The Three Seals: Burke n.d., pp. 410–13). And whenever he speaks of the 'seraglio' it is difficult not to be reminded of Montesquieu's account of the harem in *The Persian Letters*. Paradoxically, what can be given a high degree of imaginative coherence becomes, for that very reason, wholly alien, unmediated – one of the consistent problems of the trial was that of interpretation: how does one interpret the interpretation? (cf. Hastings 1948, pp. 24–7). Said's epigraph from Marx's *Eighteenth Brumaire* comes to mind:

They cannot represent themselves; they must be represented.

This is precisely what happens at the trial:

In an apostrophe the most beautiful that can be imagined, Mr Fox made the injured Cheit Sing the utterer of his own complaint to the house. – 'I was', said he, 'the Sovereign of a fertile country, happy and beloved; I endeavoured to conciliate the friendship of all around me, and as I thought with a success which impressed me with every sensation of felicity. – This was the situation of which I boasted; but what is now the reverse? I am a wretched exile, dependent on the bounty of those who were my enemies, but whose enmities are now buried in their sympathy for my distress. What have I done to deserve this punishment?' – 'You forget', replied an Englishman, 'that though a Sovereign Prince at Patna, at Benares you were but a Zemindar; in the latter character you were guilty of disobedience, and are therefore sentenced to judicial exile.' – 'Alas', rejoins the wanderer, 'I was ignorant of my crime. Why had I not an instructor to teach me the subtleties of your laws? Though to your power I was but as an atom in the view of Omnipotence, yet surely my intentions should

have been regarded, and my ignorance not construed as
guilt.'

(*The History of the Trial*, 1, 1796, p. 16)

The projection is evident: Cheit Sing becomes the hero of
romantic pastoral with gothic overtones.

Hastings will have nothing to do with the pathos of such
posturings and identifications. If the prosecution can be seen as
engaged in constructing a discourse of India that is imaginative,
romantic, theatrical and literary, then Hastings can be seen as
representing an almost diametrically opposed project wherein
the discourse of India will be technical, pragmatic, analytical
and philological. Rather than presuming to speak for India,
moreover, Hastings must be given the credit for doing all in his
power to let India speak for itself. There is already evidence for
this in his defence speeches where, as we have seen, it is the
technical precision of Islamic law that he cites in support of his
actions in India. But Hastings's major contribution to the
elaboration of this alternative discourse was his patronage of
Oriental studies. Ironically it was he who had encouraged and
in part financed Halhed's translation of *The Gentoo Code* (1776)
and Davy and White's translation of the *Institutes political and
military of Timur* (1783) which Burke was to quote from with such
authority to prove to Hastings that India did have coherent
systems of law!

Hastings also sponsored Charles Wilkin's translation of *The
Bhagvat-Geeta* which appeared in 1785, and the letter from him
to Nathaniel Smith, Chairman of the East India Company,
which prefaces that volume offers the most succinct and convenient illustration of Hastings's approach to the knowledge of
India. First there is his scholarship and evident linguistic
skill:

The Mahabbharat contains the genealogy and general history of the house of Bhaurut, so called from Bhurrut its
founder; the epithet Maha, or Great, being prefixed in token
of distinction: but its more particular object is to relate the
dissensions and wars of the two great collateral branches of
it, called Kooroos and Pandoos; both lineally descended in
the second degree from Veecheetraveerya, their common

ancestor, by their respective father Dreetrarasha and Pandoo.

> (in Marshall 1970, p. 184)

How different a discourse of India this is from Burke's account of the atrocities of Debi Sing. A few lines later Hastings counsels that we should hesitate in bringing European standards of judgement to bear on *The Bhagvat-Geeta*:

> Might I, an unlettered man, venture to prescribe bounds to the latitude of criticism, I should exclude, in estimating the merit of such a production, all rules from the ancient or modern literature of Europe, all references to such sentiments or manners as are become the standards of propriety for opinion and action in our own modes of life, and equally all appeals to our revealed tenets of religion, and moral duty. I should exclude them, as by no means applicable to the language, sentiments, manners, or morality appertaining to a system of society with which we have been for ages unconnected, and of an antiquity preceding even the first efforts of civilization in our own quarter of the globe, which, in respect to the general diffusion and common participation of arts and sciences, may now be considered as one community.

> (in Marshall 1970, p. 185)

It is this same enlightened cultural relativism, whereby he argues that Asia must be judged by Asiatic principles and standards, which Hastings will later invoke as part of his defence.

Earlier we have noted the instrumental effectivity of the myths of the 'imaginative tradition of Orientalism – the powerful excuse for conquest afforded by the construction of the other as decadent, threatening and evil – but it may well be that what seems in so many ways to be Hastings's more 'honest' or enlightened policy is in the end the more insidious and 'evil'. For while we would probably want to applaud Hastings's high regard for Islamic and Hindu culture and religion, and his correlative opposition to the establishment of Christian missions in India, it can be argued that his sponsoring of the study of the Gentoo Code and of the Koran (re-)introduced that division into Indian society between Hindu and Muslim that was to lead in 1947 to the split between India and Pakistan. Ramkrishna Mukherjee, in his exhaustively researched and documented *The Rise and Fall of the East India Company*, quotes from a British government report:

'Legislative recognition given to the differences based on religion and caste may have been responsible to some extent for holding the two major communities apart.'

(Mukherjee 1974, p. 320)

Thus, for all their incompatibility during the trial – one reason for its length, neither side understanding what the other was saying – the discourses on India of both Burke (and the Managers as a whole) and Hastings colluded in the end towards the establishment of Empire. At this level of analysis it would probably be harsh to condemn either of them: I have tended to stress the imaginative strain in Burke's speeches but it would be thoroughly reprehensible simply to dismiss his accusations and outrage as pure bluster. As we can see from Mukherjee's study of the East India Company, there was terrible suffering in Bengal in the 1770s – partly due to the appalling drought of 1770 which alone killed over three million people – and during this period Indian industry was run down and its capital drained away. To laugh at Burke, to call him mad, as so many of his contemporaries did, would be to join those who would always gloss the description of atrocities as the fantasies of a sick mind – one thinks, for example, of the reception given to Casement's reports on the Congo and Putamayo. On the other hand, it would be just as unfair to accuse Hastings of positive design in his promotion of Oriental studies towards the division of India into India and Pakistan, or to the restoration of religious practices already in decline. Though Hastings clearly recognized that knowledge was power, there is much in his regard for Indian culture which is very far from the 'knowingness' of the Orientalist specialist and scholar. In the letter to Nathaniel Smith we have already referred to there is a marvellous sense of wonder in his narrative of his experience of watching a Brahmin engaged in meditation:

The importance of this duty cannot be better illustrated, nor strongly marked, than by the last sentence with which

Kreeshna closes his instruction to Arjoon, and which is properly the conclusion of the Geeta: 'Hath what I have been speaking, O Arjoon, been heard *with thy mind fixed to one point*? Is the *distraction* of thought, which arose from thy ignorance, removed?'

(in Marshall 1970, pp. 186–7)

And Hastings goes on to ponder the significance of Brahminical meditation, of the kind of knowledge generations of contemplation might accumulate, and 'the new tracks and combinations of sentiment' that may have been discovered that could not possibly be translated into European experience. It seems to me that in this modesty and preparedness to *not* know, Hastings presents an exemplary approach to the problems of understanding another culture. The tentativeness of the early Orientalists – and the respect they paid to their originals – is to be found illustrated in Halhed's Introduction to his *Code of Gentoo Laws* when he explains his use of the word 'folly':

The folly here specified is not to be understood in the usual sense of the word in an European idiom, as a negative quality, or the mere want of sense, but as a kind of obstinately stupid lethargy, a perverse absence of mind in which the will is not altogether passive: it seems to be a weakness peculiar to Asia, for we cannot find a term by which to express the precise idea in the European languages; it operates somewhat like the violent impulse of fear, under which men utter falsehoods totally incompatible with each other, and utterly contrary to their own opinion, knowledge, conviction; and it may be added also, their inclination and intention.

(in Marshall 1970, p. 166)

I am inclined to wonder why Halhed should have been particularly fascinated by this 'folly' – 'it operates somewhat like the violent impulse of fear.' It describes an undiagnosed kind of madness but was it just 'a weakness peculiar to Asia'? In 1787 George III went mad; Francis betrays many symptoms of manic depressiveness; Hastings's sensitivity to any slight more than hints at paranoia and there is the *horror vacui* of Burke:

I do not like to see anything destroyed, any void produced in society, any ruin on the face of the land.

(Burke 1968, p. 245)

The last twenty years of the eighteenth century were a world of revolutions and madnesses, of ruins and follies. Perhaps the impeachment, with all its ceremonial, its place apart, its studied contrivance, was the greatest folly of the period, an artificial landscape where the institutions collapsing elsewhere – religion, property, chivalry, to recall the *Reflections* once more – might be shored up for a little more time. And in turn does not India, too, emerge as another folly: a place where all that has lost purchase in Europe could be reinscribed and reconstituted? The Permanent Settlement of 1793 ordered the settlement of land on the model of English improving landlordism; the restoration of Hindu and Islamic religious observances re-established the hegemonic role of religion; and the vale of Rohilcund chivalry enjoys again a last and glowing sunset.

Notes

1 See *The Times*, 15 February 1788:

> It was whimsical to hear a general remark in the Law Coffee Houses yesterday, which was, 'that during the trial of Mr Hastings, nothing would be done in the Courts of Justice'.

and 19 February:

> Mr Hastings has more to answer for than he is aware of. There were but three Bishops present at the annual meeting of the Society for the Propagation of the Gospel in Foreign Parts.

6
Bakhtin, Marxism and post-structuralism

GRAHAM PECHEY

Lucien Goldmann on Julia Kristeva on Mikhail Bakhtin: it was through this chain of scholarly hearsay that I first came across Bakhtin's name in print in 1971 (Goldmann 1967). I first read him in the following year in the context of my research on William Blake. However, it was only with the appearance of Tony Bennett's *Formalism and Marxism* in 1979 that I felt stimulated to write about Bakhtin, having already used his concepts for some years in my teaching at Hatfield Polytechnic. The paper reprinted below originated as a chapter in a (now abandoned) book project on literary theory of which Bakhtinism was to be the leading motif. Its present form is a function of two contingencies: the publication in 1981 of *The Dialogic Imagination* (which greatly extended the number of key Bakhtin texts available in English), and the evident need for Bakhtinists like myself to intervene in the contention between deconstruction and historical materialism which was then speedily moving up the agenda in the current theoretical debate. The text below is exactly the text delivered at the Essex Conference in July 1982. Nothing that has been published since has made me want to modify anything in it – not even the 'definitive' Clark/Holquist biography of 1984, with its insistence on Bakhtin's Russian Orthodox and neo-Kantian interests and its reduction of the whole range of his work on discourse to a set of variations on ethical and epistemological themes adumbrated in his (still untranslated) earliest writing. Tzvetan Todorov (1985) shows a tendency in the same direction; but at least he acknowledges that while each of Bakhtin's works 'contains . . . the whole of his thought . . . it also holds a slippage, a displacement within this same thought, at times barely perceptible yet ultimately most deserving of attention'. The journal articles I have read since this paper have been uniformly mediocre and unenlightening, especially those from North America. The exceptions are Ken Hirschkop (1985), who has attacked the tendency in American readings to 'evade the most radical aspects of Bakhtin's work'; and Allon White, whose excellent 'Bakhtin, sociolinguistics and deconstruction' (1984) pushes home the critique that I tentatively launch in my last sentence. White's piece is the perfect complement to the case that follows.

*

It may help to situate the project of this paper to say that it sets out to elaborate the implications of something I wrote three years ago. In a review of Medvedev's *The Formal Method in Literary Scholarship* I suggested that the 'other side' of this 'downright contestation' of Russian Formalism was a 'symptomatic reading' of its texts – 'an obverse of polemic determining from within the very positions from which the polemic is conducted' (Pechey 1980). The fact that I would now want to delete the 'perhaps' with which (incidentally) that statement was qualified and argue the point at length is no mere accident of autobiography: it is rather a necessity of *autocritique* forced upon me by the direction in which the debate around literary theory has shifted since then. Substitute 'deconstructive' for 'symptomatic' and the issue clarifies at once; in a moment when deconstruction appears to have a monopoly of radicalism and novelty in the theorization of discourse we need to turn from applause for the style of Bakhtinian polemic or the paraphrase of Bakhtinian themes to the deconstructive and indeed self-deconstructive activity which is the determining obverse of both. In other words, what needs now to be presented as exemplary are not the gestures of negating or positing but the textual *process* which conditions *and exceeds* these gestures. Bakhtinian theory is sometimes referred to as 'post-formalism', as if it were a question of merely being chronologically the later of two related but 'full' positions. It would be truer to characterize it as a post-structuralism coinciding with the displacement that brought about structuralism itself: a paradox from the standpoint of literal dating which usefully points to a changed meaning of the prefix, inasmuch as 'post-' now signifies not contingent succession but the status of the already-posterior which Bakhtinian theory shares with all other discourses whatever. Formed in the transformation of other texts, Bakhtinism is subject to an endless post-dating and an anticipation equally endless.

Now of course it is not only a deconstructive reading of Formalism that we read in Bakhtin; the other crucially formative encounter – with Saussurean linguistics – could also be held up as a model of such a reading. In that encounter, conducted under the signature of Voloshinov, the concept of the sign and the concept of ideology are so brought together that they transform each other, the sign taking on the historicity and ideology the materiality that would make them into concepts of historical materialism (Voloshinov 1973). To argue this case we would need to show that the replacement of the sign by the concept of the *utterance* – the real unit of social sign-production which necessarily escapes analysis into the neutral virtualities of the system of language – is in no sense a logocentric move. Appearances notwithstanding, it is the condition of a quite radical challenging of the famous Saussurean dichotomies, and in the first place of the bifurcation into *langue* and *parole*. The theory of the utterance reverses Saussure's priorities without becoming a theory of *parole*, in the manner of a stylistics. We would need to show that the Bakhtinian theory is distinct not only from stylistics, which stands to linguistics in a relation of mere parasitism and complementarity, but also from the seemingly cognate projects of Benveniste and Mukařovský, which seek to replace Saussure's bifurcation with new bifurcations (Benveniste 1971, pp. 101–12; Mukařovský 1976, pp. 50–9). An instructive parallel might be found in Gramsci's dialogue with Croce: 'politics' is rescued from the arbitrariness and irrationality to which it is condemned in Croce's text in much the same way as the domain of the utterance is rescued from Saussure's; in both cases Marxist positions are elaborated in the deconstruction of a non-Marxist antagonist. I mention these possible heads of another argument only in order to broaden the basis for discussion; the Bakhtinian reading of Formalism will be my sole concern in the rest of this paper.

I had better begin by outlining in broad terms the direction my argument will take. For this purpose I will draw on certain Bakhtinian expressions in a provisional way, recognizing their inadequacy in themselves. They are these:

'discourse in life': 'discourse in art'
　　　　　　　　　　'discourse in the novel': 'discourse in
　　　　　　　　　　poetry'

The spacing is meant to indicate a developing particularization which is only a convenience of argument; it is not meant to legislate for any genetic order in the development (so-called) of the theory. In the reversal of these two hierarchized oppositions and the transformation or redefinition of the newly privileged (left-hand) term, we have the two moments of formation of Bakhtinian theory. Bakhtin looks as it were *from* discourse in general *towards* 'artistic' discourse and then, within what Formalism calls 'verbal art' itself, he looks *from* novelistic *towards* poetic discourse 'in the narrow sense'.[1] In each case he breaks with Formalist theorizing at just those points where the latter had not broken with (or had only incoherently questioned) traditionalist presuppositions. The first of these views from outside pulls poetics back in the direction of rhetoric; the second ensures that this general theory of discourse in relation to power is no classicizing throwback but rather a theory of the non-canonical and decentring forces within ideology which was unprecedented in its time and is still not superseded. 'The novel' is Bakhtin's name for these forces in so far as they manifest themselves in the forms of writing. I hope to show that his answer to the Formalist notion of the literary as an abstracting (hypostasizing) removal from communication – the notion of the 'self-valuable' word – is not a new pragmatics of communication shorn of its prescriptive character, but a wholly new space where this theoretical see-saw no longer functions. This space is arrived at not in any external attack on the Formalist texts; it is the result of occupying these texts and inviting them to have the courage of their metaphors.

Our demonstration of all this requires that we take a lengthy detour, the first stage of which is an understanding of the deconstruction of the concept of *form* which Russian Formalism had already carried out. In an early move this concept is nominally retained on the basis of a preliminary reversal: outside becomes inside, and 'form' is undoubtedly redefined in a way that breaks with the idealism of the age-old form–content couple. On this (traditional) view, form and content are the terms of a correlation *within* the work; neither can be invoked without also invoking this internal correlation. Formalism decisively detaches 'form' from this correlation by insisting that the work is *all form*: form is 'the whole entity' (Eikhenbaum 1971, p. 12); content is non- or pre-aesthetic and can only enter the work by becoming a formal element along with the rest. Now to say that the content of the work *is* its form (as Shklovsky does in some contexts) is only to confirm the ancient dualism in a murder of definition which is anything but deconstructive. Formalism sidesteps this dead-end by setting up, in effect, two *external* correlations:

Form in general: absence of form
A particular form: other forms

In the first of these new correlations 'poetic language' stands over against an aformal (aesthetically neutral) 'practical language' in a distinction which cuts across the old generic distinction of 'poetry' and 'prose' and has all the appearance of being absolute. The 'literariness' which Formalism takes as its object is founded in this *negative* external correlation which for all its provocation has to bear the blame for the weakness of much early Formalist writing. What then takes its place is our second – *differential* rather than negative – external correlation, whereby the work cannot be understood apart from the historical succession and interaction of forms. Literary history proceeds not by the expression of new contents but by a dynamic of the replacement of old forms whose literariness has been exhausted. This firm articulation of textuality upon the movement of intertextual relations is the great strength of the Formalist case; we are not surprised to find both Bakhtinism and structuralism carrying it forward.

If we turn now to the two other key concepts of Formalism – the *device* and the *function* – we can see that their elaboration was compelled by the need to move beyond the traditional terms and abolish the inside-outside couple for good and all. The 'device' is plainly a quasi-technological riposte to the quasi-theological 'symbol' or 'image' of Symbolist discourse. Potebnya's theory of poetry as 'thinking in images' sets up a criterion at once too narrow and too broad: 'practical language' (the Formalists argued) also employed images while poetry does not need images to be poetic. Far from using different methods to the same communicative end of 'clarifying the unknown by means of the known' (Shklovsky 1965, p. 6), the two modes use the same methods to secure different ends. The Formalist notion of the peculiar signifying orientation of the 'poetic' is derived by antithesis from the Symbolist notion of familiarizing: 'forms' are 'made difficult' in order that 'objects' may be 'made strange'. Now the texts of Formalism are notoriously confusing on this issue of *defamiliarization*: what is it that the textual devices defamiliarize? Signifier, signified or referent? And if either signifier or signified, what is in question: first-order (linguistic) or second-order (semiotic) signs? Or both? Defamiliarization is also sometimes a device in its own right and sometimes the principle of all devices *per se*. Still, what we can say about this new concept of the device is that it effectively revives the old rhetorical concept of the figure – a far wider category than the image, which is ordinarily limited to lexical and punctual devices. The device extends the working of the figure further still, taking in all the levels of language and structuring: parallelism, for example – almost all the devices discussed by the Formalists are variants of this orginally purely syntactic figure – works on the phonic level to produce rhyme, assonance, alliteration; on the semantic level to produce metaphor; and on the level of narrative plotting to produce 'tautological' repetitions of events. At the same time there is a narrowing as compared with the figure: the device has nothing to do with communication; it is self-referring and asks to be 'seen'. Its defamiliarizing work effects a 'semantic shift'[2] which paradoxically effaces its own semantic nature, at once exploiting and cancelling meaning, dissolving intelligibility into 'perceptibility'. A palpable advance upon the concept of 'form', the device is none the less a somewhat problematic occupant of the conceptual field of Formalism. Born in what I have called the negative external correlation, it has a tendency to revert to the internal correlation even as it is pushed forward towards the 'strong' or differential correlation of later Formalist theorizing. It collapses into reversion to the extent that it is coupled (as it often is) with 'materials', thereby reproducing under another name the form-content dichotomy. It is then pushed forward to the extent that Formalism begins to negotiate the historical dimension of the literary – that is to say, as defamiliarization migrates to the diachronic plane, becoming for Shklovsky in particular the motor of literary history. In Shklovsky's discourse the device survives unmodified by this migration and (a related point) the extra-literary relations of the literary have no place in what is an unregenerately isolationalist argument, let alone the question of what *determines* the path taken by the lateral deviation of forms at any given juncture. The device could be said to be both condition and result of the elision of these questions, which only become frameable when the device is superseded by the function.

This supersession takes place in the later texts of Tynyanov: substituting for the early conception of the work as a 'sum of devices' the notion of a 'dynamic integration' of hierarchically ordered elements, he also sketches for Formalism a cultural theory in which the principle of the irreducible relationality of elements is no less firmly followed. For Tynyanov 'formal elements' have no substantive existence; they are functions within systems: products of a twofold interrelation, with like elements in other systems and with unlike elements in their own (Tynyanov 1971). The work as a system of 'constructive' functions can only be understood in relation to the system of 'literary' functions which makes up the current literary order, and this in turn must be referred to the system of 'verbal' functions which makes up the culture as a whole. Literary historiography is concerned with the closest cultural series to the literary system – with 'social conventions' mediated by language, their common denominator. An element originating in one of these series – what Bakhtin will later call an *ideologeme* – becomes a constructive function in the work and simultaneously a literary function beyond it, in a complex overdetermination. In short, Tynyanov thinks the whole relationship of the literary to the extra-literary in intertextual terms, as a relation of 'like to like' (Frow 1980, p. 62). The concept of the device – including the allied concept of 'motivation' and its antithesis the device 'laid bare' and unmotivated – could not, and did not, survive this move.[3]

Tynyanov in 1924 had said that devices studied without reference to the evolution of forms were 'in danger of being studied outside their functions' (quoted in Shukman and O'Toole 1977, p. 38); in 1927 the device is dropped altogether. Late Formalism, then, is the result of a steady distancing from the negative correlation and a correspondingly steady elaboration of the differential alternative. The function enables the transition to what is in effect a third correlation and the last reach of Formalist theory: that of systems. The step is taken in the Jakobson–Tynyanov theses of 1928, and with it the structuralist project is launched (Jakobson and Tynyanov 1977). Or is it? If the theses are of interest to us here as indicating the route that Bakhtinism did *not* take out of and away from Formalism, they are equally interesting for their critique of the Saussurean paradigm. On the one hand we could say that Bakhtinism catches Formalism on its way to structuralism, diverting it in a Marxist direction; on the other hand we could say that the nascent structuralism of the theses is also an inchoate post-structuralism which Bakhtin emulates and completes as much as contests. Both propositions are true, as a brief look at the theses will show.

In what sense is Jakobson–Tynyanov a structuralist text? According to Benveniste, structuralism constitutes its object as 'a system whose parts are all united in a relationship of solidarity and dependence' and, while asserting the 'predominance of the system over the elements', also defines the 'structure' of the system 'through the relationships among the elements' (Benveniste 1971, p. 83). Clearly Jakobson–Tynyanov *is* a structuralist text in so far as it uses just such a concept of *system* to oppose an atomism of the literary 'fact'; the analogy with Saussure and the linguistic 'fact' is plain enough. However, Jakobson–Tynyanov is post-structuralist – at odds with the later western European projects descending from Saussure – in so far as it proposes a quite different conception of the systemic. The Saussurean system is *closed* in the strict sense that its components are also its determinants and that it itself determines nothing else; any one such system exists only to codify random diachronic events by exploiting them in new synchronic relationships. By contrast, the late Formalist system is intended precisely to theorize both the internal dynamic of distinct cultural orders and the dynamic of their correlation, their mutation in widely diverging temporalities. Moreover, it is *open*, at once determined and determining, in both the synchronic and the diachronic dimensions. We should note that Jakobson–Tynyanov invades Saussure's own scientific heartland: in arguing that the concept of system could be used to theorize not only synchronic regularity but also diachronic productivity, this text speaks consistently of 'literature' *and* 'language'. It is of discourse in general that the theses speak when they insist that all difference is historical and all history differential, a movement of *structuring*.

So far, so good; it is when the closing theses broach the issue of what determines the particular path of 'evolution' and resolve it by appeal to the (global) 'system of systems' that the compatibility with historical materialism breaks down. These intersystemic relations are so formulated as to elide the model of dominance-subordination and of contradiction which is held to characterize relations within the textual and intertextual moments of the literary system itself. As we move from the work through genre to the literary 'series' and on to the wider reaches of the social formation, so the emphasis on the 'deforming' dominant weakens and is replaced by a contiguity of systems from which all hint of struggle and hegemony has been expelled. Bakhtinian theory is what we have when this inconsistency is overcome: the principle of intertextual contradiction is applied truly universally, instead of being forsaken half-way. The 'series' identified by Tynyanov as being in closest correlation with the literary – 'social conventions' – reappears in Bakhtinism as 'behavioural ideology', and their common implication in the verbal is reasserted. Theorizing this region of ideology at least as fully as its literary neighbour, Bakhtin then reverses Formalist procedure by viewing the latter from the vantage-point of the former. We should recall that the Bakhtinian intervention in this field was made in the context of contemporaneous attempts to synthesize Formalism and Marxism (as it were) sponsorially and organizationally: Jakobson–Tynyanov was published in *Novyi Lef* precisely with this aim in mind. The Marxism of Bakhtin's intervention diverges sharply from any strategy which confirms the two positions in their self-presence and exteriority to each other, inasmuch as it is elaborated in a realization of the critical potential of a Formalism on the verge of the structuralist mutation. The best illustration of this is *Marxism and the Philosophy of Language*, published the year after Jakobson–Tynyanov. In this text the Jakobson–Tynyanov position on synchrony and diachrony is taken up and rethought as the contest and complicity of the two great lineages of linguistic enquiry – on the one hand, the Humboldtian and on the other the Cartesian, incarnated in the twentieth century by (respectively) Vossler and Saussure. In the one tendency an objectivism is predicated upon the regularity of language, while in the other the productivity of language entails a subjectivism, a privileging of individual stylistic 'creation'.[4] Voloshinov produces his materialist alternative to both not by an external attack on either but by occupying the space of their mutual limitation. In this space he is able to think what he calls 'the objective social regulatedness of ideological creativity', thereby breaking a long historical deadlock which Jakobson–Tynyanov had made visible.

The question now arises: how exactly does Bakhtinism bring about this radical interruption and diversion of Formalist concepts? I would like to suggest that the answer lies in a reading which attends to the textuality of the Formalist texts, in turning upon *them* their own abiding preoccupation with the textual, uncovering the metaphoricity in their conceptuality. We have seen that 'device' (sometimes rendered as 'technique') is 'technological', a coinage deriving from the anti-Symbolist polemic. 'Function', for all its appearance of being at home unproblematically in late Formalist discourse, is a logico-mathematical borrowing in which the will to overcome the problems of the device generates further difficulties. More important than either, though, is the tropology of power and hierarchy with which both coexist and which borrows its terms from the class struggle: 'struggle' itself, along with 'revolt', 'conflict', 'destruction' – these terms recur throughout. Even the 'dominant', though less vivid, belongs in this field. A passage from Shklovsky may be taken as representative:

Each new school of literature is a revolution – something like the emergence of a new class. But that, of course, is only an analogy. The defeated line is not annihilated, it does not cease to exist. It only topples from the crest, drops below, for a time lying fallow, and may rise again as an ever-present pretender to the throne. Moreover, in practice, things are complicated by the fact that the new hegemony is usually not a pure instance of a restoration of earlier form, but one involving the presence of features from other junior schools, even features (but now in a subordinate role) inherited from its predecessor on the throne.[5]

'Only an analogy': Shklovsky's modest disclaimer is disarming. It is as if the *Eighteenth Brumaire* had been turned inside-out, with the textuality of revolution inverted into the (permanent) revolution of textuality – a revolution which takes place in the hermetically sealed palace of verbal art.[6] Late Formalism lives off the productivity of this trope – it unites the otherwise disparate texts of Shklovsky and Tynyanov – and is 'unthinkable' without it. What is then striking is that this 'social' tropology only operates where literary diachrony is at issue; it is glaringly *absent* when the social itself is being negotiated. Tynyanov's text of 1927, where precisely this move to the extra-literary is made, is as notable for this absence as it is for the absence of the 'device' and its associates. The rhetoric of Formalism then shifts from the metaphoric to the metonymic pole, repressing the (implicit) similarity of the social by an explicit stress on its contiguity. Now the interest in thus uncovering the 'unconscious' of Formalist theory increases when we recall that this rhetoric (in the sense of the play of tropes) is in the business of consciously revolutionizing the relationship between poetics and the *discipline* of rhetoric itself. Eikhenbaum had spoken of 'the necessity of reviving rhetoric alongside poetics' (Eikhenbaum 1971, p. 34); it would be truer to say that Formalism revives rhetoric within poetics: rhetoric achieves its occupation of the aesthetic at the cost of its wider jurisdiction within discourse in general. It is then not surprising that, in engaging the historical dynamic of the literary, Formalism calls into being a sublimated version of the articulations of discourse and power – a displaced shadow-show of power relations. The wider social or ideological dimension emerges as an inert antitype of the lively politics of discourse played out on the inside of the literary; the battle of forms fades into a ballet of functions. For Formalism, it seems, the great intertextual drama was unplayable without the 'self-valuable word' as protagonist; to accord the same role to the word of ideology was to undermine the specificity of 'verbal art'. Bakhtin, no less interested in 'specifying', does just that, re-establishing poetics within rhetoric and theorizing the literary sign and the ideological sign *together*.

The Bakhtinian transformation may now be precisely described. We may say that Bakhtinism proceeds by literalizing and applying Formalism's metaphors of the 'social' to the social 'itself'. A better formulation would be this: Bakhtin substitutively reverses Formalist procedure by using 'literary' categories in the conceptualization of the social and the ideological. This chiastic move is manifested in Voloshinov's discussion of the 'genres' of 'behavioural ideology': as early as 1926 we find him insisting that 'the potentialities of artistic form' are 'already embedded' (Voloshinov 1976, p. 98) in the latter. The title of this early Bakhtinian text – 'Discourse in life and discourse in art' – already hints at the reversal and at the need for an equal and reciprocal theorization of both domains. The text is remarkable for the passage in which the twin errors of Formalism and psychologism are analysed; both (we are told)

> *attempt to discover the whole in the part*, that is, they take the structure of a part, abstractly divorced from the whole, and claim it as the structure of the whole.

Voloshinov goes on:

> Those methods that ignore the social essence of art and attempt to find its nature and distinguishing features only in the organization of the work artefact are in actuality obliged to project the social interrelationship of creator and contemplator into various aspects of the material and into various devices for structuring the material. In exactly the same way, psychological aesthetics projects the same social relations into the individual psyche of the perceiver. This projection distorts the integrity of these interrelationships and gives a false picture of both the material and the psyche.
>
> (Voloshinov 1976, p. 97)

What appears here as a conclusion about Formalism could be read as a starting-point *in* it: a reversal of this 'projection' of social relations into the work would bring about their reinstatement in their proper locus; a synecdochic mystification only needs to be exploded for the whole to shift from the inside to the outside of the part. In a close parallel with Marx's deconstruction of the commodity, Bakhtin rescues the 'work artefact' from its fetishization by compelling the technical categories of Formalism into the rhetorical categories which they at once mimic and distort. The hierarchical relations located by Formalism within the work are rethought as the (no less hierarchical) immanently social relations in which any utterance is inscribed. In all utterances 'relations among *people* stand revealed, relations merely reflected and fixed in verbal material'; the specificity of the artistic utterance resides not in its digression from this immanent sociality but precisely in its intensification: '*a poetic work is a powerful condenser of unarticulated social evaluations* – each word is saturated with them' (Voloshinov 1976, pp. 109 and 107). A poetics adequate to the understanding of this sociality would need to be (or be a branch of) the 'sociology of discourse' sketched out in Voloshinov's text. There is no mere coincidence in the fact that in this prolegomenal text many of the oldest terms of rhetoric make their appearance, and that its keynote is the (re-)assimilation of the literary to the more 'public' ideological discourses, notably the juridical and the political. The historical significance of this move cannot be too strongly underlined. In the Romantic mutation the condition of the specificity of 'art' had been its assimilation to 'everyday' ideology conceived as a private domain – an area of freedom for the subject outside institutions, of unconditioned privacy in which the writ of the more public discourses does not run – and the very notion of the 'aesthetic' took shape in the conceptual space thus hollowed out. Now to contest the expressivism or mimeticism raised on this basis (as Formalism consistently does) is to leave the aesthetic itself undeconstructed. The term 'aesthetic' in Bakhtinian discourse has been redefined out of all recognition, inasmuch as it realizes the 'potentialities' of an everyday-ideological domain which is always already structured like the juridico-political, always already *written*. Formalism had only gone as far as to bracket-out the authorial 'psyche' as a cause of the work; Bakhtinism takes the more radical step of theorizing this 'cause' as an effect of the same (discursive) order as the work itself. The upshot is a thorough-going deconstruction of the aesthetic in which the formal possibilities are read back into ideological domains whose bifurcation into public and private had given birth to it in the first place.

So much for the first of our 'two moments of formation of Bakhtinian theory': the second moment makes good a great and potentially disabling absence in the first as it is (in more than one sense) classically represented in the text of 1926. This is the lack of any reference either to the *unofficial* 'lower' strata of 'discourse in life' or to their counterpart in 'discourse in art': namely, the novel. The project of 1926 was at bottom a neo-rhetorical and indeed even classicizing project which would have left Bakhtinism roughly where 'speech-act theory' is fixed today. (We recall that Bakhtin was trained as a classicist.) The difference and the relationship between the two moments may be measured in the distance between this early essay and one of 1934–5 which appeared in English translation in 1981 under the title 'Discourse in the novel'; doubtless the crucial nexus here was the path-breaking work on Dostoevsky which inter-vened: no neo-rhetoric could survive unmodified an engage-ment of that depth with the peculiar productivity of novelistic discourse.[7] As with the first moment, my procedure will be to isolate the Formalist concept(s) in the transformation of which the Bakhtinian position is produced. What did Formalism make of the novel? Formalism theorizes the prose genres only *after*, and then *by analogy with*, those of poetry. Two strategies are adopted: fiction is held to reproduce in its repetitive sequences the linguistic devices (such as rhyme) of the same order in poetry; or the language of fiction is itself investigated for its quasi-poetic textuality. In both cases fiction is admitted to the canon of 'verbal art' only in so far as these effects are more or less foregrounded, deflected from the referential. Only the second strategy will concern us here. The rubric under which Formal-ism develops it is that of *skaz* – that form of prose writing which (allegedly) displays in its style an 'orientation' towards 'oral speech'. Bakhtin takes his cue from this problem of the (idiosyncratic) narrator in fiction, not only reformulating it in itself but also elaborating out of it those great themes of *dialogue* and *carnival* which transgress all disciplinary boundaries.

Skaz is a preoccupation of early Formalism and of Eikhenbaum in particular.[8] However, in this instance Bakhtin has the advantage of a prior critique *within* Formalism, or at least on its periphery. Victor Vinogradov's reformulation of the problem is the decisive enabling condition of Bakhtin's move (Vinogradov 1975). Let us take Eikhenbaum first. *Skaz* for him 'departs in principle from the written language and makes the narrator as such into a real figure', thereby freeing the prose genres from the joint domination of 'plot' and of 'a culture geared to writing and printing'. Happily the mixed mode of realist fiction was now undergoing a process of fission into its constituent forms and of these forms those that were oriented towards 'voice' were pushing an already devitalized novel genre into obsolescence. Eikhenbaum concludes: 'our relationship to the word has become more concrete, more sensitive, more physiological' (Eikhenbaum 1975, pp. 214, 223). In other words, Formalism sees in *skaz* the pure presence of speaking uncontaminated by writing and anterior to all institution. The problem of other speech in the authorial context is mooted only to be dropped, forgotten in the rush to embrace the fullness of orality. Vinogradov's assault on Eikhenbaum is directed at the latter's polarization of speech and writing and at the myth of the unity and purity of speaking. *Skaz* is redefined as a form of (prose) writing which is oriented not towards the undifferentiated phonicity of 'oral speech' but towards a particular oral genre – the 'narrative monologue' – which is distinguished (among other things) by 'having as its goal the forms of the written language'. It is 'an artistic construction taken to the second power', an orientation towards a spoken form which is itself always-already oriented towards the forms of writing. Beyond this, it displays 'whimsical forms of a multilingual mixture' and 'a conscious blending of various linguistic spheres' (Vinogradov 1975, pp. 242, 240 and 244). The *skaz* which mimics this genre assumes and exploits the existence of distinct linguistic practices within one and the same national language; it could not arise otherwise. Predicated upon this multilinguality, indefinable apart from it – no mere linguistic markers can fix a phenomenon so variable socially and historically – *skaz* is also the great operator of multilingualism in the whole field of prose writing. Formalism had tended to privilege the short story over the novel as the special locus of *skaz* effects; in Vinogradov's text *skaz* is the means by which non-canonical discourses subvert the 'conservative dogmas' of prose in general and 'create anew the whole world'. The dialogue of characters can (and does) accommodate such discourses, but with nothing like the effect that is generated by their permeation of the narrative itself. The effect of 'free verbal play' is possible only when other speech is not subordinated to plot or characterization but is itself rather the context of dialogue: a context without a placing pretext or 'motivation' in the Formalist sense. Such, then, is *skaz*: a context of narration not only without pretext but also refusing the status of a pretext for other texts; unmotivated and unmotivating, non-unified and non-unifying, it 'usually absorbs' the speech of characters or at least 'struggles with it' (Vinogradov 1975, p. 248).

Bakhtin's response to this powerful deconstruction of Formalist phonocentrism is to take it further still in the same direction. Vinogradov's sweeping generalization of the work of *skaz* becomes in Bakhtin that ubiquitous phenomenon of prose writing which he calls the 'double-voiced' or 'dialogical' word, of which *skaz* proper is only one of the types; parody, stylization and polemic share with it the dialogism which arises when two or more speech-acts of equal semantic weighting come together in a dynamic and internal relation.[9] Novelistic 'polyphony' is what we have when this play of voices is the textual dominant and when the finalizing forces of plot and of authorial authority are more or less subordinated. Single-voiced discourse is exemplified in the direct voice of the author with its claim on referential transparency and in the speech of characters which has been reduced to a mere theme or 'object' of authorial intentions, a manipulated transparency ignorant of its own service of those intentions. Now it is in Vingradov's formulation of this (so to speak) priority-finality of the authoritative single voice that we can locate the point of departure for Bakhtin's most productive – his most decisively deconstructive – move. The passage in which this formulation appears is worth quoting at length:

In those epochs when the forms of written, literary, artistic speech experience a revolution, it is *skaz* which helps language break with the past. Indeed *skaz* is psychologically limited only when it is attached to the image of a person or his designated representative, that is, to a verbal label. Then to some extent the illusion of an everyday situation is also created, even if object accessories of the illusion are not indicated. The amplitude of lexical oscillations grows narrow. The stylistic motion leads a secluded life within the narrow confines of a linguistic consciousness that is dominated by the social mode of life that is to be presented. Meanwhile *skaz*, proceeding from the author's 'I', is free. The writer's 'I' is not a name but a pronoun. Consequently, one can conceal under it whatever one wants to. It is able to conceal forms of speech appropriated from constructions of various bookish genres and from *skaz*-dialectal elements. An integral psychology is a superfluous burden for the writer. The writer's broad right to transform has always been acknowledged. In the literary masquerade the writer can freely change stylistic masks within a single artistic work. To be able to do this he needs only a large and heterogeneous linguistic workshop. Such an artist, a reformer of the literary language, transforms his work into a motley garment, woven from variations of different written *skaz* forms, from declamatory-oratorical speech, and even from the introduction of verse or forms close to it. It is natural that the element of *skaz* becomes the main reservoir from which new aspects of literary speech are drawn. The conservatism of the written literary language is overcome by infusing into it living, varied dialectal elements and their individual, artificial imitations through the means of *skaz*, the transmissive instance between the artistic element of oral creation and the stable tradition of the literary stylistic canon.

(Vinogradov 1975, pp. 248–9)

There can be no doubt that in this distinction between a *skaz* bound to 'the image of a person' and a 'free' *skaz* of the authorial 'pronoun' we have an early stage of Bakhtin's broader distinction between the singleness of 'objectivized' social-typical discourse and the doubleness of those manifold discourse types which *institute the priority of other speech*. But this is not all that this extraordinary passage can be made to yield: the textuality of this celebration of textuality needs to be brought out if we are to see what Bakhtin made of it. Consider the fields of metaphor on which it draws: how it 'reminds' mainstream Formalism of the two tropologies it seems curiously to have 'forgotten' in its theorization of *skaz*. 'Workshop' and 'reservoir' connote the technological and adumbrate an aesthetic of 'production' just as 'device' does within early Formalism. 'Revolution', 'break with the past', 'transform', 'conservatism' apply implicitly political metaphors to cultural practice. Outrunning these tropologies, though – exerting irresistible pressure upon them – is a third, exemplified in 'literary masquerade', 'stylistic masks' and 'motley garment': a tropology, in short, of *carnival*. The anonymous (pronominal) writing subject is an analogue of the reveller who is (as Kristeva puts it) 'neither nothingness nor anybody' (Kristeva 1980, p. 74). The *skaz* text conceived as endlessly mutable 'garment' revives the very etymology of 'text' itself. (We are not far here from Peirce's thesis of the primacy of the pronominal over all nomination whatever.) In 'free' *skaz* the textual garment is not secondary to a given identity; it is itself the production of identities.

To take stock of the yield of Vinogradov's text, we need to look first back to Eikhenbaum and then forward to Bakhtin. In bracketing-out the authorial subject, reducing it to nothingness – refusing to think the problem of the authorial *position* by expelling the subject so prematurely and undialectically – Formalism frees the category of the subject for the mischief it so plainly makes when *skaz* is discussed. The radical and multiple otherness of other speech is cancelled in the *oneness* of so-called 'oral speech', the quasi-physical substance of a secular Word in which the play of even the most outrageous *skaz* is subject to closure. Vinogradov not only seizes on this repressed problem of the author but also finds himself thinking of it as an anti-type of the sacerdotal: the metaphor of the carnivalesque spectator-participant counters Eikhenbaum's virtual priesthood of the spoken word with the ambivalence of writing. Bakhtin for his part isolates this metaphor of the author-as-anonym from its competitors in Vinogradov's text (artisan and revolutionary) as the one most capable of escaping altogether the logic of presence and absence, the 'one' and the 'nought'. This irreducible double of the author as verbal reveller is then – and it is this move that is decisive – *applied to the other participants in the textual transaction*. Read back into everyday ideology, the metaphor of the verbal reveller produces the new theoretical object of carnival signification. Speaker, spoken-about and spoken-to are themselves quite openly texts or signifiers – 'masks' with no claim (as Bakhtin himself puts it) to an 'authentic incontestable face' (Bakhtin 1981, p. 273). Author, hero and reader have the same status in that equally new theoretical object: the polyphonic novel. Both are, of course, also firmly historical phenomena, and Bakhtin's mature work is given over to an exploration of the historical relationship between them. Carnival does not abolish the immanently social and hierarchical relations in which the ideological sign is inscribed; only the terms of these relations are none of them out of play as signifieds in a transcendence. Carnival is the permanent possibility within everyday ideology of inverting hierarchies, dissolving their absolutism in relativity. It is what we have when the social relations in which the sign is constituted are flagrantly intertextual, its terms (participants) interchangeable anonyms. Now it is worth recalling that the text of 1926 – the text of our first 'moment' – had described these relations as 'relations among *people*, relations merely reflected and fixed in verbal material'. Carnival and polyphony are clearly *unthinkable* under this definition of the sign (work, utterance): however helpful it had been in pushing beyond Formalism, this description could not survive the passage to the second 'moment'; its supersession is the index of the *self*-deconstruction forced upon Bakhtin as the limits of his neo-rhetorical project are revealed. The 'people' of which it speaks appear to transcend 'relations' which in turn transcend a (dispensable) 'verbal material'. Carnival undermines such transcendences in Bakhtinian theory with the same summary justice that it exercises on their counterparts in history.

This brings us, finally, to the new perspective in which Bakhtinism places poetic discourse by viewing it from 'outside' – from its 'own' historical outside, to be precise: the other because and in spite of which it exists at all. What is this other? In engaging this issue Bakhtin speaks not of carnival and polyphony but (respectively) of 'the novel' and 'heteroglossia', their less exceptional correlatives. These are broader categories: where carnival discourse is *anti*-official, heteroglossia is the multiplicity of *un*official linguistic practices in general; likewise the novel with its dialogism is the general case of which polyphony is the most uncompromising realization. It is in their orientations towards this heteroglot intertext that poetic and novelistic discourse most sharply diverge. The novel is that order of discourse which is open to and echoes – by exploiting – the rich multilingualism of 'social heteroglossia', whereas poetic discourse classically behaves as if it were not surrounded by the latter in all its writings and rewritings, and its only dealings were immediately with its object. Historically, poetry is bound up with the politically and culturally centralizing forces within ideology, while the novel participates in those *de*centralizing forces against which any unitary language has always and everywhere to *posit itself*. Both poetry 'in the narrow sense' and the system of linguistic norms are predicated upon a tacit *exclusion* of these forces. This is not to say that the verse genres are inherently hostile to dialogism or that monologism does not have its way in the prose genres; on the contrary. There are no monological texts properly speaking – only monological readings. The very disciplines of discourse themselves ensure these readings, complicit as they are with the whole centralizing and unifying project as it has unfolded historically. More than anything else it is the separation of poetics and rhetoric, with their strictly segregated fields of competence, that has guaranteed the invisibility of dialogism in the forms of writing, first dichotomizing 'prose' and 'verse' and then (when the prose genres come to be canonized) theorizing prose with the categories devised for the canon of poetic writing. We have seen the Formalists taking rhetoric up into poetics on the latter's terms only to fail what Bakhtin calls the 'acid test' posed by novelistic discourse (Bakhtin 1981, p. 261). We have seen Bakhtin in his first 'moment' taking poetics up into rhetoric largely on rhetoric's terms only to move on to a new terrain altogether, beyond both. It is a terrain which our contemporary theorists of discourse have yet to occupy.

Notes

1 By 'poetry in the narrow sense' Bakhtin means the discourse of the 'straightforward' canonical genres (epic, lyric, tragedy). There is no correlation here with the 'verse' genres as opposed to 'prose' in the purely technical-compositional distinction: *Don Juan* and *Eugene Onegin* are instances of novelistic discourse on Bakhtin's terms. The phrase is used throughout 'Discourse in the novel' and elsewhere in *The Dialogic Imagination* (Bakhtin 1981).

2 Shklovsky 1965, p. 21. Lemon and Reis use the phrase 'unique semantic modification'. 'Semantic shift' is used in the translation quoted by Fokkema 1976, p. 159.

3 Tynyanov historicizes the concept of 'motivation' in the 1927 text (Tynyanov 1971), citing as an example 'nature descriptions in old novels': whereas we might read such descriptions as mere motivation for 'transitions or retardation' (a characteristically Shklovskian move), 'in a different literary system' they might be the 'dominant element' with the 'story' providing the motivation for *them*. It is worth noting that Tynyanov continues to use the concept of the 'device' in another text of 1927 (Tynyanov 1982) where the devices of film are held to enjoy an independence of 'naturalistic "motivation in general"'. Evidently Tynyanov saw no danger in using the concept in a *synchronic* account of *contemporary* cultural production.

4 See Voloshinov 1973, pp. 45–63. There is a clear parallel here with Derrida's critique of the competing explanatory schemes of structuralism and phenomenology: see the useful summary in Norris 1982, pp. 50–5.

5 This passage appeared first in *Rozanov* (1921) and then again in *Theory of Prose* (1925). The translation used here is from a longer passage quoted in Matejka and Pomorska 1971, p. 32.

6 Nobody seems to have noticed that Shklovsky's famous thesis of the 'legacy' in literary history passing 'not from father to son but from uncle to nephew' (enunciated in the same text) reproduces another motif from the *Eighteenth Brumaire*.

7 There is no translation of the 1929 version of Bakhtin's monograph on Dostoevsky; my statement is made on the basis of a reading of the revised and expanded edition (Bakhtin 1973).

8 The first and best-known of Eikhenbaum's articles on *skaz* is of course 'How Gogol's "overcoat" is made' (Eikhenbaum 1974). The positions of this article are assumed in what follows, even though it is not directly quoted.

9 See the extract from the Dostoevsky book reproduced as 'Discourse typology in prose' in Matejka and Pomorska 1971, pp. 176–96. In this study of discourse types Bakhtin explicitly contests Eikhen-

baum's definition of *skaz* proper: *skaz* is characterized in the first place by an 'orientation towards another speech-act'; its 'oral' character is adventitious, a mere consequence of this primary orientation. 'Orientation towards oral speech' – Eikhenbaum's conception – is adequate only in the case of the (single-voiced) phenomenon of a narrative discourse delegated to a 'literary' narrator whose speech is 'enlivened' by 'oral intonations'. This is nothing more than compositional convenience and has nothing to do with the special productivity of *skaz*; it is a disguise covering an authorial identity rather than a guise constructing one; not an interorientation of two signifiers but a signifier portending a signified. Bakhtin cites Turgenev as an example.

7
National language, education, literature

RENÉE BALIBAR

To begin with, my paper brings to mind the need felt by French academics in the 1970s and 1980s for theoretical concepts. At the time when I read this paper, I had just completed my contribution to *Histoire de la langue française 1880–1914* (Balibar 1985a) concerning national French, and I was writing a book, *L'Institution du Français-Essai sur le colinguisme, des Carolingiens à la République* (Balibar 1985b). In search of the principle of literary production in the twentieth century, I had traced the founding document of official written French (the Compacts of Strasbourg, 14 February 842), and I had analysed the revolutionary events of 1789 from a new point of view.

I had ascertained a paradoxical fact: literary criticism in the Republican era had refused to consider the relationship between literature and the history of the linguistic institution. Literature was not seen as a reflection of the practice of the national language. Criticism, while claiming allegiance to Marxism or Freudianism, was mainly preoccupied with analysing the symbolic relation between literary fiction on the one hand, and general politics and capitalism or sexuality in general and the family on the other. These considerations are of undeniable importance, but what was systematically ignored, in Balzac, in Ionesco, was the imaginary representation of the tortured institutional practice of the French language.

The hypothesis I put forward to try to understand this taboo is that the embryonic condition of Republican French has made a conscious criticism (*critique consciente*) impossible until now. So long as the first achievements of primary school French, along with those of the literature in which it bathes, had not been fully put into effect, it has been impossible, for two hundred years, to define the problems of the new synchronia (*synchronie*). Only today are we beginning to understand the stakes and the grounds of the conflicts.

All the conflicts interlock around the *power of translation*, a legacy of medieval scholars now exercised, unequally but jointly, by both the masses and the élite in our present-day democracies.

At the level of the languages of the state, reasoned translation – organized by grammarians and scholars – between a classical language and a modern language on the one hand, and among national languages on the other, provides the key to linguistic 'elementation', and therefore to abstract conceptions and cultural depths. I have called this *colinguism* and carefully distinguished it from bilinguism, plurilinguism, etc. These latter activities have their own requirements and give access to other languages while avoiding as far as possible reflection and theory. Colinguism is, however, a theoretical practice associated with political thinking.

My paper presents a concrete example of colinguism: the fruitful encounter during the revolutionary years of *Lessons for Children* by Anna-Laetitia Barbauld and *The Library for Villages* by Arnaud Berquin. These two books, inheritors of European humanism, forged the first model for the learning of democracy.

*

Although the title sounds quite broad and general, what I intend to offer is, in effect, a brief historical survey of very precise and concrete facts.

But, first of all I wish to make clear, as briefly as possible, the scope and place of my 'research works', of my 'articles' and my 'published books', using, for this purpose, one or two French textbooks. I have selected these books from among other works of critical analysis, because they are currently used as reference books in French higher education. Indeed my personal views are not what is to be considered. What I am concerned with is to propound the terms I am using, i.e. 'national French', 'fictional

French languages', 'colinguistic practice' and 'grammatization', with a view to raising certain problems regarding the relation of literature to literacy.

I had two books published in 1974: *Le Français national* and *Les Français fictifs*. They were in a series created by Althusser, 'Analyses', in which only three titles have been published: *Positions*, by Althusser, and my two books. In 1977 the Editions du Seuil published *Histoire littérature* by Gerard Delfau and Anne Roche. Delfau (who was responsible for the chapter dealing with *Les Français fictifs*) discusses the 'theory of ideology' which Althusser launched, and he considers that *Les Français fictifs* is

> an initial assessment of Althusserianism as far as literary criticism is concerned, both on account of the application, to specific works, of the working hypotheses contained in Althusser's article on 'The Ideological State Apparatuses', and also because of the long introduction written by Etienne Balibar and Pierre Macherey, essentially focused upon the theme of 'Literature as an ideological form'.
>
> (Delfau and Roche 1977, pp. 299–300)

I do not wish to enter into a controversy about the words 'application of Althusser's working hypotheses', which seem to give primacy to theory over actual literary practice. I would rather take up the following sentence:

> Let's confess our perplexity in front of the meagreness of the results attained.
>
> (Delfau and Roche 1977, p. 300)

I would like to make a note of the 'benefits expected' – in Delfau's own words – either by himself or by Althussereans, ranging from 'restoring the capacity of Marxism for opening up onto the social sciences' to 'throwing a light, in passing, upon the Marxist position on art'. Delfau is disappointed by the 'timidity' of the 'Althusserean school' in comparison with

> the great adventure of criticism, that of a man like Sartre who got engrossed in Flaubert to the point of almost losing some of his own identity.
>
> (Delfau and Roche 1977, p. 302)

One feels at liberty to have a different view on critical venturesomeness! Nevertheless, Delfau considers that the best Althusserean works – the most convincing ones, he says, being mine – restore to the work of art

part of its autonomy. From being 'pure reflection' [of reality], the work of art becomes the place and state of a specific form of class struggle fought within the sphere of influence of the 'Ideological State Apparatuses', namely: academies, salons, schools, universities, etc.

(Delfau and Roche 1977, p. 303)

I am keeping in mind that, in connection with my books, Delfau recognizes the existence of an 'ideological formative action' in which literary fiction takes shape; a specific formation that cannot occur without apparatuses or institutions. The linguistic aspect of that formation will be recognized later, but it was overlooked by Delfau, although the titles of my books did announce analyses concerning 'French', and the historical struggle in the field of language.

In 1978 a textbook widely circulated in institutions of higher education – *La Critique* (*Criticism*) by Roger Fayolle (Fayolle 1978) – makes favourable mention, among the 'currents' of Marxist criticism, of

the research works undertaken and published under the leadership of Renée Balibar, which represent the most important contribution . . . in that direction [the direction indicated by Althusser's analysis of ideological apparatuses and formative actions]. The point here is to lead us to understand the illusions on which our habitual conceptions and practices of what we call 'literature' are based. Are we not inclined to recognize the presence of literature only providing that we exclude and cast out into some mechanically separated exterior region, the relationship of literary effects to education and the history of schools, to the national language and the history of that language, to the struggles among social classes and the history of those struggles?

(Fayolle 1978, pp. 200–3)

Having said this, Fayolle wonders if it is possible to extend such methodological principles to those centuries that preceded the nineteenth. And besides, he thinks that Marxist literary critical research is often very different from these 'avant-garde methodological explorations'.

Let me point out that it is mainly commentators on my work (whether Delfau and Fayolle, or Etienne Balibar and Pierre Macherey) who have concerned themselves with general Marxist theory: my only pretension has been to introduce the history of literary production into the history of the national language, in fact, to call back to mind that French literature is written in French, and that the creative work of writers moves in the field where institutions and linguistic apparatuses interplay. This does, of course, fall within the province of historical materialism and ties up with Marxist research on the state and ideological formative actions.

In 1979, Nathan published *Sociocritique* (Duchet 1979), a collection of texts presented at a symposium organized by the University of Paris-VIII and New York University. In that book Jacques Dubois describes 'the literary institution' which, since the Revolution of 1789, has given literary practice its two-fold character: official and sacred. Dubois mentions my book *Les Français fictifs* and says this:

> Thus literature appears to us as being submitted, in most cases, to a threefold determination: linguistic, educational and imaginary.

And he concludes:

> Strongly articulated, this thesis strengthens the foundation one wishes to give to the institutional analysis of literary practices. It has the special merit of inscribing the set named 'literature' within a concrete pattern of historical determinations, and, in the last resort, of relating it to a State power. We believe however that, by subordinating that set 'wholly' to the educational apparatus, it leads to the paradoxical consequence of eliminating the specific apparatus instituting literature, and of neglecting the role it plays.
>
> (Duchet 1979, p. 171)

Perhaps, in order to understand better the special function of the literary institution, we ought to separate out the role of the linguistic apparatus within the educational institution.

But I shall not carry on any longer with such abstract considerations. I am now going to set out a few results of recent research and I hope that, in doing so, my notions about the relationship between the French fictional languages and the national language, as well as the concept of colinguistic practice, will not deserve the blame expressed in the famous phrase: 'What is simple is not accurate, and what is complex is incomprehensible.'

The English may not be aware of the historical event called *Les Serments de Strasbourg*, the Compacts of Strasbourg, which took place in the ninth century, more precisely, on 14 February 842. Theoretically, the French should have heard about it when in primary school. In any case, I believe that I have drawn some conclusions (so far unpublished) from the history of the French language and the general history of the early middle ages in Europe.

Here is a summary of the facts, according to F. Brunot:

Two sons of Louis the Pious (who died in 840), Louis the Germanic and Charles the Bald, in revolt against the pretensions of their brother Lothair, had just won the battle of Fontanet (841) over the latter. As the war was not over, they met in Strasbourg, on February 14th, 842, to strengthen their union and they pledged themselves to an alliance with each other. In order that the armies who were present might be witness of their solemn compact, Louis the Germanic swore his oath in the language of his brother and of the Franks from France, i.e. in French 'Roman' (late vulgar Latin), and Charles repeated the same oath as his elder brother in the Germanic language. And in their turn, the soldiers swore too, in their respective languages.

A historian of the time, Nithard, himself a grandson of Charlemagne, recorded those oaths, the original copies of which he may have had under his eyes, in his *History of the divisions between the sons of Louis the Meek* (Louis le Débonnaire). . . . We present below a facsimile of the page of the unique manuscript (from the end of the tenth or beginning of the eleventh century) which has preserved, with Nithard's chronicle, this text, the first one written in French and one of the first written in old German.

[. . .] In 860 peace was proclaimed at Coblentz, in French 'Roman' and in Germanic, but the wording of the declaration has not come down to us.

F. Brunot translated the contents of the compacts into present-day French. I give here an adaptation of it in English:

The wording of the king's oaths:
For the love of God and for the common good of the Christian people and of ours, from this day on, as long as God gives me knowledge and power, I will support my brother Charles with my assistance and in all things, as one must justly support one's brother, provided he does the same for me, and I shall never make any arrangement with Lothair that, by my will, may be to the detriment of my aforesaid brother Charles.

The wording of the soldiers' oaths:
If Louis keeps his pledge to his brother Charles, and Charles, my lord, for his part, does not keep his, in the event of my being unable to dissuade him, I, for one, shall not lend him any help, nor shall any one I shall be able to dissuade from doing so.

(Brunot 1968, pp. 143–95)

The spontaneous interpretation of present-day Europeans is suggested by the way the above story is told: Louis the Germanic had expressed himself in 'Roman' (i.e. French of *langue d'oil*, northern French) – it is suggested – in order to be understood by Charles the Bald and his 'French' army; and Charles the Bald had expressed himself in Germanic to recipro-cate. The 'soldiers' are supposed to have warned their respec-tive kings that they would abide by the compact, if necessary against their lord. And such is indeed the meaning laid down by the teaching of French history since 1880 in Republican France. This is a fabulous historical misinterpretation; a wonderful ideological vision of things, of vital importance in the nineteenth century and still so nowadays in modern French society. Let us now have a look at the real state of affairs in the ninth century.

According to the historical documents, the first Carolingian kings spoke Germanic '*Tudesque*'. Neither Charlemagne nor his grandsons Louis the Germanic and Charles the Bald spoke rustic 'Roman'. So it was not in order to be understood by his brother that Louis the Germanic took his oath in the 'Roman' language. He must have recited a text he had learned by heart, or repeated word for word a text whispered to him, a text totally strange and unfamiliar to the ancient noble practice of the two kings' family. Neither did Louis the Germanic utter his solemn oath in Roman so as to make himself clearly understood by an army that would have been 'French'. The two camps gathered under each of the kings two sets of vassals singly bound to them by personal vassalic pledges. On both sides the most powerful lords, no doubt the spokesmen for their inferiors, also spoke Germanic '*Tudesque*'. As for the lower class of vassals – down to the men-at-arms who had no vassals of their own and ruled over the peasantry and the serfs on their small estates – they had oral practices which were multilingual and confused. They were able to speak in rustic language with the Galloromans of various estates in the territories inherited by Charles; and they could also speak, on occasion, with the men-at-arms of the opposite party. Far from having established a direct communication between the participants in the Strasbourg alliance, the proclamation of the oaths in the form of a twofold speech delivered in vernacular languages by the two kings must have created some obscurity and originated new distances. In this way certain objectives were effectively attained, so effectively that nowadays such a situation seems natural to us.

What objectives? This is where the *clerks* come in. The clerks of the royal chancelleries were not gathered on the field with the men-at-arms; nor were they standing on the dais with the kings. They were penmen not swordsmen, dignitaries of the Church, relatives of the kings and experts in law and in rhetoric. They had discussed at length among themselves the alliance between Louis and Charles against Lothair, drawn up the Compacts and worked out the staging of a sacramental event: the outcome of long experience in a centuries-old apparatus.

In the ninth century, in the Carolingian kingdoms, churchmen, 'clerks', were in full possession of their heritage ('*cleros*' in Greek) which set them apart and gave them their share of power: the exclusive control of the written word, and consequently of teaching, recording and translating. This monopoly had been instituted in the territorial divisions of the Roman Empire since the Emperor Constantine had recognized the Church. Thus the bishops' administration had duplicated in written official Latin the administration of local magistrates. During the period of the invasions, the Church became more rural and preached the gospel in the vernacular languages of the different lands: Irish, Galloroman, Anglo-Saxon, Germanic. The Church was recognized anew as an official power by the Merovingian Franks who wished to cast their conquests into Galloroman administrative modes, and again by Charlemagne, two centuries later, when he tried to establish his centralizing power. Throughout this time the Church managed to keep up its classical written Latin, a factor of universality, while developing its local linguistic implantation. Only the Church had the power to channel down the doctrine and the law from the scriptures into oral commentaries and injunctions in the vernacular languages.

This power was used in an original way by the clerks of Strasbourg to consolidate their own inheritance and, at the same time, that of the kings. They reversed the translating operation which, until then, they had performed only from the written Latin text into various oral vulgarized versions, and produced two written texts in two tongues derived from oral languages, in such a way that each one of those texts might be rendered with rigorous accuracy in the other and in Latin, thus producing versions of the same discourse. We shall not go into the details of the operation but just point out what it was aiming at: the creation of two state languages, each as valid as Latin for use in diplomatic recording and yet distinct from each other as signs of two different territories.

The spoken languages typical of territorial divisions had just been recognized by the Church for the purposes of evangelization at the Council of Tours in 813, one year before Charlemagne's death. In Strasbourg, those languages became symbols of the territories inherited by Charlemagne's grandsons: to one went the lands where the people obeyed in Germanic, to the other the lands where the people obeyed in Roman French. And from then on the changes brought about by land apportionments and vassalage obligations could not affect the situation. The *King's Language* now existed within stable linguistic boundaries regulated by bishops and abbots as well. A few years after the Compacts of Strasbourg, Charles the Bald took advantage of the linguistic channel provided by the bishops when he asked them to make his royal edicts known to the people in their own tongues.

This brings us back to the power of the kings. It was they who gave the phrasing of the oaths, when it issued through their charismatic lips, the value of a sacred sign. In accordance with their divine right, the kings of Strasbourg recognized each other as being entitled to fix as a national language the distinctive language of the land each one had inherited. If, as it happened, neither of them had ever spoken the French language in that manner, since they were ignorant of the various Roman dialects, the inauguration, the consecration and the acknowledgement of the new linguistic practice were all the more revealing of their power. Each set of vassals swore loyalty to the sharing out that had been accomplished, expressing himself in the language of his own king. The vassalic pledge put each subordinate under an obligation to defend personally the sacred linguistic boundary. There was an immediate political consequence: in spite of the Treaty of Verdun (843) which gave Lothair a third, intermediate kingdom, the Strasbourg alliance entered into by the two kings succeeded in depriving the land of Lorraine of the linguistic sign which would have been the mark of its particular unity.

Thus the Compacts of Strasbourg closely associated two apparatuses (royal and clerical) and three tongues (a classical one and two new ones) with very precise functions: to legitimate and to separate. I have coined the term colinguistic practice to designate this historical association. Since 842 the national French tongue has preserved its classical Latin dimension and its modern foreign dimension.

I shall now turn to what the appropriately named French Revolution of 1789 created in the structure of its apparatuses and languages, in opening up the era of Republican French, that is, school French, after the eras of clerical royal French, of university royal French, and of academic monarchical French. At the same time we will see the strategic place occupied by literature in the history of a national language.

Everybody knows that the Revolution of 1789 changed institutions in France; that it abolished feudal rights on the land; that it abolished the king's power by divine right; that it created middle-class property rights, and the right of citizens to participate by voting in the government of the nation. But the revolution in the state language – the abolition of the divine right of the king's language, and the creation of a state language common to all citizens – has not been studied seriously enough.

In 1789, the *Declaration of the Rights of Man and the Citizen*, Article XI, proclaimed:

The free communication of thoughts and opinions is one of the most precious rights of Man; any citizen can then speak, write and print freely.

The right to free expression was linked to the right of all citizens to state education (Article XXII of the Constitution of Year I). The practice of the national language which used to be the privilege of the king and the literate belonged, from then on, to all citizens from the first level of the new schooling system.

This revolution in the language assimilated the right of expression to the individual right of free communication. Privilege implies a power of authoritarian expression, whereas the right to writing, in a republic, presupposes the sharing of the power of expression so that linguistic exchange can have the communicative character of equality. Far from legislating a vacuum, all the Declarations, Reports and Decrees on free communication issued by the revolutionary assemblies were accompanied by the abundant publication of books, newspapers, periodicals of various types, etc., which historians have called a 'deluge of papers'. It is intellectually convenient for us that the revolutionary principles were first enunciated through phrases in institutional texts. But we cannot ignore the fact that those formulations could not have existed without playing a role in the field of practice.

In particular, among the papers printed at the time, it is of interest to bring to light a text the practical importance of which has not been sufficiently recognized. In 1790, during the campaign which preceded the elections for the Legislative Assembly, there took place the publication of *La Bibliothèque des Villages* by Arnaud Berquin, a series of small booklets which were issued every month from 1 July onwards:

> The subscription to the ten volumes delivered in all villages, postage paid, amounts to *6 livres*. Each volume sold separately, 12 *sols*.

Each booklet contained several short narratives or dialogues inspired by the ideas of *The Society of the Friends of the Constitution*. For example:

The Happiness of Country Folk
M. Rancey, Matthieu

M. Rancey – Well, Matthieu, how are things with you?

Matthieu – Oh, sir, do you really have to ask? Things are always bad with people in our station. Happiness is not for us.

M. Rancey – Who is it for, then, can you tell me?

Matthieu – That's a question gentlemen from the town may very well ask.

M. Rancey – So you think we are happier than you people are?

Matthieu – I'd like to see you lead our life for just a month. You would soon see what you yourselves would answer.

At the end of the story, the farmer, won over to the new ideas, gets involved in political life:

> Look, M. Rancey went on, take this piece of writing that a worthy member of the National Assembly has just addressed to his fellow citizens, read the pages I have marked ... Matthieu took the paper home with him and, after having read it with attention, he ran, transported with joy, and communicated it to the parish priest who immediately summoned the inhabitants of the village in order to read it to them. ... The country people all renewed in their hearts the oath they had already taken: to maintain at the risk of their lives a constitution so favourable to their felicity.

In another story in the *Library for Villages* ('Honour', in Vol. V), Arnaud Berquin presents three farmers, brothers, two of whom are sinking into routine, whereas the third one is in favour of new things: potatoes, artificial meadows, the teaching of writing and arithmetic. This man, Julian, has to face hardships:

> To be mayor of his village, in preference to him, they had elected a worthless intriguer who had gone as far as paying a fortune to buy votes all over the district.

But in the end:

> There is no doubt that, in the next election, Julian will be made one of the administrators of his district. I even know of many people who intend to make him become a member of the next legislature, in which I am confident that he will distinguish himself by his disinterestedness, his love of the public good, the extent of his knowledge in rural affairs, and the soundness of his views on all sorts of things.

What was the circulation of these booklets? What was their impact on the population? I shall deal with this shortly. But may I first remind you that at the beginning of the French Revolution only a small number of the literate were capable of writing, having been trained in Latin grammar and rhetoric by ecclesiastics in the *Collèges*, and in the king's language in public offices, at court, and in the academies. In the *petites écoles* of the parish schools, when reading was taught, it was to decipher A and B in the Latin text of the Lord's Prayer and Hail Mary, or to make out as a whole such signs as '*Au Cochon Rôti*', '*Au Lion d'Or*'. As a rule, during the first electoral campaign of the revolutionary period, either the parish priests would serve as interpreters into the provincial vulgar languages, when they were in favour of *les lumières* (enlightenment), or else well-meaning notables, wealthy farmers like Matthieu. As all media of expression, whether oral or written, were meant to establish discriminations and hierarchies, anyone who wanted to write in order to address the new citizens on an ideally equal footing had to invent a medium for communication, to coin a style, to write in an imaginary French that could overcome the obstacles. A text for revolutionary propaganda had to hold the attention of the citizens at whose approval it was aiming, by calculating the risk of being misunderstood or betrayed – or else given an advantage – by its translations and by the circulation of rumours about it.

Under such conditions, the texts which were trying to establish revolutionary communication come, I think, under three main types of style which correspond to as many attitudes, as many ideological and political positions. Some texts proceeded with a wealth of Franco-Latin rhetoric; others in a coarse fictively oral style; and others in a fictively simple and conventional French, as was the case with the *Library for Villages*.

Apart from the great tribunes, the leaders of the parties in the assemblies, who often fired the spirit of the people of Paris who had come to listen to them, thanks to their theatrical personalities, their voices, and the dramatic circumstances of the great Days of the Revolution, it is paradoxical that those revolutionaries who were politically the most advanced on account of their republican spirit (the Jacobins, the Montagnards of the Convention) were the weightiest latinists, conservative in the field of rhetoric, users of high-flown language, unable to get away from their own writing habits. There is nothing inexplicable in this if one remembers that for the most part they were lawyers, they belonged to the middle class, and they were convinced they must use the trump card of their literary education against the old nobility and the courtiers. In the most successful cases they attained their aims and fashioned the great abstract texts of the declarations, reports, decrees, when their grandiloquence yielded to the demands of juridical precision. Later Stendhal was to make famous this modern literary style when he tried to write *comme le code civil* (like the civil code).

The camp that adopted the '*poissard*' (fishwife) style – the term used at the time – was, in the beginning, that of the counter-revolutionary propagandists who published several series of lampoons in 1790, *The Acts of the Apostles*, which are full of dialogues that make the Parisian rabble speak fictitiously and that drag the people's representatives through the mud. Coarse words created a link between, on the one hand, illiterate aristocrats whose swear words in the absence of well-argued speeches scandalized the Assembly, on the other, the workers from the central food market of Paris, and in between, characters of all conditions who delighted in violating interdictions. Very soon this enormous potential clientèle is being aimed at by the journalists of the extreme left in the publications of the *Père Duchesne*. Most of the time Father Duchesne and his imitators in

Paris or in the provinces had no difficulty outclassing the productions of the extreme right. The leftist journalists had a great variety of linguistic means at their disposal, ranging from classical Latin to the languages used in the salons and the trades. They also had newer and stronger ideas. After the Revolution, in the reign of Louis-Philippe, Balzac was to write a serial, *Les Paysans* (*Country Folk*), for a rightist paper, and he created a terrifying image of the rural classes by making his fictional rustics speak the '*poissard*' language of the Parisian revolutionary lampoons. Such are the complexities of literary realism!

Finally there was the third camp, that in which from a linguistic point of view Berquin's *Library for Villages* is to be situated. This is the group that was banking on state education, aimed in the short term at well-to-do peasants who were capable of taking advantage of changes in the way of tilling their lands, and in the long run at all the citizens who had been through primary schooling. Berquin was a first-class journalist. He belonged to the staff of the *Moniteur Universel*, the best of the period, and he also wrote in *La Feuille villageoise* (*The Village Sheet*), a publication which had a very large print-run and an extensive circulation in all the newly created *départements* at the beginning of the French Revolution. He was also close to the staff of *La Feuille du cultivateur* (*The Husbandman's Sheet*), an organ for the popularization of agronomic science, a link between the most enlightened of the farmers and members of the former *Societies of Agriculture*. During the terrible years when it was so hard to provide the population and the army with good supplies, *La Feuille du cultivateur* published articles about fodder plants, the three-year rotation of crops and the like, while it also discussed the problems of the nomenclature of plants, tools and farming skills. For in that domain as well as in others, nothing could be improved in communications without an effort to standardize the language. It should be remembered here that it was possible to subscribe to those booklets issued by Berquin 'in all post offices'. The *Library for Villages* marked the end of the chapbooks of the former regime, and the beginning of the written informative literature centralized and circulated thanks to modern means of transmission. Letters, orders and money had to be sent to Paris, at this address: Rue de l'Université No.

28, at the *Bureau de l'Ami des Enfants* (the offices of the *Children's Friend*). That site was the very fulcrum of the lever that was to move the world, the place where a new French language was being created in another colinguistic practice. But to sum up the process briefly, it is now necessary to comprehend its European dimensions and, first of all, to go over to England.

Twelve years earlier, in 1778, there had appeared in London the first primer for learning the language, an instrument directly suited to the needs of children from aristocratic and upper middle-class families; a sort of book that relegated hornbooks and ancient alphabet primers to an archaic past, and one which no longer belonged to Utopian literature as did those written by the theoreticians of education. It was *Lessons for Children*, the work of Anna-Laetitia Barbauld. Anna-Laetitia was then thirty-four and belonged to a family that was perfectly typical of liberal culture in England: they were important cloth makers in large-scale European trade and great scholars of the classical humanities; they were dissenters, excluded from certain ecclesiastical offices; and they were interested in education, being founders, together with other members of the elite, of Warrington Academy (1757). Anna-Laetitia made a name for herself as a poet, a writer of odes. Some scholars have thought that she was wasting her talent in *Lessons for Children*, and in her *Hymns in Prose* (1781) – a work designed to provide texts for the first steps in religious and moral education in English in parallel with biblical texts. But these books aroused a tremendous interest among the general public. They were immediately translated into other European languages and were constantly republished. They created a universal demand in middle-class families. Mrs Barbauld opened a school in Palgrave, which soon became a place famous for training gentlemen of a new type. At the same time, her brother John became a physician, a humanist, the literary editor of the *Monthly Magazine*, and the founder, in association with his sister and his daughters, of the recreational and educational publication *Evenings at Home* (1793–6). Years later Lamb, in a letter to Coleridge, made the remark that because of Mrs Barbauld and her imitators, geography and natural history had replaced old wives' tales for children.

At the same time Arnaud Berquin made a name for himself in London as well as in Paris as a writer of elegies and romances.

He belonged to the same generation as Anna-Laetitia Barbauld, the two Chéniers, Germaine Necker de Staël and Joachim-Henri de Campe. He immediately adapted *Lessons for Children* into French, and he also founded a periodical publication, *L'Ami des enfants*, made up of narratives and dialogues which were so well suited to the foundation of teaching French within families that it established a new French word, a common noun – a '*berquinade*' – that was to designate that kind of writing for more than a century. *L'Ami des enfants* was in its turn translated into English with great success. Berquin, without creating a school as Mrs Barbauld had done, became the friend and adviser on pedagogical matters to prominent liberals and to liberally minded families such as the Malesherbes. He was also considered as a possible primary tutor to the heir apparent to the throne, although his death in 1791 prevented him from taking up that position. The German Joachim-Henri de Campe, born in 1746, was a year older than Berquin and two years younger than Mrs Barbauld. He was a European lexicographer and humanist, Adviser for Schools to the Duke of Brunswick, and author of the *Small Instructive Library for Children or Hamburg Almanach for Children* (1779–84). He also rewrote Defoe's novel under the title of *Young Robinson* (Hamburg, 1780), the starting point of the book's universal fame in modern times.

On the one hand these books became firmly rooted among the international aristocratic bourgeoisie. They were even intended to revive the elite descended from the *ancien régime*, thanks to their boldly realist views on education and instruction. But on the other hand, they impugned the old structure of privileges, aiming to share the means of expression of the state language with the lower classes. Those who were literate believed they could establish general communication by providing every child with the means to appropriate, through practice, the grammatical rules followed when writing in the national language. To their minds, *Evenings at Home*, by winning for itself a wide public, was in keeping with the development of a new type of public spirit: 'The morality they inculcate is not that of children merely, but of men and citizens.' The French Revolution provided the political circumstances for that evolution of ideas, along with the possibility of carrying them out. Grammarians, philosophers, teachers, journalists from all the

European capitals often became in Paris honorary citizens of the French nation. It was then that Berquin entered the election campaign for the constitution in the French style of *L'Ami des enfants*.

The national–international aspect of the new instructive publications is obvious. It has been one of the fundamental structures of European colinguistic practice since the Compacts of Strasbourg. But here the mutual translation of living languages from one into another excludes from the outset the authority of a Latin model. In *Lessons for Children*, Barbauld created images of everyday life in an English house in the country. For instance in the lesson entitled *Tea-Time*:

> Bring the tea-things.
> Bring the little boy's milk.
> Where is the bread and butter?
> Where is the toast and the muffin?
> Here is some bread for you.
> Little boys should not eat butter.
> Sop the bread in your tea.

It would never occur to anybody to try and translate this type of discourse straight into Latin. On the other hand, it is of interest to find out how the linguistic and culturally distinctive features of the English tongue can pass into French. For example, in the following 'new translation illustrated with pretty printed pictures, Geneva and Paris 1854':

> *Apportez le thé.*
> *Apportez le lait du petit garçon.*
> *Ou est le pain et le beurre?*
> *Ou sont les rôties et les gaufres?*
> *Voici du pain pour vous.*
> *Trempez votre pain dans votre thé.*

Swiss consciousness could not write such nonsense as '*Les petits garçons ne doivent pas manger de beurre*'. But, in the *Library for Villages*, English readers will be able to recognize at once a fictional French farmer named Matthieu with double *t* like Matthew in English, a man from the middle classes named Rancey (= Ramsay in English), and an episode pertaining to British mores (the farmer stakes his best cow in a bet) which would be a preposterous fantasy in French. From then on everything which in the colinguistic practice of previous days had stemmed from an Imaginary fed on Latin mythology (*Telemachus*) and on Roman history was to be the product of modern folklore, almost wholly Anglo-Saxon.

Now the same linguistic revolution that had invented general communication between all citizens, invented state education with different levels (*degrés*). Latin, which had been discarded from the common training for written expression in the national tongue, had gone out through the door and come back through the window. It survived under a different form in the '*degré secondaire*' (at the high-school level): it was no longer spoken or even fluently written but it was, as it still is nowadays, essential to the appropriation of really rationalized, really theorized comparative grammar; and it is essential also for the appropriation of a European culture founded on Greco-Latin classical literature and on comparative criticism, both having firm roots in the history of 'western' European peoples.

In *Lessons for Children*, Barbauld depicts the family of a wealthy landowner, Mr Dodwell, and one of his farmers, Matthew. The farmer is the target of Roger's – Mr Dodwell's son – jeers: he smells of manure. But the landowner takes advantage of the occasion to educate his son, to make him see that manure earns a man his bread – which Latin does not – and that it brings income to the owner of the land as well. So it is a duty to honour the farmer and his manure, especially when one enjoys the invisible power conferred by the knowledge of Latin.

The English grammarians, journalists, literary men of a new type, were bringing to the linguistic revolution the centuries-old experience of their education based on the official English version of the Bible. In the same way, the Germans had been using Luther's Bible for a long time. But the French elite could bring in the Port Royal Grammar (the work of *their* dissenters) and the *Traité des Tropes*, an aristocratic language which was extremely sophisticated as far as effects of 'simplicity' were concerned (e.g. in the Romances written by Arnaud Berquin the *poète de salon*), and finally Lhomond's double volume of Franco-Latin elementary grammar for the lower forms of secondary schools (of which the Convention subsequently took the French part and had it used separately in primary schools).

Modern French literature has always been less 'credible' than English when written in fictional plain style; but it has constantly reinvested its classical Latin heritage in the French national language.

In the exposition of historical facts and in the synthetic observations I have been submitting to you, literature has often been mentioned. And it is a fact that the practice of a written language, recognized and taught by the state, cannot be dissociated from literary practice. Training in written expression cannot take place except in the presence of texts, considered as *examples*, which are the starting point and the final result of abstract work. These texts are made up by grammarians according to their theoretical needs in particular cases. But as soon as a global impression of the discourse is required, grammarians draw their material from large-scale verbal structures by which a language idealizes its unity and, by its own means only, recreates the equivalent of lived realities. The imaginary dimension is vital, even and especially when the grammatical exercise is asserting its own conventions. Thus sentences like 'Bring the tea-things' and 'The earth is blue like an orange' have a twofold existence: once as examples of simple sentences having to do with literacy, that is to say, examples of simple communication, of elementary grammatical convention in a republican situation; and second, as linguistic imaginings, having to do with literature written in fictional English, in fictional French, dreaming that they are either establishing or cutting communication.

Most of the time, in present-day France, nonsensical terms or phrases function as a way of asserting the solidity of instituted syntax, paradoxically, and all the more forcibly, by creating daydreams, rather than by appealing to common sense. In fictive French 'the earth is blue like an orange', the incongruity of the terms 'blue' (like an orange) makes the syntactic structure authoritative, for only that structure is capable of making the sentence stand up, i.e. capable of being written French. But through the breaches opened up by the imaginary, there sneak in all the individual phantasms linked with the appropriation of the written language. The threefold determination of literary production mentioned at the beginning of this paper – linguistic, educational and imaginary – is to be found on the plane of subjective experience, on the border line with the unconscious, as much as on the plane of the state institutions. Far from stifling art, general scholarization generalizes literary practice; it creates, in every individual, the frustrations and the delights of power of expression in the state language, that is to say, the conditions of literary calling. 'Poetry must be made by all' is a fictional French sentence coined by Lautréamont in the reign of Napoleon III which has become more and more expressive of literary ideology in a republican situation.

With that sentence I will conclude considerations that were meant only to draw attention to the complexities of the linguistic practices which create simplicity in national languages. To take leave with the help of a concrete quotation, I wish to pay tribute to that great writer in the English language, Anna-Laetitia Barbauld. In one of her 'lessons' she describes the death of a hare that a pack of hounds has just hunted down. I would like this quotation to become the symbol of the primary school texts, so vigorous and so full of hope, which have been captured, devoured, digested, forgotten by all European children:

> Then the hounds come up and tear her and kill her. Then, when she is dead, her little limbs which moved so fast, grow quite stiff, and cannot move at all. A snail could go faster than a hare when it is dead and its poor little heart that beat so quickly, is quite still and cold; and its round full eyes are dull and dim; and its soft, furry skin is all torn and bloody. It is good for nothing now but to be roasted.

Bibliographical note

I have not referred in my paper to the issue of *Praxis* (5, 1981) on 'Art and ideology' where the problems of materialist literary criticism are very well explained, especially in relation to my own work in the opening article by Claude Bouché (Bouché 1981). This is partly because such an important publication cannot be dealt with adequately in a few lines and partly because I have deliberately situated my contribution within the professional context of the French school system. This does not prevent me from thinking that the positions such as those expounded in *Praxis*, 5, have a great international future. My paper is precisely intended to show that French language and literature exist only in relation to English language and literature, within their respective historical apparatuses.

Each page of the paper could well carry numerous notes and bibliographical references. I simply list here a small number of books which, in addition to those cited above, were particularly useful: Marc Bloch's *La Société féodale* (Bloch 1968); Jacques Le Goff's *Pour un autre Moyen-Age* (Le Goff 1977); Perry Miller's *The New England Mind* (Miller 1968), especially Chapter XII, 'The plain style'; and Betsy Rodgers' *Georgian Chronicle* (Rodgers 1958).

8
The other question: difference, discrimination and the discourse of colonialism

HOMI K. BHABHA

The genesis of this essay is diverse and discontinuous; its long march of critical contestation tracks my attempts to clear a space for the 'other' question. To pose the colonial question is to realize that the problematic representation of cultural and racial difference cannot simply be read off from the signs and designs of social authority that are produced in the analyses of class and gender differentiation. As I was writing in 1982, the conceptual boundaries of the west were being busily reinscribed in a clamour of counter-texts – transgressive, semiotic, sem-analytic, deconstructionist – none of which pushed those boundaries to their colonial periphery; to that limit where the west must face a peculiarly displaced and decentred image of itself 'in double duty bound', at once a civilizing mission and a violent subjugating force. It is there, in the colonial margin, that the culture of the west reveals its 'différance', its limit-text, as its practice of authority displays an ambivalence that is one of the most significant discursive and psychical strategies of discriminatory power – whether racist or sexist, peripheral or metropolitan.

It is the force of ambivalence that gives the colonial stereotype its currency: ensures its repeatability in changing historical and discursive conjunctures; informs its strategies of

individuation and marginalization; produces that effect of prob-
abilistic truth and predictability which, for the stereotype, must
always be in *excess* of what can be empirically proved or logically
construed. The absence of such a perspective has its own history
of political expediency. To recognize the stereotype as an
ambivalent mode of knowledge and power demands a theoretical and political response that challenges deterministic or
functionalist modes of conceiving of the relationship between
discourse and politics, and questions dogmatic and moralistic
positions on the meaning of oppression and discrimination. My
reading of colonial discourse suggests that the point of intervention should shift from the *identification* of images as positive or
negative, to an understanding of the *processes of subjectification*
made possible (and plausible) through stereotypical discourse.

  My essay is indebted to traditions of post-structuralist and
psychoanalytic theory, especially in their feminist formulation.
Equally important is its theoretical reorientation, effected
through my reading of the work of Frantz Fanon and Edward
Said. Fanon's insights into the language of the unconscious, as it
emerges in the grotesque psychodrama of everyday life in
colonial societies, demands a rethinking of the forms and forces
of 'identification' as they operate at the edge of cultural authority. Said's work – especially *Orientalism* (1978) and *The Question
of Palestine* (1980) – dramatically shifts the locus of contemporary theory from the Left Bank to the West Bank and beyond,
through a profound meditation on the myths of western power
and knowledge which confine the colonized and dispossessed to
a half-life of misrepresentation and migration. For me, Said's
work focused the need to quicken the half-light of western
history with the disturbing memory of its colonial texts that
bear witness to the trauma that accompanies the triumphal art
of Empire.

  Edward Said concludes his essay, in this volume, with a
perspective on the state of the art, which is both informative and
interdisciplinary. Three recent publications which are representative of developments in the analysis of 'otherness' are :
Europe and Its Others (Barker *et al.* 1985); 'Race, "writing" and
difference' ('Race' 1985) and *Black Literature and Literary Theory*
(Gates 1984).

*

To describe the racist discourse of colonial power as constructed around a 'boundary dispute' is not merely to pun the political with the psychoanalytic. It is the object of my talk today to suggest that the construction of the colonial subject in discourse, and the exercise of colonial power through discourse demands an articulation of forms of difference – racial and sexual. Such an articulation becomes crucial if it is held that the body is always simultaneously inscribed in both the economy of pleasure and desire and the economy of discourse, domination and power. I do not wish to conflate, unproblematically, two forms of the marking – and splitting – of the subject nor to globalize two forms of representation. I want to suggest, however, that there is a theoretical space and a political space for such an articulation – in the sense in which that word itself denies an 'original' identity or a 'singularity' to objects of difference, sexual or racial. If such a view is taken, as Feuchtwang argues in a different context (Feuchtwang 1980, p. 41), it follows that the epithets racial or sexual come to be seen as modes of differentiation, realized as multiple, cross-cutting determinations, polymorphous and perverse, always demanding a specific and strategic calculation of their effects. Such is, I believe, the moment of colonial discourse. It is the most theoretically underdeveloped form of discourse, but crucial to the binding of a range of differences and discriminations that inform the discursive and political practices of racial and cultural hierarchization.

Before turning to the construction of colonial discourse, I want briefly to discuss the process by which forms of racial/cultural/historical otherness have been marginalized in theoretical texts committed to the articulation of *différance*, *signifiance*, in order, it is claimed, to reveal the limits of western metaphysical discourse. Despite the differences (and disputes) between grammatology and semiology, both practices share an anti-epistemological position that impressively contests western modes of representation predicated on an episteme of presence and identity. In facilitating the passage 'from work to text' and stressing the arbitrary, differential and systemic construction of social and cultural signs, these critical strategies unsettle the idealist quest for meanings that are, most often, intentionalist and nationalist. So much is not in question. What does need to be questioned, however, is the *mode of representation of otherness*, which depends crucially on how the 'west' is deployed within these discourses.

The anti-ethnocentric stance is a strategy which, in recognizing the spectacle of otherness, conceals a paradox central to these anti-epistemological theories. For the critique of western idealism or logocentrism requires that there is a constitutive discourse of lack imbricated in a philosophy of presence, which makes the differential or deconstructionist reading possible, 'between the lines'. As Mark Cousins says, the *desire* for presence which characterizes the western episteme and its regimes of representation, 'carries with it as the condition of its movement and of the regulation of its economy, a destiny of non-satisfaction' (Cousins 1978, p. 76). This could lead, as he goes on to say, 'to an endless series of playful deconstructions which manifest a certain sameness in the name of difference'. If such repetitiousness is to be avoided, then the strategic failure of logocentrism would have to be given a displacing and subversive role. This requires that the 'non-satisfaction' should be specified *positively* which is done by identifying an anti-west. Paradoxically, then, cultural otherness functions as the moment of *presence* in a theory of *différance*. The 'destiny of non-satisfaction' is fulfilled in the recognition of otherness as a *symbol* (not sign) of the presence of *significance* or *différance*: otherness is the point of equivalence or identity in a circle in which what needs to be proved (the limits of logocentricity) is assumed (as a destiny or economy of lack/desire). What is denied is any knowledge of cultural otherness as a differential *sign*, implicated in specific historical and discursive conditions, requiring construction in different practices or reading. The place of otherness is fixed in the west as a subversion of western metaphysics and is finally appropriated by the west as its limit-text, anti-west.

Derrida, for example, in the course of his *Positions* interview (Derrida 1981a), tends to fix the problem of ethnocentricity repeatedly at the limits of logocentricity, the unknown territory mapped neatly on to the familiar, as presuppositions inseparable from metaphysics, merely another limitation of metaphysics. Such a position cannot lead to the construction or exploration of other discursive sites from which to investigate the differential materiality and history of colonial culture. The interiority and immediacy of voice as 'consciousness itself', central to logocentric discourse, is disturbed and dispersed by the imposition of a foreign tongue which differentiates the gentleman from the native, culture from civilization. The colonial discourse is always at least twice-inscribed and it is in that process of *différance* that denies 'originality', that the problem of the colonial subject must be thought.

To address the question of ethnocentricity in Derrida's terms, one could explore the exercise of colonial power in relation to the violent hierarchy between written and aural cultures. One might examine, in the context of a colonial society, those strategies of normalization that play on the difference between an 'official' normative language of colonial administration and instruction and an unmarked, marginalized form – pidgin, creole, vernacular – which becomes the site of the native subject's cultural dependence and resistance, and as such a sign of surveillance and control.

Finally, where better to raise the question of the subject of racial and cultural difference than in Stephen Heath's masterly analysis of the chiaroscuro world of Welles's classic *A Touch of Evil*. I refer to an area of its analysis which has generated the least comment, that is, Heath's attention to the structuration of the border Mexico/USA that circulates through the text affirming and exchanging some notion of 'limited being'. Heath's work departs from the traditional analysis of racial and cultural differences, which identifies stereotype and image, and elaborates them in a moralistic or nationalistic discourse that affirms the *origin* and *unity* of national identity. Heath's attentiveness to the contradictory and diverse sites within the textual system which *construct* national/cultural differences in their deployment of the semes of 'foreignness', 'mixedness', 'impurity', as transgressive and corrupting, is extremely relevant. His attention to the turnings of this much neglected subject, as sign (not symbol or stereotype) disseminated in the codes (as 'partition', 'exchange', 'naming', 'character', etc.), gives us a welcome sense of the circulation and proliferation of racial and cultural otherness. Despite the awareness of the multiple or cross-cutting determinations in the construction of modes of sexual and racial differentiation, there is a sense in which

Heath's analysis marginalizes otherness. Although I shall argue that the problem of the border Mexico/USA is read too singularly, too exclusively under the sign of sexuality, it is not that I am unaware of the many proper and relevant reasons for that 'feminist' focus. The 'entertainment' operated by the realist Hollywood film of the 1950s was always also a containment of the subject in a narrative economy of voyeurism and fetishism. Moreover, the displacement that organizes any textual system, within which the display of difference circulates, demands that the play of 'nationalities' should participate in the sexual positioning, troubling the law and desire. There is, nevertheless, a singularity and reductiveness in concluding that:

> Vargas is the position of desire, its admission and its prohibition. Not surprisingly he has two names: the name of desire is Mexican, Miguel . . . that of the Law American Mike. . . . The film uses the border, the play between American and Mexican . . . at the same time it seeks to hold that play finally in the opposition of purity and mixture which in turn is a version of Law and desire.
>
> (Heath 1975, p. 93)

However liberatory it is from one position to see the logic of the text traced ceaselessly between the Ideal Father and the Phallic Mother, in another sense, in seeing only one possible articulation of the differential complex 'race-sex' it half colludes with the proffered images of marginality. For if the naming of Vargas is crucially mixed and split in the economy of desire, then there are other mixed economies which make naming and positioning equally problematic 'across the border'. For to identify the 'play' on the border as purity and mixture and to see it as an allegory of law and desire reduces the articulation of racial and sexual difference to what is dangerously close to becoming a circle rather than a spiral of différance. On that basis, it is not possible to construct the polymorphous and perverse collusion between racism and sexism as a *mixed economy* – for instance, the discourses of American cultural colonialism and Mexican dependency, the fear/desire of miscegenation, the American border as cultural signifier of a pioneering, male 'American' spirit always under threat from races and cultures beyond the border. If the death of the Father is the interruption on which the narrative is initiated, it is through that death that miscegenation is both possible and deferred; if, again, it is the purpose of the narrative to restore Susan as 'good object', it also becomes its project to deliver Vargas from his racial 'mixedness'. It is all there in Heath's splendid scrutiny of the text, revealed as he brushes against its grain. What is missing is the taking up of these positions as also the *object(ives)* of his analysis.

The difference of other cultures is other than the excess of signification, the *différance* of the trace or trajectory of desire. These are theoretical strategies that may be necessary to combat 'ethnocentricism' but they cannot, of themselves, unreconstructed, represent that otherness. There can be no inevitable sliding from the semiotic or deconstructionist activity to the unproblematic reading of other cultural and discursive systems. There is in such readings a will to power and knowledge that, in failing to specify the limits of their own field of enunciation and effectivity, proceed to individualize otherness as the discovery of their own assumptions.

What is meant by colonial discourse as an apparatus of power will emerge more fully as a critique of specific, historical texts. At this stage, however, I shall provide what I take to be the minimum conditions and specifications of such a discourse. It is an apparatus that turns on the recognition and disavowal of racial/cultural/historical differences. Its predominant strategic function is the creation of a space for a 'subject peoples' through the production of knowledges in terms of which surveillance is exercised and a complex form of pleasure/unpleasure is incited. It seeks authorization for its strategies by the production of knowledges of colonizer and colonized which are stereotypical but antithetically evaluated. The objective of colonial discourse is to construe the colonized as a population of degenerate types on the basis of racial origin, in order to justify conquest and to establish systems of administration and instruction. Despite the play of power within colonial discourse and the shifting positionalities of its subjects (e.g. effects of class, gender, ideology, different social formations, varied systems of colonization, etc.), I am referring to a form of governmentality that in marking out a 'subject nation', appropriates, directs and dominates its various spheres of activity. Therefore, despite the play in the colonial system which is crucial to its exercise of power, I do not consider the practices and discourses of revolutionary struggle as the under/other side of 'colonial discourse'. They may be historically co-present with it and intervene in it, but can never be 'read off' merely on the basis of their opposition to it. Anti-colonialist discourse requires an alternative set of questions, techniques and strategies in order to construct it.

Through this paper I shall move through forms of colonial discourse or descriptions of it, written from the late nineteenth century to the present. I have referred to specific historical texts in order to construct three theoretical problems which I consider crucial. In Temple's work the circulation of power as knowledge; in Said's the fixation/fetishization of stereotypical knowledge as power; and in Fanon's the circulation of power and knowledge in a binding of desire and pleasure.

The social Darwinist problematic of Charles Temple's 'The native races and their rulers' [1918] (Temple 1971) enacts the tension between 'the free and continual circulation' that natural selection requires and the effects of colonial power which claims to assist natural selection by controlling racial degeneracy but, through that intervention, must necessarily impede free circulation. The colonial system then requires some justification other than mere material necessity; and if justification is understood as both vindication and correction, then we can see in this text a crucial adjustment in the exercise of colonial power. In the face of an ambitious native 'nationalist' bourgeois, Temple's text marks the shift in the form of colonial government, from a juridical sovereign exercise of power as punitive and restrictive – as harbinger of death – to a disciplinary form of power.

Disciplinary power is exercised through indirection on the basis of a knowledge of the subject-races as 'abnormal'. They are not merely degenerate and primitive but, Temple claims, they also require the 'abnormality' of imperialist intervention to hasten the process of natural selection. If 'normalization' can imply even the faint possibility of an absorption or incorporation of the subject-races then, like mass rule at home, this must be resisted in the colonies. The natives are therefore 'individualized', through the racist testimony of 'science' and colonialist administrative wisdom, as having such divergent ethical and mental outlooks that integration or independence is deemed impossible. Thus marginalized or individualized, the colonial subject as bearer of racial typologies and racist stereotypes is reintroduced to the circulation of power as a 'productive capacity' within that form of colonial government called 'indirect rule'.

The co-option of traditional elites into the colonial administration is then seen to be a way of harnessing the ambitious life-instinct of the natives. This sets up the native subject as a site of productive power, both subservient and always potentially seditious. What is increased is the visibility of the subject as an object of surveillance, tabulation, enumeration and, indeed, paranoia and fantasy. When the upward spiral of natural selection encounters differences of race, class and gender as potentially contradictory and insurrectionary forces, whose mobility may fracture the closed circuit of natural selection, social Darwinism invokes what Temple calls 'the decrees of all-seeing Providence'. This agency of social control appeals in desperation to God instead of Nature to fix the colonized at that point in the social order from which colonial power will, in Foucault's specification, be able simultaneously to increase the subjected forces and to improve the force and efficacy of that which subjects them.

Colonial power produces the colonized as a fixed reality which is at once an 'other' and yet entirely knowable and visible. It resembles a form of narrative in which the productivity and circulation of subjects and signs are bound in a reformed and recognizable totality. It employs a system of representation, a regime of truth, that is structurally similar to realism. And it is in order to intervene within that system of representation that Edward Said proposes a semiotic of 'Orientalist' power, which in raising the problem of power as a question of narrative introduces a new topic in the territory of colonial discourse.

Philosophically, then, the kind of language, thought, and vision that I have been calling Orientalism very generally is a form of radical realism; anyone employing Orientalism, which is the habit for dealing with questions, objects, qualities and regions deemed Oriental, will designate, name, point to, fix what he is talking or thinking about with a word or phrase, which is then considered either to have acquired, or more simply to be, reality. . . . The tense they employ is the timeless eternal; they convey an impression of repetition and strength. . . . For all these functions it is frequently enough to use the simple copula is.

(Said 1978, p. 72)

But the syllogism, as Kristeva once said, is that form of western rationalism that reduces heterogeneity to two-part order, so that the *copula* is the point at which this binding preserves the boundaries of sense for an entire tradition of philosophical thinking. Of this, too, Said is aware when he hints continually at a polarity or division at the very centre of Orientalism (Said 1978, p. 206). It is, on the one hand, a topic of learning, discovery, practice; on the other it is the site of dreams, images, fantasies, myths, obsessions and requirements. It is a static system of 'synchronic essentialism', a knowledge of 'signifiers of stability' such as the lexicographic and the encyclopaedic. However, this site is continually under threat from diachronic forms of history and narrative, signs of instability. And, finally, this line of thinking is given a shape analogical to the dream-work, when Said refers explicitly to a distinction between 'an unconscious positivity' which he terms *latent* Orientalism, and the stated knowledges and views about the Orient which he calls *manifest* Orientalism.

Where the originality of this account loses some of its interrogative power is in Said's inadequate engagement with alterity and ambivalence in the articulation of these two economies which threaten to split the very object of Orientalist discourse as a knowledge and the subject positioned therein. He contains this threat by introducing a binarism within the argument which, in initially setting up an opposition between these two discursive scenes, finally allows them to be correlated as a congruent system of representation that is unified through a political–ideological *intention* which, in his words, enables Europe to advance securely and *unmetaphorically* upon the Orient.

This seems to be a rather peremptory resolution to a problem posed with remarkable insight. It is compounded by a psychologistic reduction when, in describing Orientalism through the nineteenth century, Said identifies the *content* of Orientalism as the unconscious repository of fantasy, imaginative writings and essential ideas; and the *form* of manifest Orientalism as the historically and discursively determined, diachronic aspect.

To develop a point made above, the division/correlation structure of manifest and latent Orientalism leads to the effectivity of the concept of discourse being undermined by what I will call the polarities of intentionality. This is a problem fundamental to Said's use of the terms *power* and *discourse*. The productivity of Foucault's concept of power/knowledge is its refusal of an epistemology which opposes form/content, ideology/science, essence/appearance. 'Pouvoir/Savoir' places subjects in a relation of power and recognition that is not part of a symmetrical or dialectical relation – self/other, Master/Slave – which can then be subverted by being inverted. Subjects are always disproportionately placed in opposition or domination through the symbolic decentring of multiple power-relations which play the role of support as well as target or adversary. It becomes difficult, then, to conceive of the *historical* enunciations of colonial discourse without them being either functionally overdetermined or strategically elaborated or displaced by the *unconscious* scene of latent Orientalism. Equally, it is difficult to conceive of the process of subjectification as a placing *within* orientalist or colonial discourse for the dominated subject without the dominant being strategically placed within it too. There is always, in Said, the suggestion that colonial power and discourse is possessed entirely by the colonizer, which is an historical and theoretical simplification. The terms in which Said's Orientalism are unified – which is, the intentionality and undirectionality of colonial power – also unifies the subject of colonial enunciation.

This is a result of Said's inadequate attention to representation as a concept that articulates the historical and fantasy (as the scene of desire) in the production of the 'political' effects of discourse. He rightly rejects a notion of Orientalism as the misrepresentation of an Oriental essence. However, having introduced the concept of 'discourse' he does not attend adequately to the problems it makes for the instrumentalist use of power/knowledge that he sometimes seems to require. This problem is summed up by his ready acceptance of the view that

Representations are formations, or as Roland Barthes has said of all the operations of language, they are deformations.
(Said 1978, p. 273)

This brings me to my second point, that the closure and coherence attributed to the unconscious pole of colonial discourse, and the unproblematized notion of the subject, restricts the effectivity of both power and knowledge. This makes it difficult to see how power could function productively both as incitement and interdiction. Nor would it be possible without the attribution of ambivalence to relations of power/knowledge to calculate the traumatic impact of the return of the oppressed – those terrifying stereotypes of savagery, cannibalism, lust and anarchy which are the signal points of identification and alienation, scenes of fear and desire, in colonial texts. It is precisely this function of the stereotype as phobia and fetish that, according to Fanon, threatens the closure of the racial/epidermal schema for the colonial subject and opens the royal road to colonial fantasy.

If Said's theory disavows that *mise-en-scène*, his metaphoric language somehow prefigures it. There is a forgotten, under-developed passage which, in cutting across the body of the text, articulates the question of power and desire that I now want to take up. It is a process that has the power to reorientate our representation and recognition of colonial 'otherness'.

Altogether an internally structured archive is built up from the literature that belongs to these experiences. Out of this comes a restricted number of typical encapsulations: the journey, the history, the fable, the stereotype, the polemical confrontation. These are the lenses through which the Orient is experienced, and they shape the language, perception, and form of the encounter between East and West. What gives the immense number of encounters some unity, however, is the vacillation I was speaking about earlier. Something patently foreign and distant acquires, for one reason or another, a status more rather than less familiar. One tends to stop judging things either as completely novel or as completely well-known; a new median category emerges, a category that allows one to see new things, things seen for the first time, as versions of a previously known thing. In essence such a category is not so much a way of receiving new information as

> it is a method of controlling what seems to be a threat to some established view of things. . . . The threat is muted, familiar values impose themselves, and in the end the mind reduces the pressure upon it by accommodating things to itself as either 'original' or 'repetitious'. . . . The Orient at large, therefore, vacillates between the West's contempt for what is familiar and its shivers of delight in – or fear of – novelty.
>
> (Said 1978, pp. 58–9)

What is this other scene of colonial discourse played out around the 'median category'? What is this theory of encapsulation or fixation which moves between the recognition of cultural and racial difference and its disavowal, by affixing the unfamiliar to something established, in a form that is repetitious and vacillates between delight and fear? Is it not analogous to the Freudian fable of fetishism (and disavowal) that circulates within the discourse of colonial power, requiring the articulation of modes of differentiation – sexual and racial – as well as different modes of discourse – psychoanalytic and historical?

The strategic articulation of 'co-ordinates of knowledge' – racial and sexual – and their inscription in the play of colonial power as modes of differentiation, defence, fixation, hierarchization, is a way of specifying colonial discourse which would be illuminated by reference to Foucault's post-structuralist concept of the *dispositif* or apparatus. In displacing his earlier search for discursive regularity as *episteme*, Foucault stresses that the relations of knowledge and power within the apparatus are always a strategic response to an *urgent need* at a given historical moment – much as I suggested at the outset, that the force of colonial discourse as a theoretical and political intervention was the *need*, in our contemporary moment, to contest singularities of difference and to articulate modes of differentiation. Foucault writes:

> the apparatus is essentially of a strategic nature, which means assuming that it is a matter of a certain manipulation of relations of forces, either developing them in a particular direction, blocking them, stablizing them, utilizing them, etc. The apparatus is thus always inscribed in a play of power, but it is always also linked to certain coordinates of knowledge which issue from it but, to an equal degree, condition it. This is what the apparatus consists in: strategies of

relations of forces supporting and supported by, types of knowledge.

(Foucault 1980a, p. 196)

In this spirit I argue for the reading of the stereotype in terms of fetishism. The myth of historical origination – racial purity, cultural priority – production in relation to the colonial stereotype functions to 'normalize' the multiple beliefs and split subjects that constitute colonial discourse as a consequence of its process of disavowal. The scene of fetishism functions similarly as, at once, a reactivation of the material of original fantasy – the anxiety of castration and sexual difference – as well as a normalization of that difference and disturbance in terms of the fetish object as the substitute for the mother's penis. Within the apparatus of colonial power, the discourses of sexuality and race relate in a process of *functional overdetermination*, 'because each effect . . . enters into resonance or contradiction with the others and thereby calls for a re-adjustment or re-working of the heterogeneous elements that surface at various points' (Foucault 1980a, p. 195).

There is both a structural and functional justification for reading the racial stereotype of colonial discourse in terms of fetishism.[1] My rereading of Said establishes the *structural* link. Fetishism, as the disavowal of difference, is that repetitious scene around the problem of secondary castration. The recognition of sexual difference – as the pre-condition for the circulation of the chain of absence and presence in the realm of the symbolic – is disavowed by the fixation on an object that masks that difference and restores an original presence. The functional link between the fixation of the fetish and the stereotype (or the stereotype as fetish) is even more relevant. For fetishism is always a 'play' or vacillation between the archaic affirmation of wholeness/similarity – in Freud's terms: 'All men have penises'; in ours: 'All men have the same skin/race/culture; and the anxiety associated with lack of difference' – again, for Freud: 'Some do not have penises'; for us: 'Some *do not* have the same skin/race/culture'. Within discourse, the fetish represents the simultaneous play between metaphor as substitution (making absence and difference) and metonymy (which contiguously registers the perceived lack). The fetish or stereotype gives access to an 'identity' which is predicated as much on mastery and pleasure as it is on anxiety and defence, for it is a form of multiple and contradictory belief in its recognition of difference and disavowal of it. This conflict of pleasure/unpleasure, mastery/defence, knowledge/disavowal, absence/presence, has a fundamental significance for colonial discourse. For the scene of fetishism is also the scene of the reactivation and repetition of primal fantasy – the subject's desire for a pure origin that is always threatened by its division, for the subject must be gendered to be engendered, to be spoken. The stereotype, then, as the primary point of subjectification in colonial discourse, for both coloniser and colonized, is the scene of a similar fantasy and defence – the desire for an originality which is again threatened by the differences of race, colour and culture. My contention is splendidly caught in Fanon's title *Black Skin White Masks* where the disavowal of difference turns the colonial subject into a misfit – a grotesque mimicry or 'doubling' that threatens to split the soul and whole, undifferentiated skin of the ego. The stereotype is not a simplification because it is a false representation of a given reality. It is a simplification because it is an arrested, fixated form of representation that, in denying the play of difference (that the negation through the other permits), constitutes a problem for the *representation* of the subject in significations of psychic and social relations.

When Fanon talks of the positioning of the subject in the stereotyped discourse of colonialism, he gives further credence to my point. The legends, stories, histories and anecdotes of a colonial culture offer the subject a primordial Either/Or (Fanon 1970, pp. 78–82). *Either* he is fixed in a consciousness of the body as a solely negating activity *Or* as a new kind of man, a new genus. What is denied the colonial subject, both as colonizer and colonized, is that form of negation which gives access to the recognition of difference in the symbolic. It is that possibility of difference and circulation which would liberate the signifier of skin/culture from the signifieds of racial typology, the analytics of blood, ideologies of racial and cultural dominance or degeneration. 'Wherever he goes', Fanon despairs, 'the negro remains a negro' – his race becomes the ineradicable sign of negative difference in colonial discourse. For the stereotype impedes the circulation and articulation of the signifier of 'race' as anything other than its *fixity* as racism. We always already know that blacks are licentious, Asiatics duplictious. . .

There are two 'primal scenes' in Fanon's *Black Skin White Masks*: two myths of the origin of the marking of the subject within the racist practices and discourses of a colonial culture. On one occasion a white girl fixes Fanon in look and word as she turns to identify with her mother. It is a scene which echoes endlessly through his essay 'The fact of blackness': 'Look, a negro . . . Mamma, *see* the Negro! I'm frightened. Frightened.' 'What else could it be for me', Fanon concludes, 'but an amputation, an excision, a haemorrhage that splattered my whole body with black blood' (Fanon 1970, p. 69) Equally, he stresses the primal moment when the child encounters racial and cultural stereotype in children's fictions, where white heroes and black demons are proffered as points of ideological and psychical identification. Such dramas are enacted *every day* in colonial societies, says Fanon, employing a theatrical metaphor – the scene – which emphasizes the visible – the seen. I want to play upon both these senses which refer at once to the site of fantasy and desire and to the site of subjectification and power.

The drama underlying these dramatic 'everyday' colonial scenes is not difficult to discern. In each of them the subject turns around the pivot of the 'stereotype' to return to a point of total identification. The girl's gaze returns to her mother in the recognition and disavowal of the negroid type; the black child turns away from himself, his race, in his total identification with the positivity of whiteness which is at once colour and no colour. In the act of disavowal and fixation the colonial subject is returned to the narcissism of the Imaginary and its identification of an ideal-ego that is white and whole. For what these primal scenes illustrate is that looking/hearing/reading as sites of subjectification in colonial discourse are evidence of the importance of the visual and auditory imaginary for the *histories* of societies (Metz 1982, pp. 59–60).

My anatomy of colonial discourse remains incomplete until I locate the stereotype as an arrested, fetishistic mode of representation within its field of identification, which I have identified in my description of Fanon's primal scenes, as the Lacanian scheme of the Imaginary. The Imaginary^2 is the transformation that takes place in the subject at the formative mirror phase, when it assumes a discrete image which allows it to postulate a series of equivalences, samenesses, identities, between the objects of the surrounding world. However, this positioning is itself problematic, for the subject finds or recognizes itself through an image which is simultaneously alienating and hence potentially confrontational. This is the basis of the close relation between the two forms of identification complicit with the Imaginary – narcissism and aggressivity. It is precisely these two forms of 'identification' that constitute the dominant strategy of colonial power exercised in relation to the stereotype which, as a form of multiple and contradictory belief, gives knowledge of difference and simultaneously disavows or masks it. Like the mirror-phase 'the fullness' of the stereotype – its image *as* identity – is always threatened by 'lack'.

The construction of colonial discourse is then a complex articulation of the tropes of fetishism – metaphor and metonymy – and the forms of narcissistic and aggressive identification available to the Imaginary. Stereotypical racial discourse is then a four-term strategy. There is a tie-up between the metaphoric or masking function of the fetish and the narcissistic object-choice and an opposing alliance between the metonymic figuring of lack and the aggressive phase of the Imaginary. One has then a repertoire of conflictual positions that constitute the subject in colonial discourse. The taking up of any one position, within a specific discursive form, in a particular historical conjuncture, is then always problematic – the site of both fixity and fantasy. It provides a colonial identity that is played out – like all fantasies of originality and origination – in the face and space of the disruption and threat from the heterogeneity of other positions. As a form of splitting and multiple belief, the stereotype requires, for its successful signification, a continual and repetitive chain of other stereotypes. This is the process by which the metaphoric 'masking' is inscribed on a lack which must then be concealed, that gives the stereotype both its fixity and its phantasmatic quality – the same old stories of the negro's animality, the coolie's inscrutability or the stupidity of the Irish which *must* be told (compulsively) again and afresh, and is differently gratifying and terrifying each time.

In any specific colonial discourse the metaphoric/narcissistic

and the metonymic/aggressive positions will function simultaneously, but always strategically poised in relation to each
other; similar to the moment of alienation which stands as a
threat to Imaginary plenitude and 'multiple belief' which
threatens fetishistic disavowal. Caught in the Imaginary as they
are, these shifting positionalities will never seriously threaten
the dominant power relations, for they exist to exercise them
pleasurably and productively. They will always pose the problem of difference as that between the pre-constituted, 'natural'
poles of black and white with all its historical and ideological
ramifications. The *knowledge of the construction* of that 'opposition'
will be denied the colonial subject. He is constructed within an
apparatus of power which *contains*, in both senses of the word, an
'other' knowledge – a knowledge that is arrested and fetishistic
and circulates through colonial discourse as that limited form of
otherness, that fixed form of difference, that I have called the
stereotype.

My four-term strategy of the stereotype tries tentatively to
provide a structure and a process for the 'subject' of colonial
discourse. I now want to take up the problem of discrimination
as the political effect of such a discourse and relate it to the
question of 'race' and 'skin'. To that end it is important to
remember that the multiple belief that accompanies fetishism
does not only have disavowal value; it also has 'knowledge
value' and it is this that I shall now pursue. In calculating this
knowledge value it is crucial to try and understand what Fanon
means when he says that:

> There is a quest for the Negro, the Negro is a demand, one
> cannot get along without him, he is needed, but only if he is
> made palatable in a certain way. Unfortunately the Negro
> knocks down the system and breaks the treaties.
>
> (Fanon 1970, p. 114)

What this demand is, and how the native or negro is made
palatable requires that we acknowledge some significant differences between the general theory of fetishism and its specific
uses for an understanding of racist discourse. First, the fetish of
colonial discourse – what Fanon calls the epidermal schema – is
not, like the sexual fetish, a secret. Skin, as the key signifier of
cultural and racial difference in the stereotype, is the most

visible of fetishes, recognized as common knowledge in a range of cultural, political, historical discourses, and plays a public part in the racial drama that is enacted every day in colonial societies. Second, it may be said that the sexual fetish is closely linked to the 'good object'; it is the prop that makes the whole object desirable and lovable, facilitates sexual relations and can even promote a form of happiness. The stereotype can also be seen as that particular 'fixated' form of the colonial subject which *facilitates* colonial relations, and sets up a discursive form of racial and cultural opposition in terms of which colonial power is exercised. If it is claimed that the colonized are most often objects of hate, then we can reply with Freud that

> affection and hostility in the treatment of the fetish – which run parallel with the disavowal and acknowledgement of castration – are mixed in unequal proportions in different cases, so that the one or the other is more clearly recogniz-able.   (Freud 1981, pp. 357ff.)

What this statement recognizes is the wide range of the stereotype, from the loyal servant to Satan, from the loved to the hated; a shifting of subject positions in the circulation of colonial power which I tried to account for through the mobility of the metaphoric/narcissistic and metonymic/aggressive system of colonial discourse. What remains to be examined, however, is the construction of the signifier 'skin/race' in those regimes of visibility and discursivity – fetishistic, scopic, imaginary – within which I have located the stereotypes. It is only on that basis that we can construct its 'knowledge-value' which will, I hope, enable us to see the place of fantasy in the exercise of colonial power.

My argument relies upon a particular reading of the prob-lematic of representation which, Fanon suggests, is specific to the colonial situation. He writes:

> the originality of the colonial context is that the economic substructure is also a superstructure . . . you are rich because you are white, you are white because you are rich. This is why Marxist analysis should always be slightly stretched every time we have to do with the colonial problem.
>
>   (Fanon 1969, p. 31)

Fanon could either be seen as adhering to a simple reflectionist or determinist notion of cultural/social signification or, more interestingly, he could be read as taking an 'anti-repressionist' position (attacking the notion that ideology as miscognition, or misrepresentation, is the repression of the real). For our purposes I tend towards the latter reading which then provides a visibility to the exercise of power; gives force to the argument that skin, as a signifier of discrimination, must be produced or processed as visible. As Abbott says, in a very different context:

> whereas repression banishes its object into the unconscious, forgets and attempts to forget the forgetting, discrimination must constantly invite its representations into consciousness, reinforcing the crucial recognition of difference which they embody and revitalizing them for the perception on which its effectivity depends. . . . It must sustain itself on the presence of the very difference which is also its object.
>
> (Abbott 1979, pp. 15–16)

What 'authorizes' discrimination, Abbot continues, is the occlusion of the preconstruction or working-up of difference:

> this repression of production entails that the recognition of difference is procured in an innocence, as a 'nature'; recognition is contrived as primary cognition, spontaneous effect of the 'evidence of the visible'.
>
> (Abbott 1979, p. 16)

This is precisely the kind of recognition, as spontaneous and visible, that is attributed to the stereotype. The difference of the object of discrimination is at once visible and natural – colour as the cultural/political sign of inferiority or degeneracy, skin as its natural 'identity'.

Although the 'authority' of colonial discourse depends crucially on its location in narcissism and the Imaginary, my concept of stereotype-as-suture is a recognition of the *ambivalence* of that authority and those orders of identification. The role of fetishistic identification, in the construction of discriminatory knowledges that depend on the *presence of difference*, is to provide a process of splitting and multiple/contradictory belief at the point of enunciation and subjectification. It is this crucial splitting of the ego which is represented in Fanon's description of the construction of the colonial subject as effect of stereotypical discourse: the subject primordially fixed and yet triply split between the incongruent knowledges of body, race, ancestors. Assailed by the stereotype

> The corporeal schema crumbled, its place taken by a racial epidermal scheme. . . . It was no longer a question of being aware of my body in the third person but a triple person. . . . I was not given one, but two, three places.
>
> (Fanon 1970, p. 79)

This process is best understood in terms of the articulation of multiple-belief that Freud proposes in the essay 'Fetishism'. It is a non-repressive form of knowledge that allows for the possibility of simultaneously embracing two contradictory beliefs, one official and one secret, one archaic and one progressive, one that allows the myth of origins, the other that articulates difference and division. Its knowledge-value lies in its orientation as a defence towards external reality, and provides, in Metz's words.

> the lasting matrix, the effective prototype of all those splittings of belief which man will henceforth be capable of in the most varied domains, of all the infinitely complex unconscious and occasionally conscious interactions which he will allow himself between believing and not-believing.
>
> (Metz 1982, p. 70)

It is through this notion of splitting and multiple belief that, I believe, it becomes easier to see the bind of knowledge and fantasy, power and pleasure, that informs the particular regime of visibility deployed in colonial discourse. The visibility of the racial/colonial other is at once a *point* of identity 'Look at a negro' and at the same time a *problem* for the attempted closure within discourse. For the recognition of difference as 'imaginary' points of identity and origin – such as black and white – is disturbed by the representation of splitting in the discourse. What I called the play between the metaphoric – narcissistic and metonymic – aggressive moments in colonial discourse – that four-part strategy of the stereotype – crucially recognizes the prefiguring of desire as a potentially conflictual, disturbing force in all those regimes of the 'originary' that I have brought together. In the objectification of the scopic drive there is always the threatened return of the look; in the identification of the Imaginary relation there is always the alienating other (or mirror) which crucially returns its image to the subject; and in that form of substitution and fixation that is fetishism there is always the trace of loss, absence. To put it succinctly, the recognition and disavowal of 'difference' is always disturbed by the question of its re-presentation or construction. The stereotype is, in fact, an impossible object. For that very reason, the exertions of the 'official knowledges' of colonialism – pseudo-scientific, typological, legal-administrative, eugenicist – are imbricated at the point of their production of meaning and power with the fantasy that dramatizes the impossible desire for a pure, undifferentiated origin. Not itself the object of desire but its setting; not an ascription of prior identities but their production in the syntax of the scenario of racist discourse; colonial fantasy plays a crucial part in those everyday scenes of subjectification in a colonial society that Fanon refers to repeatedly. Like fantasies of the origins of sexuality, the productions of colonial desire mark the discourse as

> a favoured spot for the most primitive defensive reactions such as turning against oneself, into an opposite, projection, negation.
>
> (Laplanche and Pontalis 1980, p. 318)

The problem of origin as the problematic of racist, stereotypical knowledge is a complex one and what I have said about its construction will come clear in this illustration from Fanon. Stereotyping is not the setting up of a false image which becomes the scapegoat of discriminatory practices. It is a much more ambivalent text of projection and introjection, metaphoric and metonymic strategies, displacement, overdetermination, guilt, aggressivity; the masking and splitting of 'official' and fantasmatic knowledges to construct the positionalities and oppositionalities of racist discourse:

> My body was given back to me sprawled out, distorted, recoloured, clad in mourning in that white winter day. The Negro is an animal, the Negro is bad, the Negro is mean, the Negro is ugly; look, a nigger, it's cold, the nigger is shivering because he is cold, the little boy is trembling because he is

afraid of the nigger, the nigger is shivering with cold, that cold that goes through your bones, the handsome little boy is trembling because he thinks that the nigger is quivering with rage, the little white boy throws himself into his mother's arms: Mama the nigger's going to eat me up.

(Fanon 1970, p. 80)

It is the scenario of colonial fantasy which, in staging the ambivalence of desire, articulates the demand for the negro which the negro disrupts. For the stereotype is at once a substitute and a shadow. By acceding to the wildest fantasies (in the popular sense) of the colonizer, the stereotyped other reveals something of the fantasy (as desire, defence) of that position of mastery. For if 'skin' in racist discourse is the visibility of darkness, and a prime signifier of the body and its social and cultural correlates, then we are bound to remember what Karl Abraham (Abraham 1978) says in his seminal work on the scopic drive. The pleasure-value of darkness is a withdrawal in order to know nothing of the external world. Its symbolic meaning, however, is thoroughly ambivalent. Darkness signifies at once birth and death; it is in all cases a desire to return to the fullness of the mother, a desire for an unbroken and undifferentiated line of vision and origin.

But surely there is another scene of colonial discourse; where the subverting 'split' is recuperable within a strategy of social and political control. It is recognizably true that the chain of stereotypical signification is curiously mixed and split, polymorphous and perverse. The black is both savage (cannibal) and yet the most obedient and dignified of servants (the bearer of food); he is the embodiment of rampant sexuality and yet innocent as a child; he is mystical, primitive, simple-minded and yet the most worldly and accomplished liar, and manipulator of social forces. In each case what is being dramatized is a separation – *between* races, cultures, histories, *within* histories – a separation between *before* and *after* that repeats obsessively the mythical moment of disjunction. Despite the structural similarities with the play of need and desire in primal fantasies, the colonial fantasy does not try to cover up that moment of separation. It is more ambivalent. On the one hand, it proposes a teleology – under certain conditions of colonial domination and control the native is progressively reformable. On the other, however, it effectively displays the 'separation', makes it more visible. It is the visibility of this separation which, in denying the colonized capacities of self-government, independence, western modes of civility, lends authority to the official version and mission of colonial power. Colonial fantasy is the continual dramatization of emergence – of difference, freedom – as the beginning of a history which is repetitively denied. Such a denial is the clearly voiced demand of colonial discourse as the legitimization of a form of rule that is facilitated by the racist fetish. In concluding, I would like to develop a little further my working definition of colonial discourse given at the start of this paper.

Racist stereotypical discourse, in its colonial moment, inscribes a form of governmentality that is informed by a productive splitting in its constitution of knowledge and exercise of power. Some of its practices recognize the differences of race, culture, history as elaborated by stereotypical knowledges, racial theories, administrative colonial experience, and on that basis institutionalize a range of political and cultural ideologies that are prejudicial, discriminatory, vestigial, archaic, 'mythical' and, crucially, are recognized as being so. By knowing the native population in these terms, discriminatory and authoritarian forms of political control are considered appropriate. The colonized population is then deemed to be both the cause and effect of the system, imprisoned in the circle of interpretation. What is visible is the *necessity* of such rule which is justified by those moralistic and normative ideologies of amelioration recognized as the 'civilizing mission' or the 'white man's burden'. However, there coexists within the same apparatus of colonial power, modern systems and sciences of government, progressive western forms of social and economic organization which provide the manifest justification for the project of colonialism – an argument which, in part, impressed Karl Marx. It is on the site of this coexistence that strategies of hierarchization and marginalization are employed in the management of colonial societies. And if my deduction from Fanon about the peculiar visibility of colonial power is acceptable to you, then I would extend it to say that it is a form of governmentality in which the ideological space functions in more openly collaborative ways with political and economic exigencies. The barracks stand by the church which stands by the schoolroom; the cantonment stands hard by the 'civil lines'. Such visibility of the institutions and apparatuses of power is possible because the exercise of colonial power makes their *relationship* obscure, produces them as fetishes, spectacles of a naturalized racial pre-eminence. Only the seat of government is everywhere – alien and separate by that distance upon which surveillance depends for its strategies of objectification, normalization and discipline.

Notes

1 See Freud 1981, pp. 345ff.; for fetishism and 'the Imaginary signifier' see Metz 1982, Chapter 5. See also Neale 1979/80.
2 For the best account of Lacan's concept of the Imaginary see Rose 1981.

9
Images of the sixteenth and seventeenth centuries as a history of the present

SIMON BARKER

The polemic contained in my contribution to the 1983 *Confronting the Crisis* conference arose from two principal sources. First, there was the unwillingness (or rather the tactical inability) of the Labour opposition to contest the organic national history so readily evoked by the war cabinet over the issue of the Falklands – a history quietly projected on to the subsequent general election. Second, it seemed that while the victims of these two conflicts were being buried – the war dead with an expensive ceremony not extended to the undeserving unemployed – the academic left was content with a post-Derridean 'freeplay of meaning' game in which it hardly mattered that nobody could win, since nothing was at stake.

Since 1983 a number of critics have usefully addressed that singular authority of the Shakespearean 'Golden Age' so powerfully articulated through the educational system and within a wider context. Several volumes have appeared which 'politicize' the drama of the period in order to confront its 'organicism'. These include Dollimore (1984), Barker *et al.* (1984), Dollimore and Sinfield (1985), Drakakis (1985) and Belsey (1985). An extended account of the *Mary Rose* phenomenon is contained within Wright (1985).

As these volumes were being prepared, Margaret Thatcher's 'enemy without' was displaced by the 'enemy within' with whom the government fought a year-long battle over the issue of colliery closures. It became safe to parody the Falklands War and even to question its excesses, yet extremely dangerous to recover a history which was narrative, yet oppositional, in that it foregrounded such dates as 1926. The Conservative press was forced to efface this history with a concerted organicist rhetoric in the pursuit of 'peace and order' which made the miners, and particularly their leaders, mere criminals. In the context of these confrontations it seems there is still a case for a 'partial' history constructed on the basis of *implications* beyond the 'freeplay and text' liberalism found within some institutions which are themselves vulnerable to, at the very least, partial closure.

*

In this paper I want to discuss a particular 'history of the present' which is constructed through representations of the sixteenth and seventeenth centuries as a 'Golden Age' of 'civilization'.[1] I want to argue that, to some extent at least, these representations underpin the ideology characterized by the now familiar Conservative slogan 'the resolute approach'. But I think it is important that the notions of determined government, self-reliance and 'no alternative' evinced by this slogan should not be over-emphasized as defining the actual behaviour of the present Conservative government. I would argue, in fact, that there is little fundamental difference between Thatcher's regime and previous governments, both Tory and Labour. If Thatcher was 'resolute' in 'holding out' against the health workers, and in sending the Task Force to the South Atlantic, then a succession of Labour cabinets have been no less ruthless in their deployment of troops against workers in the British Isles. Quite apart from the case of Ireland there are numerous examples of such resolution, ranging from Attlee's use of the army against dock workers in 1945 to Callaghan's introduction of military scab labour during the firemen's dispute of 1977–8. In fact the success of Thatcherism partly depends upon a factor of consent which is largely secured by the existence within the labour movement of a bureaucracy of full-time trade union officials and Labour Party politicians committed to the reconciliation of labour and capital. Thatcher's 'resolute approach' is extremely severe in its evocation of national pride, restraint and a curious kind of puritanism; yet, stripped of its 'resolution', the 'approach' is all too familiar. The slogan is simply a new standard to raise above a set of policies which have been justified in terms of 'the national interest' by every shade of government since the establishment of bourgeois democracy, and especially during times of recession in the capitalist mode of production. At the present time, in the face of an extremely reactionary government, mass unemployment and the prospect of wage cuts, there exists a distinct lack of confidence among those sections of the social formation which have most interest in resisting the state. During such a downturn the kind of history which I want to describe is most effectively persuasive, helping to neutralize what little resistance there is.

The 'history of the present' which represents the sixteenth and seventeenth centuries in a particular way is important for two reasons. First, it is highly pervasive; its power is distributed across a wide range of institutions in order to offer a variety of people a notion of smooth historical continuum. The effect is to make the present crisis appear within 'our' control, so long as 'we' react according to the evidence of 'our' history. Opposition to the order of things is neutralized through the participation of people in such seemingly disparate practices as watching television, reading books and newspapers and, crucially, I want to suggest, studying literature. The history offered through these practices must offer hope – an ideal reward for our submission to images of the present inscribed in the representations of the past.

Second, this history is important because it most powerfully conveys exactly that sense of 'the national interest' and 'resolution' which frames a variety of popular consents to a form of government which includes among its policies such nationalistic planning as immigration control, limits on importation, and nuclear 'defence', as well as acts of international aggression such as the sinking of the *General Belgrano*.

The paper is in three sections. In the first I shall examine a small selection of contemporary texts which construct an ideology of the present through specific representations of the sixteenth and seventeenth centuries. These representations will indicate just how pervasive the discourse is, since they are, in many ways, more powerful, and certainly less equivocal (perhaps because of their comparative historical 'distance' from popular experience) than those of a Victorian world which were summoned and fought over during the general election of 1983.

Second, I shall address the educational institution, and English studies in particular, in order to show how powerfully linked it is to the wider context through which these images are presented. Indeed, it might be argued that however 'sound' one's rereading of English may be, to regard the educational institution and its critical practice in isolation from a wider context can itself constitute something of a neutrality.

Last, I shall suggest some ways of resisting these histories by the production of a knowledge of the sixteenth- and seventeenth-century epoch as a period of crisis and rapid change. Such a knowledge offers a disruption of the smooth continuum of history and the naturalness of consent. If things have changed in the past, they can change again. If nationalism is a bourgeois ideology fostered by myths of the past, then it can be demythologized in the name of internationalism.

To start at the top, so to speak, I shall begin by discussing the Queen's *Message to the Commonwealth* which was broadcast on Christmas Day 1982.[2] With the possible exception of the World Cup Final, which is relayed throughout the eastern bloc, no other broadcast is available to such a massive and literally global audience. It offers a classic use of 'history' made to reinforce contemporary values. As Her Majesty is anxious to point out, she is speaking from the Library at Windsor Castle, 'a room once occupied by Queen Elizabeth 1'. This is a significant situation since the theme of the message is (as ever) the unity of the Commonwealth, and 'it was the voyages of discovery by the great seamen of Queen Elizabeth's day which laid the foundations of modern trade . . . [and] . . . discovery and trade in their turn laid the foundation of the present-day Commonwealth.' Moreover, 'the members of the Commonwealth which evolved from Britain's seafaring history have acquired an affinity through sharing a common philosophy of individual freedom, democratic government and the rule of the law.' Since these values were disseminated, apparently individually, by 'such names as Drake, Anson, Frobisher, Cook, Vancouver and Phillip', they must be eternal values because they also inspired 'our sailors, soldiers and airmen to go to the rescue of the Falkland Islanders eight thousand miles across the ocean; and to reveal the professional skills and courage that could be called on in the defence of basic freedoms'.

In the face of all this history, the 'difficulties' experienced in the Commonwealth during the twentieth century, due to its component nations becoming multiracial and multireligious, are of little importance and may be overcome partly through 'a sense of tolerance' and also, it seems, through events such as the Commonwealth Games which 'stand out as a demonstration of the better side of human nature'. In the closing sentences of the speech this spirit of harmony and tolerance is linked through a quotation from the seventeenth-century poet John Donne ('No man is an island . . .') to the message of Christ who

> attached supreme importance to the individual . . . amazed the world in which he lived by making it clear that the unfortunate and the underprivileged had an equal place in the Kingdom of Heaven with the rich and powerful . . . but . . . also taught that man must do his best to live in harmony with man.

As a 'history of the present', the Christmas *Message* depends upon a negation of history itself. It is not simply that what is said is not true, but that all the values of the Elizabethan epoch are recognizable because they are vital, and demonstrative because they produce a material practice in the form of the South Atlantic war effort. Furthermore, their substance is an individual responsibility. The great seamen of the past can be named, as can the poet who encapsulated their enduring experience. Similarly, Britain can be named individually as a nation, the centre and eternal distributor of all this peace and tolerance. By contrast, the Commonwealth is simply a conglomerate. It may be 'an association of free and independent nations' but it is not *English*. It was discovered, but can discover nothing for itself. Since the Commonwealth is both multiracial and multireligious, it has, according to Her Majesty, a distinct potential for 'argument, disagreement and violence'. Its only hope lies in the 'better side of human nature' carried to its many shores by an endless flotilla of Elizabethan values.

One Tudor seafarer who did not get quite as far as his contemptoraries was Sir George Carew, the unfortunate commander of Henry VIII's flagship, the *Mary Rose*. The *Mary Rose* sank in Portsmouth harbour before it could play a part in the war between England and France (1543–51) for which it was built. Having survived plans to blow it up during the nineteenth century (when it was significant to Portsmouth seafarers as an undersea hazard), the vessel was raised to the surface within hours of the so-called Falklands Victory Parade. Like the parade itself, the emergence of the hulk was witnessed by a television audience of millions. What is interesting about the *Mary Rose* is the way that the sixteenth and twentieth centuries were conjoined in order to offer a distinct coexistence in terms of 'Englishness'; from what might seem a rather inauspicious start, the second coming of the *Mary Rose* has seen it laden with a significance based upon entirely transhistorical and nationalistic values. Television viewers were invited by a series of 'expert' commentators not only to marvel at the technology of the recovery, but also to take comfort from the peculiarly English eccentricity of the whole event and the sense of national pride and heritage which seeped from between the Tudor timbers. Similarly, most of the texts which narrate the raising (or rescue) of the ship, which might colloquially be described as 'coffee table' volumes, invite a sense of historical continuum which, in ideological purpose, is quite as powerful as the Falklands Parade itself. In the most comprehensive and technical of the popular volumes, the leader of the *Mary Rose* project, Margaret Rule, offers this acknowledgement:

> What can I say of the inspiration and involvement of His Royal Highness Prince Charles, Prince of Wales, President of the Mary Rose Trust, scuba diver, archaeologist, and heir to the throne of the United Kingdom of Great Britain and Northern Ireland? Our confidence in and our loyalty to our president can only equal that of Henry VIII's Admiral to his king who wrote 'I submit all this to the order of your most noble Grace who, I pray God preserve from all adversity and send you as much victory of your enemys as ever had any of your noble ancestry'.

(Rule 1983, acknowledgements)

This invites the reader to recognize a timeless and individual worth which is shared between Charles and his distant ancestor. Nothing has really changed because time changes nothing.

Like Henry, Charles is the 'Renaissance man', a rounded and accomplished individual invested with a multiplicity of talents and boundless confidence in every project upon which he gazes.

Charles himself, in a foreword to the same book, describes the usefulness of the *Mary Rose* excavation with disarming clarity:

> The result of all this hard work and expertise is that future generations, we hope, will be able to glimpse a small part of Britain's maritime heritage; will be able to see history 'come alive' and to step, as it were, into the shoes of a Tudor seaman in the reign of Henry VIII. The only real way of understanding and coping with the present is, I believe, through an adequate knowledge and interpretation of the past. From that point of view we are able, at once, to transform a contemporary naval disaster into a victory in terms of human awareness.
>
> (Rule 1983, preface)

Allowing the reader to cope with the present is, in fact, precisely the work of such texts. *The True Glory*, one of the numerous volumes published in the aftermath of the South Atlantic War, folds the recent fighting into a general account of Britain's military past and includes the *Mary Rose* debacle in some detail. Again, the practice of modern warfare is made intelligible because the reader is encouraged into an 'awareness' of the values which over-reach time itself. And just as quotations from Shakespeare find their way into a number of the *Mary Rose* volumes, this text's title is given a validity because it is derived from the letters of Sir Francis Drake. The foreword explains that:

> Now that the age of materialism shows signs of drawing to a close, with earlier and more noble values being in part restored, I hope that this partial record of British seamen, their successes, their failures, their characters, their reliability and their steadfastness in the face of great odds may inspire in those with a feeling for the sea a possible drawing together or at least an increased understanding of a story remarkable by any criterion. This I venture to call *The True Glory* after the prayer concocted from Drake's letters home whilst blockading Cadiz in 1587. This prayer, which General

Montgomery pinned up in his caravan throughout the desert campaign of the Second World War serves well as the keynote to all that follows. . . . 'Oh! Lord God, when thou givest to thy servants to endeavour any great matter, grant us to know that it is not the beginning but the continuing of the same until it be thoroughly finished which yieldith the True Glory' [sic.].

(Tute 1983, foreword)

What we are dealing with in these kinds of texts is a set of peculiarly English values such as steadfastness, loyalty, character and so on, which might by synthesized as a 'resolute approach'. On the one hand, these values are almost tangible because we can observe their manifestation in the actual battles which the histories narrate. But, at the same time, such values rise above materialism, that cancer which is held at bay only by a treatment which involves recognition of the truly timeless values of human existence. And, in order to assimilate these values, those of us unfortunate enough not to make history, but only to read of it, must be attuned to human awareness, have a 'feeling for the sea' perhaps, and understand and interpret correctly.

Great literature, it seems, can help. It certainly stands as a substantial component in the overall presentation of the sixteenth and seventeenth centuries as a 'Golden Age'. The canon of great works, and especially those secured by that most potent signifier of Englishness, William Shakespeare, is aimed across a range of institutions whose business is not primarily the analysis and interpretation of the words on the page. That work is done for them elsewhere. The discourse of the 'Golden Age' is presented through institutions which simply require a consent based upon the 'evidence' of a high level of cultural activity. The pages of *Hansard*, for example, fairly bristle with allusions to the former epoch, particularly when 'Englishness' is threatened by a 'national emergency'. Shakespearean language provides a suitable medium through which to articulate the gravity of the present moment, against which 'we' are armed, as a nation, with the imminent rediscovery of 'our' Elizabethan selves.

The host of television and film productions which arose during the troubled period of the early 1970s are worth some consideration; these centred the sixteenth and seventeenth centuries on the lives of a chain of 'glamorous' individuals, beginning with Henry VIII and his six wives, and moving towards the later Stuarts by way of a recuperated Oliver Cromwell whose regicidal tendencies were more than adequately mitigated by the message at the end of the 1970 screen production. The interregnum, it seems, was a mere 'hiccup' in the course of an English history which has served to secure our present freedom and democracy; the word is restoration not revolution.[3]

Such productions are entirely appropriate both to the ideology of Thatcherism and to the educational institutions' representation of history. As far as the former is concerned, Thatcher's message to student voters which was sent to the National Union of Students newspaper *National Student* (and reproduced in most local union journals) is almost wholly concerned with an image of the present in terms of a mythologized past:

> the choice before the nation is stark. Either to continue our present steadfast progress towards recovery, or to follow policies more extreme and more damaging than those ever put forward by any previous opposition. I believe that Britain has recovered confidence and self-respect. We have regained the regard and admiration of other nations. We are seen today as a people with integrity, resolve, and the will to succeed . . . our history is the story of a free people – a great chain of people stretching back into the past and forward into the future. All are linked by a common belief in freedom, and in Britain's greatness. All are aware of their own responsibility to contribute to both, none more so than young people. Our past is witness to their enduring courage, honesty and flair and to their ability to change and create. Our future will be shaped by those same qualities.[4]

As far as institutions of higher education are concerned, the young people who read Mrs Thatcher's election address start their courses having already been most deliberately drawn into a particular conjunction of literature and history. Almost without exception, history books for children evaluate the sixteenth and seventeenth centuries in terms of the profusion of literary works and then link this to colonial expansion. The literary works, after all, hold the key to 'what it felt like' to be involved in such adventuring, the same critical mode developed by the Queen in her *Message to the Commonwealth*. Many examples of this conjunction can be found in the present series of Ladybird Books:

> Queen Elizabeth reigned over England for forty-five years. When she came to the throne England was poor. When she died England was rich, prosperous, united and happy. Her reign saw the beginnings of what came to be the British Empire. The fighting sailors of her reign, and the great victory over the Spanish Armada made England one of the greatest countries in Europe.
>
> (Du Garde Peach 1958, p. 50)

> The reign of Elizabeth has been called the Golden Age of English Literature. This means that as well as the great sailors and explorers there were living at that time men who wrote some of the most wonderful poems and plays in our language.
>
> (Du Garde Peach 1958, p. 42)

It is hardly surprising that students, and especially students of literature, should recognize themselves in this history and that such a recognition should effectively neutralize their practices both in terms of struggle within the institutions and in the wider context. For it is within these institutions, and particularly within departments of English, that this history is distilled, using the raw material of a canon which is rigorously defended for any number of reasons, but in the end best produces a knowledge of the timeless values and truths which can be recognized in the texts I have outlined. This is not so much a conspiracy as an effect of the sublime status which criticism has achieved in relation to other branches of the humanities.

The political power of criticism lies in the considerable distance which exists between itself and vulgar political discourse. Very few critics of Tudor and Stuart drama are politically active, and it is rare for Shakespeare's plays to cause riots in the streets. Nor have I heard of any critics prepared to undertake active service in defence of the Falklands. Yet it is exactly their work upon the texts which fosters the kind of history available to the ideological apparatus of the state in general. The link between criticism and the wider context may be glimpsed during those periods of crisis when an *overt* use of 'literary' texts may occur in order to secure a sense of national identity. It seems to me that the history of the present constructed through representations of the sixteenth and seventeenth centuries over the last decade bears some relation to a general decay in the 'body' of British society. Notions of a regainable organic world have grown as a *general* palliative (though not the cure, as I suggested earlier), for a sickness which took hold in the west from the mid-1960s onwards as the post-war boom withered away. In Britain, concrete struggles took place against sexual and racial inequalities, the war in Vietnam, the military occupation of the north of Ireland, the Industrial Relations Bill and, to some extent, against trade union bureaucracy. The late 1970s saw mass organization on the streets against fascism and, more recently, against the bomb. It was these activities which succeeded the more ephemeral and now largely mythologized 'spirit of the sixties'; and if they did not cohere into a mass revolutionary practice, they at least disrupted the 'one nation' ideology which has regained a hold during the last few years.

As a general palliative, criticism may produce its histories and its knowledges of human nature and organization over a long period. This was the case with the *Scrutiny* group of critics whose project has been closely associated with the threat to 'Englishness' posed by revolution in Europe and the growth of Marxism in the British labour movement and intelligentsia during the 1920s and 1930s. To a large extent the present-day purveyors of the sixteenth and seventeenth centuries as an organic and homogeneous social order are in debt to the *Scrutiny* group. These critics worked hard on Shakespeare's texts in order to produce a knowledge of his times in terms of this ideal, as well as to define their own discipline as the protector of this vision in the face of the moral and cultural bankruptcy which haunted Europe during the inter-war years. And the long-term success of the *Scrutiny* group can be measured by the way that their resulting works of criticism have given both shape and purpose to curricula around the world.

Yet, as I suggested, there are moments of relatively *overt* participation by criticism in matters of national concern. This is especially true when 'national identity' is sufficiently susceptible to external threat or internal instability for the guise of apoliticality to be jettisoned almost entirely. The best-known examples of this extrusion were the wartime productions of Shakespeare's history plays for stage, radio and film, including Laurence Olivier's *Henry V*. As Derek Longhurst has remarked, the years 1939–45 also saw the publication of some of the most persistent works of criticism by E. M. W. Tillyard, whose work, although registering a marked departure from the *Scrutiny* group through a concern with 'extra-textual' material, none the less regarded Shakespeare as the supreme advocate of an ordered but hierarchical world.[5] In these critics' publications, the groundwork was done for exactly the ideology of heroic patriotism in which the wartime productions were framed.

Almost forty years of Shakespeare criticism and some very radical appropriations of Shakespearean texts in the theatre have done little to eclipse the potential the canon holds for reinsertion into just such a framework of ideas. In the book *Authors Take Sides on the Falklands* an opinion was sought from the critic G. R. Wilson Knight concerning the war in the South Atlantic. Wilson Knight had been most active in the Second World War when his rather closet life-style as an academic gave new meaning to the term 'reserved occupation'. Years of textual analysis were finally invested in a number of stage productions which confirmed Shakespeare's unique contribution to the British war effort. And since the values discovered in Shakespeare's texts are self-evident and timeless, Wilson Knight's own contribution to the debate on the South Atlantic War is given as though entirely motivated by Shakespeare's eternal prompting:

Britain's response to the Falklands' crisis was ratified by all three parties in Parliament, and I accordingly would not presume to register any complaint. However I feel that behind the astounding speed, energy, resource, expense and brilliant organization in what seems, taking a long view, a hazardous cause, there may be reasons unknown to me and the general public. As for the future, I can only assess our prospects by stating my own convictions. I have for long accepted the validity of our country's historic contribution, seeing the British Empire as a precursor, or prototype, of world order. I have always relied on the Shakespearean vision as set forth in my wartime production *The Sceptred Isle* at the Westminster Theatre in 1941 (described in *Shakespearean Production*, 1964). This theme I also discuss in various writings collected under the title *The Sovereign Flower* in 1958. Our key throughout is Cranmer's royal prophecy at the conclusion of Shakespeare's last play, *Henry VIII*, Shakespeare's final words to his countrymen. This I still hold to be our one authoritative statement, every word deeply significant, as forecast of the world-order at which we should aim. Though democratic, it involves not just democracy alone, but democracy in strict subservience to the crown as a symbol linking love to power and the social order to the divine. For world-order, this symbol, or some adequate equivalent, must be supposed.

(Woolf and Moorcroft Wilson 1982, p. 67)

The extraordinary feature of Wilson Knight's contribution lies beyond his unreserved acceptance of parliament's decision (which was tellingly shared by some sections of the left), or even his anachronistic assertions concerning the British Empire; what is at stake here is the *future* inscribed in the Shakespearean text for all time as a prophecy which reaches over the mere discussions and voting of parliament and the United Nations. The power of Shakespeare's contribution to the history of the present and a practice for the future lies in the greater truth of Shakespeare *vis-à-vis* an 'expanding British tradition'. It would be easy to be sceptical of Wilson Knight's tenacious commitment to the 'word' of Shakespeare; yet quite apart from the fact that the tenor of his remarks is exactly that of his criticism, which remains a powerful current in the field of Shakespearean studies, he is by no means alone in his celebration of the Shakespearean 'word' as bearing a conspicuous relevance to the present state of the nation. His contribution to *Authors Take Sides on the Falklands* is dated 9 June 1982.

Exactly a year later, on 9 June 1983, the Royal Shakespeare Company gave its first performance of a new production of *Henry VIII* at the Royal Shakespeare Theatre in Stratford-upon-Avon.

Apart from all the general comments that can be made about the Stratford enterprise, such as its role as a signifier of 'Englishness', its concern with the mutuality of 'culture' and big business, and the curious fictioning of a biography for Shakespeare himself, the notable features of this particular production were the timing and the programme which the RSC had published. The latter displays an over-riding concern with the play's textuality. Extracts from the Penguin edition are reproduced together with a selection of other printed material ranging from Holinshed, the source, to part of a *Woman's Own* article concerning the fortunes of Anne Boleyn. The effect is to determine for the play a rightful place within that distinctive body of writing which is English literature. Offering the play as a special kind of writing is, of course, wholly inappropriate to seventeenth-century notions of writing. It is unlikely that any of Shakespeare's plays in folio form would have enjoyed the kind of privilege afforded by the RSC above and beyond a spectrum of other forms of writing. By impressing the assumption of *text* as origin for performance, the Stratford programme secures the fixed category of literature while suggesting the flexibility of other kinds of writing which append themselves to the text over the years.

The programme masquerades as a 'Prompt Copy', which explains the supposedly handwritten elucidations presented alongside the printed extracts. The contrast between the printed word of Shakespeare and the pencilled additions is complete; print and scrawl, text and meaning. The programme reproduces part of Wolsey's speech in the first act in which he is defending his policy of high taxation in the pursuit of the war against France. The Queen is doubtful and expresses her fears of unemployment and civil disorder, to which Wolsey replies:

> If we shall stand still,
> In fear our motion will be mock'd or carp'd at,
> We should take root here where we sit,
> Or sit state-statues only.

It comes as small surprise to discover alongside this the ironic handwritten slogan, 'the Resolute Approach – hard measures necessary "THERE IS NO ALTERNATIVE"'.[6]

These examples show something of the extent to which

images of the sixteenth and seventeenth centuries are reproduced in a variety of institutions in order to construct a distinctive history of the present. The service which this history offers
to the ideology of the state in general is an impressive one. The
past is presented as a seamless discourse of eternal verities
which are thoroughly nationalistic in character and provide an
ideal which may be easily apprehended, simply through the
individual consenting to a whole series of practices exercised by
the state in the name of 'the national interest'. Sometimes, as in
the present context, the state may mediate its crisis through a
more profound conjunction of past, present and future; a new
layer of appeal conveyed by such determinations as 'the resolute
approach' is only as successful as the layers beneath, cemented
into place as much by reformist Labour politicians as by the
monetarists of the present regime. The unique value of a
sixteenth- and seventeenth-century history to the current
appeal is yielded partly through a fictionalized temporal relativity; but also through the extraordinary range of meanings
available from the components which are understood as the
whole. The epoch pre-dates capitalism, yet can invite a knowledge of capitalism's mechanisms in an heroic way; trade and
expansion, enterprise and reward, all signify in the present
context, yet are 'innocent' in the Elizabethan age of, say, their
nineteenth-century connotations. The era pre-dates socialism
and is largely built upon a list of proper nouns which confront
notions of collectivity and class struggle. And the particular
'history' speaks to us a truth of events which took place over
three hundred years ago. This 'space', which is no space at all,
encourages consensus and submission to an historical truth and
a modern discursive power.

To some extent the interest paid by the left to the sixteenth
and seventeenth centuries reflects the concerns of liberal
humanism. It seems that left-wing historians and critics have
felt safer dealing with modes of production in the capitalist
epoch. If we accept for a moment the usual distinction between
'history' and 'criticism' (as separate disciplines), the former has
seen little work done in terms of developing theory beyond the
seminal work of Christopher Hill. The right, on the other hand,
has been more than busy here for decades, and I need only
mention Hugh Trevor-Roper in this context. Indeed, the

Marxist historian Norah Carlin has remarked that 'it is hardly surprising that defending Hill should come to be almost a significant activity in itself' (Carlin 1980, p. 107). With the exception of the work started at the Essex Conference in 1980, and in some other arenas, few assaults have been mounted against the kind of criticism produced in the 1930s, which continues to hold great sway within the educational institutions. In the face of this neglect the task confronting both historians and critics on the left is immense, yet imperative, given the power of these histories in a popular context.

As far as this paper is concerned I can only suggest a few areas of activity which might combine in order to resist this particularly pervasive history of the present. Considering the range of institutions through which it is broadcast, our engagement should be multilayered. For example, it might well be developed in the area of education within the organized left, and this project is well under way in some quarters.[7] Yet since I have suggested that criticism plays a leading role in shaping this history, and the established canon provides a buttress to its popular appeal, I want to suggest some areas of discussion in terms of our concerns as students and teachers.

The aim must be to disrupt the continuum of history and to produce a knowledge of the sixteenth and seventeenth centuries as a period of crisis and rapid change. Another history is required which engages the present crisis by confronting the construction of a whole range of values as eternal and exclusive, natural and national. The history we produce should be partial to our concerns as socialists in order to confront the 'impartiality' and 'completion' of the seamless knowledge produced by the opposition.

The areas which could combine to achieve this effect might include the examination of what 'writing' means in the sixteenth and seventeenth centuries. It is important to undermine the privilege given to Shakespearean drama and bourgeois criticism's wholly inappropriate sense of value and biography, as well as notions of writing as a private realm. This confronts the textuality imposed upon the plays as well as allowing for the alignment of various forms of writing. It would lead to an examination of seventeenth-century theatre itself, which is often framed by the assumption that in many respects it was as illusionary as the theatre of later periods and that our 'experience' at Stratford or the Barbican is essentially a historical one.

Furthermore the relations between the theatrical and critical institutions should be examined in order to show how the knowledges produced in criticism have developed in the wider context throughout history and how sixteenth- and seventeenth-century writing has been separated into particular realms of, say, fact and fiction, truth and experience. Criticism itself is the major concern – what is its object and effect in terms of education? How has it used particular texts and not others, and what governs the selection?

Finally, it seems absolutely crucial that this politicization of writing and the production of an alternative history for our present should avoid being sealed off, so to speak, from our everyday practices. The great problem with liberal humanism is that it readily assimilates radicalism and that Marxism thus becomes simply another 'approach', and is finally given a status as sublime and removed as bourgeois criticism itself. Unless the alternative is agitational and wholly linked to everyday struggle in the wider context, it risks becoming guilty of aiding and abetting the present downturn in the struggle for socialism.

Notes

1 I am grateful to Catherine Belsey and David Goldwater for commenting on an earlier draft of this paper.
2 The Queen's *Message to the Commonwealth* for 1982 was not published. Copies of the script are available from Buckingham Palace on request.
3 *Cromwell*, directed by Ken Hughes, 1970.
4 Reproduced in *Gair Rhydd*, no. 156 (Cardiff, 1983).
5 Longhurst 1982. Although new schools of Shakespearean criticism have come and gone since the war, I would argue that the framework of ideas produced by Tillyard and the *Scrutiny* group has not only influenced these later groups, but also survived intact in a variety of educational institutions. Their books still enjoy republication and regularly appear on school and university reading lists.
6 Programme for the Royal Shakespeare Company Summer Season, 1983.
7 For example, Socialists Unlimited, *The First English Revolution* (London, 1983).

10

Towards a grammatology of America: Lévi-Strauss, Derrida and the native New World text

GORDON BROTHERSTON

No literary approach to the texts of the New World can avoid the problem of 'grammatology' raised by Derrida in his book of that title (1967, trans. 1976). Incisive as it is, however, in exposing the covert ethnocentricity of Lévi-Strauss and Saussurean structuralism, with its dream of pure speech, this study has little to offer in the way of practical help when it comes to treating the New World in terms of its 'visible language' systems, its alphabetization, and ultimately the order of cultural integrity championed on other grounds in Lévi-Strauss' *Mythologiques* (1964–71). Drawing out these sets of differences between Lévi-Strauss and Derrida, in what amounts to a syllogism, provides a new and comprehensible framework for the concept of native American literature.

Elaborated in my *Image of the New World. The American Continent portrayed in Native Texts* (1979a), this framework is also implicit in a number of case studies destined to form part of the *Book of the Fourth World*, currently in preparation. These range from questions of native chronology, script and genre, through native adaptation of Old World texts (e.g. the Aztec translation of Aesop), to the incorporation of New World literature by such writers as Roger Williams in the seventeenth century and

Antonin Artaud in ours, each the subject of a previous Sociology of Literature conference paper (Brotherston 1979b and 1981).

*

In his essay 'L'Efficacité symbolique' (1949), later a chapter in *Anthropologie structurelle* (trans. 1977), Lévi-Strauss turned to the Cuna nation of Panama, picking out an item of their literature known by the title Mu Igala. Published two years previously by Holmer and Wassen (1947), this Cuna work is described by Lévi-Strauss as 'the first important South American magico-religious text to be known [to us]'. Though bibliographically this is questionable, given the South American texts published decades previously by Preuss and others, there can be no doubt that the Mu Igala (or Ikala) indeed amounts to a major example of American literary shamanism (see Figure 1).[1]

Over its 535 phrase-images the Mu Ikala represents the 'way' (ikala) of countering the dark and dangerous forces of Mu during a difficult childbirth; and Lévi-Strauss's analysis of how it does so shows him at his best. He draws out the multiple meanings of 'way', as psychic procedure and actual uterine road; and he precisely diagnoses the contest between the journeying shaman and the retentive Mu. He is particularly

Figure 1   Native America towns and nations

adept at revealing the ploys and rhythms of the text as sung rhetoric, allowing us too to feel the powers of its persuasion, and the 'effectiveness' of its symbols. Of the slow-motion preliminaries he says:

> Everything occurs as though the shaman were trying to induce the sick woman – whose contact with reality is no doubt impaired and whose sensitivity is exacerbated – to relive the initial situation through pain, in a very precise and intense way, and to become psychologically aware of its smallest details;

by contrast over the next ten pages we find,

> in breathless rhythm, a more and more rapid oscillation between mythical and physiological themes, as if to abolish in the mind of the sick woman the distinction which separates them, and to make it impossible to differentiate their respective attributes.
>
> (Lévi-Strauss 1977, p. 193)

Then, from textual criticism of this kind he goes on to illustrate his structuralism as such, by comparing Cuna shamanism with western psychoanalysis, matching their respective appeals to controlling 'myth', memory and time.

Yet, as close as his attention to the Cuna text undoubtedly is, nowhere does Lévi-Strauss actually mention that it is not just sung but written down; still less, that it is written down in characters especially developed by the Cuna to record their ikala and other canonical literature. At first sight the omission appears the stranger since, ranged in their boustrophedon lines, certain of these characters register, visually and immediately, just those qualities in the text which Lévi-Strauss, by referring only to the 'song', has to argue the harder for. For example, the slow pace of the preliminaries is physically evident in the ponderous four-square paragraphing of the opening lines, while the excitement of the conflict with Mu's beasts can actually be seen in the rapid repetition and postures of the animal images in question. Also the details of some individual characters make explicit such factors as the angles of the shaman's approaches, the entire coverage of the iron nets used to seal the uterus against re-entry, and the time-element in the neka or houses of

the cosmic directions. In addition, the sheer boustrophedon progress of the reading itself is designed to match the
shifts in the shaman's position as at the start of successive
lines he faces one way then the other, weaving his therapeutic
web.

In his recent analysis of the Mu Ikala, Helbig (1984)
has pointed to the inadequacy of Lévi-Strauss's approach in
similar terms. Especially striking is the way he appeals to details
of the written text in order to justify his rectifying Lévi-Strauss's
narrowly psychological and physiological reading. For
instance, in arguing that the body guarded by Mu and the
shaman's road refer likewise to an exterior territory of sea and
underworld, in an astronomical paradigm that is in fact found
throughout the Americas, he focuses on the corresponding
pictographic semi-circle (*halbgerundete Erde*). Then, broadening
the argument, we may note how at a more general sociological
level, seeing the Mu Ikala as a written as well as a performed
text leads us to consider the function of writing as such among
the Cuna, within what Fritz Kramer has called their paideuma,
in his *Literature among the Cuna Indians* (1970, pp. 113–16). Drawing on Wassen, Holmer, Nordenskiöld and other members
of the remarkable Göteborg group who, like his own mentor
Karl Nowotny, have never lost sight of the historicity of native
American literature, Kramer explores the Mu and other ikala
as distillations of a common experience in time, making important links between this order of therapy and the epic genre; and
he relates the fact of their being recorded to their pedagogic
transmission, in schools like those celebrated by Ernesto
Cardenal, in his poem to the Cuna shaman leader Nele de
Kantule (*Homage to the American Indians*, 1973). And he aims all
this to make good Lévi-Strauss's synchronism and negligence of
script.

Odd as it may seem in 'L'Efficacité symbolique', Lévi-
Strauss's failure to mention the fact of Cuna literacy proves on
inspection to be far from casual or accidental. On the contrary,
it may be held as symptomatic of his whole approach to native
America, notably in the four volumes of his *Mythologiques* (1964–
71). In this work of continental scope, Lévi-Strauss contrives to
build up for us a frame for the mythology of all native America.
Moving from the Brazilian lowlands, where he has concen-

trated his own fieldwork as an anthropologist (Vol. 1, *Le Cru et le cuit*), to the north-west coast of North America (Vol. 4, *L'Homme nu*; also the main setting for the more recent *La voie des masques*, 1975–9), he constructs the boldest of parallels over the widest of spaces. Yet this is done almost entirely on evidence said to derive from oral rather than any written sources in the New World; indeed one can detect a positive avoidance of those geographical areas which, in these terms, might have proved an embarrassment, above all Middle America, that millennial focus of book-making and literacy. Correspondingly, though he openly proposes millennia as the proper time-perspective for so vast an intellectual phenomenon (*'schèmes communs aux deux hémisphères . . . dont l'âge ne saurait se chiffrer en décennies, mais en millénaires'*, Vol. 3, p. 191), he explicitly eschews all reference to material history which, like script, is consigned to an order of lesser and less desirable knowledge.

Before looking at the reasons Lévi-Strauss gives, which he does freely, for his aversion to script and the idea of a literate and historically conscious New World, it is worth emphasizing that in this attitude he by no means stands alone. For generations of Americanists have fostered the same prejudice or ideal, as have those students of script or grammatologists, if we may prematurely introduce Derrida's convenient term, who have bothered to cast their eye in the direction of America. Apart from anything else, this much is clear from the fact that only very recently have any serious and systematic attempts been made to account for the main scriptual and literary tradition of the continent, 'its visible language', or even to cense and catalogue texts *extant*. Before the Aschers (1981), true successors to Nordenskiöld, began their survey and analyses of the Andean quipu, that recording system was regularly derogated as some kind of mere mnemonic or rosary; while in northern America Howard provided the first census of Winter Counts as late as 1979 and Dewdney's census of Ojibway scrolls (1975) was the first to establish a firm bibliographical home and focus for the Mide sign-system. As for Middle America, it was only with the appearance of the *Handbook* (Glass and Gibson 1975) that the many hundreds of texts from that area extant in native script, hieroglyphic and iconographic, were adequately listed and described. Or going back a century or so one could point to the model case of *The Library of Aboriginal American Literature*, eight volumes of which were published in Philadelphia by D. G. Brinton between 1882 and 1890; for in Vol. 5, which includes the *Walam Olum* of the Lenape and seems in retrospect the most significant, we find Brinton entirely subordinating the Mide pictographic version of this text to an oral gloss and even wilfully altering the latter in order to discredit the former as the true original (1884, p. 170). Over the decades many further examples of such script-aversion could be found in the work of other no less eminent Americanists.

When it comes not so much to Americanists as to those who as historians and theoreticians have devoted their scholarly powers to the phenomenon of script in general, the story is no less dismal. The widely cited *A Study of Writing* by I. J. Gelb (1963) typifies that crass evolutionism which sees the alphabet, like the wheel, as the definitive 'invention'; and in such an argument there is clearly little room for America, except here and there at the benighted start. In David Diringer's otherwise meticulous *The Alphabet: A Key to the History of Mankind* (1968), pre-Columbian scripts are not in any way related to each other; and the quotation from a Maya hieroglyphic text is somewhat marred by the fact that it is upside down. Still less acceptable is what has happened as a result of certain attempts to apply sociological rigour to the question. Jack Goody's remarks on the Maya in his *Literacy in Traditional Societies* (1968, p. 6) amount to something like an insult: 'it is not clear who was ever literate in that language', he announces, (to whom? was? we might reply); and his footnote, distinguished by its fondness for 'almost exclusively' carries on in the same vein, apparently in total ignorance of the Yucatec tradition of *Chilam Balam* or Community Books (cf. Barrera Vasquez and Rendón 1948). Against such a background it becomes easier to understand the continued appearance of works like Tzvetan Todorov's recent and lamentable *La Conquête de l'Amérique. La question de l'autre* (1982); as some preposterous 'other' of ourselves, native Americans are here presented effectively as illiterate and therefore mindless, and in any case incapable of recording and reflecting upon their own history for themselves. All told, we seem not to have moved very far from that highly interested account of the New World given, shortly after its 'discovery', by Montaigne, who spoke of its typical inhabitant as 'so new and infantine, that he is yet to learn his A.B.C'.

To return to Lévi-Strauss: in his case, script-aversion is something that he has taken the trouble to justify extensively on theoretical grounds. When, in 1954, he changed the title of the lecture course he gave at the Parisian École Practique des Hautes Études, by replacing *'Religions des peuples non-civilisés'* with *'Religions comparées des peuples sans écriture'*, he explained the switch from uncivilized to illiterate as follows:

> It is true that the new title, referring to non-literate peoples, also evinces a privative character. But, even disregarding that it is a statement of fact which does not imply a value judgement, the absence of writing in the societies we study seems to us – and this is indeed an essential theme of our thinking – to exercise a sort of regulatory influence on a tradition which is to remain oral. Better than our traditions, whose transformation accelerates with the ever increasing mass of knowledge accumulated in books, these traditions lend themselves to an experimental research which requires a relative stability in its object.
>
> (Lévi-Strauss 1978, p. 61)

Nothing could be clearer: in this version of events nothing acts for an anthropologist as a destabilizing factor, a lapse from grace as unwelcome as the thing that Lévi-Strauss assures us literature has become in our modern world.

Diagnosis of this order is thoroughly confirmed by an episode during his own Brazilian fieldwork which Lévi-Strauss has seen fit to report in several versions, notably as the chapter 'La Leçon d'écriture' in *Tristes Tropiques* (1955). Here we are told of his encounter with a Nambikwara Indian who comes to exploit his fellows simply as a result of his 'writing lesson' and his skill at appearing to possess white man's capacity to write. There can be no other conclusion, paradoxical as it must seem in one so deeply literate as Lévi-Strauss: literacy is undesirable not just because it destabilizes but because it corrupts, as instantly and decisively as fruit from the tree of knowledge.

So ingrained in Lévi-Strauss and his method is the need for this categorical divide between oral and written that at moments it leads him into unwitting inconsistency. A fine instance of this occurs in *Mythologiques* where he enquires into colour sequences and relates the waves of human perception to the notion of writing (Vol. 1, p. 331). A first example is found in the snake Muyusu, who brings script to the natives of Brazil: '*Les Mundurucu évoquent le même règne des petits intervalles en termes graphiques et acoustiques, quand ils racontent que le serpent Muyusu, c'est-à-dire l'arc-en-ciel, désireux d'enseigner l'écriture aux hommes, les attira en imitant la voix de toutes sorts d'animaux.*' A second, in the wavy lines, duly illustrated, which his Nambikwara Indian traced on a piece of paper: '*Il est frappant, en effet, que des indigènes cherchant à imiter l'écriture s'y prennent en traçant des lignes ondulées, comme si elle consistait, non pas en caractères opposés par la forme, mais en une suite de fluxions.*' So plausibly is this put that we could be forgiven for forgetting that the whole point of the Nambikwara anecdote was that that nation could be so easily exploited by one of their number, precisely because they were so integrally innocent and ignorant of the nature and function of script. Yet only one line previously, exactly the opposite of that graphic ignorance is presupposed in the evocation of the serpentine script-bringer common to South America and matched further north in the 'plumed serpent', Quetzalcoatl, who is shown giving his decidedly pre-Colombian 'writing lesson' in more than one Mesoamerican screenfold book. One might argue that the types of script in question differ substantially, yet Lévi-Strauss himself removes that distinction; and in any case the script-consciousness implied is in principle the same. We have here, in fact, a significant case of particular evidence being neutralized by the power of the overall model of an oral America.

For an exhaustive critique of the handling of script typified by Lévi-Strauss, its intellectual roots and ideological charge, we can do no better than turn to Jacques Derrida. Indeed, in Derrida's *De la Grammatologie* (1967, transl. 1976) making this critique is synonymous with habilitating the very concept, indispensable for our purposes, announced in his title. As a main reference point, Derrida takes the much-cited Nambik-wara episode: meticulously deconstructing and comparing Lévi-Strauss's various versions of what happened, he reveals a whole range of ambiguities in the author as both narrator and participant, and gradually elicits from the text its underlying philosophical suppositions. For example, he shows how in *Tristes Tropiques* (1955) Lévi-Strauss suppressed the notes he had dedicated in *La vie familiale et sociale des Indiens Nambikwara* (1948) to the graphic designs or ierkariukedjutu incised by these people on their gourds and other objects, when these clearly had the script function associated earlier both with the snake Muyusu and, as part of that blatant self-contradiction, with the alphabetic practice 'suddenly and disastrously' grasped by one of their number.

So thorough and radical is Derrida's approach in *Of Grammatology* that it goes to 'the root of all sciences', since 'reflection on the essence of mathematics, politics, economics, religion, technology, law etc., communicates most intimately with the reflection upon and information surrounding the history of writing' (Derrida 1976, p. 88). In other words it would be quite out of the question here to follow his whole thesis, even if we stuck to the New World context provided for us by Lévi-Strauss. His line of argument on ethnocentricity is, however, of direct concern.

In the history of western philosophy, the aversion to script typified by Lévi-Strauss is taken by Derrida as far back as Plato's *Phaedrus*; and less remotely to Rousseau's *Essay on the Origin of Languages* and to Saussure's *Cours de linguistique générale* (1915, trans. 1959). Through Rousseau we are shown how the 'fall' occasioned by script corresponds to the need for agency and re-presentation within the earliest (Ur) communities, like those of the American 'savages'. So that once out of the earshot of each other, a phrase evidently relished by Derrida and indeed by his translator in English, Gayatri Spivak, humans began to cede the pristine qualities of language as speech, a notion then taken up by Herder in his pioneering anthology of primitive, i.e. oral poetry of the earth's different nations, including for the first time those of the New World (*Stimmen der Völker in Liedern* 1778, 1807). Referring this forward to Lévi-Strauss, in particular his essay on 'The place of anthropology in the social sciences', Derrida says:

The ideal profoundly underlying this philosophy of writing is therefore the image of a community immediately present to itself, without difference, a community of speech where all the members are within earshot. . . . Writing is here defined as the condition of *social inauthenticity*.

(Derrida 1976, p. 136)

Rather, he says, the supposed 'degeneration' fostered by script can more readily be understood in terms of social structuring generally; and, as with the Nambikwara, the script function can be detected as such even in models that are quite restricted in geography and technologically. With Saussure we move another step, towards a notion not just of purer, more pristine speech, but of the whole phenomenon of language (*langue*) as something spoken rather than written. Setting up a system that would prove decisive for structuralism as a whole, Saussure went so far as to posit the norms of this language as synchronic, that is immune to history, and in any one instance as a closed national phonetic system, e.g. 'French', when as a matter of political fact writing has most often been essential to the production of such norms in the first place (cf. Brotherston 1981).

In summing up this intellectual heritage of Lévi-Strauss's, Derrida refers to it as a 'phonologism', which 'is undoubtedly the exclusion or abasement of writing' (Derrida 1976, p. 102). And he goes on further to characterize it as 'a profound ethnocentrism' which in fact privileges the model of phonetic writing, 'a model that makes the exclusion of the *graphie* easier and more legitimate':

It is, however, an ethnocentrism *thinking itself* as anti-ethnocentrism, an ethnocentrism in the consciousness of a liberating progressivism. By radically separating language from writing, by placing the latter below and outside, believing at least that it is possible to do so, by giving oneself the illusion of liberating linguistics from all involvement with written evidence, one thinks in fact to restore the status of authentic language, human and fully signifying language, to all languages practised by *peoples whom one nevertheless continues to describe as 'without writing'*.

Finally, he sets out at length the two sides of this ambiguity, as the lead into his close reading of 'Writing lesson'. In this analysis, and contrary to first appearances, Lévi-Strauss's characterization of the New World as some preferable other turns out itself to be exploitative in its way, yet another chapter in the long history of an imperialism of and within which alphabetic script has in practice been a main agent of dogma and repression.

Turning now to what, in this perspective, we should positively understand writing to be, Derrida again offers valuable pointers. Reviewing European answers to the question 'what is writing?', he establishes in sequence: that theologism whereby the Judeo-Christian god personally traced man's first characters with his finger; the would-be universal rationalism of the Enlightenment, both ideogrammatic, with Leibniz, and hieratic, with Warburton; the racist evolutionism of the nineteenth century, plus certain more recent accounts, like those of Freudian psychology. In attempting his own answer, he puts his finger on a key dilemma: we need a prior, systematic definition of writing in order to recognize and trace its possible history, at the same time as we need to ground such a definition in an adequately global history. In practice, Derrida's most useful comments and recommendations, that is in addition to the terminology and perspective he provides us with, come piecemeal; they may be listed threefold, as follows. We should beware of denying some inner systemic principle to even the most primitive-seeming graphie, and by the same token should use judiciously if at all such catch terms as 'pictographic' or mnemonic. The encoding process synonymous with script is likewise intimately allied to the problem of proper names and nouns, figures that can be at once general and individually specific, so that speech and gesture themselves may be regarded as 'arch' script. Phoneticism in script, whatever its type, can never be entirely absent or entirely present.

The fact that Derrida's own comments on script are isolated is due not just to the enormity of the question but to his overall approach. For in the end he is less interested in script as such, its materiality, its particular social and political functions and so forth, than he is in using it to diagnose the larger ills of western culture and philosophy. And this has certain profound and unfortunate effects on his otherwise revolutionary and liberating enquiry.

At a sheer technical level, the occasional interpretation he himself offers of 'what is known [about script], thanks to unquestionable and abundant information' can be bizarre. For example, he insists on a highly questionable universal link between 'the birth of script' and what he calls 'genealogical anxiety' (Derrida 1976, p. 124). More notably, he has obviously taken little trouble with just those New World cultures that have so preoccupied his contemporary object of criticism, Lévi-Strauss. For all its brilliance, his argument about phoneticism, proper names and so on, issues into a most unsatisfying account of the Middle American 'Aztec' and Maya scripts, which Derrida in fact fails to connect with each other despite their common fund of iconography and numerology. And he does not mention the Andean quipu at all, an omission that is the more surprising since this knotted string device excellently exemplifies his claim for the functional equivalence of script in society, above and beyond particular media; and it is also historically the case that the quipu has been transcribed into alphabetic Quechua and Spanish. By the same token, when it comes to those New World nations not so much avoided by Lévi-Strauss as misrepresented by him as purely oral, he fails to explore how the encoding process synonymous with script and visible language may in his own terms operate within spoken language itself, with the known graphie as a correlative: the encoding in question here is often into some esoteric, time-resistant and condensed (= poetic) form that stands at the opposite pole to Saussure's norms. Witness, for example, the Carib charter known as *Watunna*, recently published by the French anthropologist de Civrieux who offers his own implicit refutation of Lévi-Strauss's method:

The *Watunna* is in its essence a secret teaching restricted to the circle of men who undergo the initiations of the *Wanwanna* festivals. But there is another, popular *Watunna* which belongs to everyone regardless of sex or age, and this is the *Watunna* which is told daily outside the ritual dance circle. It is an exoteric *Watunna* told in everyday language, a profane reflection of that of the sacred space. . . . These variations, altered and abbreviated, subject to personal interpretations and the teller's level of knowledge and memory, still fulfill the *Watunna*'s essential role of teaching the tribe's history and

spreading its ethical and social ideals. More concerned with
the anecdotal aspects of the *ademi* however, these popular
versions are unable to preserve the symbolic structure
created by their secret language. The phonetic games and
mental associations which are such an important part of the
sacred dance cannot be translated into profane language.

(Civrieux 1980, pp. 16–17)

For himself, in diagnosing a western aversion to or exclusion
of script, Derrida may indeed be said to concern himself more
with its ideological force within his and our tradition than with
any other reality it may have effectively displaced. And this
view is well confirmed by his other work on writing and
dissemination, notably *L'Écriture et la différance* (trans. 1978),
published in the same year as *De la Grammatologie*, and more
recently *La Dissémination* (1972, trans. 1981b). In the former
volume, his tendencies and choice of task are neatly summed up
in the two subjects who, unlike any of the others, are honoured
with double essays: the surrealist Antonin Artaud, whose last
major project was to go to Mexico in search of her Indian soul;
and Edmond Jabès, *par excellence* the poet of 'the book'. With
Artaud he persistently by-passes the writer's vision of '*la révolu-
tion indienne*', humanity's last chance derived from a reading of
Mexico's 'living hieroglyphs' (cf. Brotherston 1979b): Artaud is
de-Americanized and his discourse on script and theatre is
referred back to an exclusively Old World debate. In Jabès, as a
Jew also one of the '*peuple écrit*', he finds the solace of a soul
brother. In kabbalistic vein, signing himself with anagrams of
his own name, Derrida descants here on how script prefigures
reality and, when it comes right down to it, has but one
true historical source: the master text of the Judaic biblical
books. Throwing care to the winds and reverting to the
most 'genealogical', not to say racial of models, he brings
himself to reduce all the planet's history and truth to this
'fold':

The only thing that begins by reflecting itself is history. And
this fold, this furrow, is the Jew. The Jew who elects writing
which elects the Jew, in an exchange responsible for truth's
thorough suffusion with historicity and for history's *assignment*
of itself to its empiricity.

difficulty of being a Jew, which coincides with the difficulty of writing: for Judaism and writing are but the same waiting, the same hope, the same depletion.

(Derrida 1978, p. 65)

Here, Derrida's focus has become obsessively narrow and curbs his liberating argument. Given this, and the deprecation he shows not just for Lévi-Strauss's method but for its object and the whole notion of a New World culture independent of his semitic axis, it seems likely Lévi-Strauss had him in mind in the finale of his *Mythologiques* where, returning the charge of ethnocentrism, he contrasts the palpable cultural wealth of native America with the self-enclosing sterility of a certain western philosophy.

By this third stage of the argument we can appeal to syllogism and use the differences between Lévi-Strauss and Derrida not so much for mutual negation as to suggest a possible grammatology (Derrida) of America (Lévi-Strauss). In the first place this involves firmly establishing the New World as a term in its own right, beyond its role as a mere correlative for European philosophy. Few have done this better than Lévi-Strauss, in a famous paragraph from 'Race and history' which deserves to be cited entire:

The example of America shows convincingly enough that this cumulative history is not the exclusive privilege of one civilization or one period of history. This immense continent doubtlessly saw men arrive in small groups of nomads moving over the Behring Strait in the course of the last ice age, at a date which modern archaeological knowledge tentatively sets around the twentieth millenium BC. During this period, these men achieved one of the world's most astonishing demonstrations of cumulative history. They explored thoroughly the resources of a new natural environment. Besides the domestication of some animal species, they cultivated the most diverse vegetable forms for their food, their remedies, and their poisons. And – something unequalled anywhere else – they adapted such poisonous substances as cassava plants to the role of basic food; they used other plants as stimulants or anaesthetics; they collected certain poisons or narcotics according to the way they affected certain animal species; finally, they perfected to the highest degree certain industries such as weaving, ceramics, and the working of precious metals. In order to appreciate this immense accomplishment, it is enough to measure the contribution of America against the civilizations of the Old World. In the first place, there are potatoes, rubber, tobacco, and coca (the basis of modern anaesthetics) which, in various ways, constitute four pillars of Western culture; there are corn and ground nuts, which were to completely transform the African economy before becoming widespread in the alimentary diet of Europe; then cocoa, vanilla, tomatoes, pineapples, pimentos, several types of beans, cotton, and gourds. Finally, the zero, basis of arithmetic (and, indirectly, of modern mathematics), was known and used by the Maya's at least half a millennium before being discovered by Indian scholars, from whom Europe received it through the Arabs. For this reason perhaps, their calendar was then more accurate than that of the Old World. Much ink has been spilled about the question whether the political regime of the Incas was socialist or totalitarian. In any case it fell within the most modern formulae and was many centuries ahead of European phenomena of the same type. The recent revival of interest in curare should call to mind, if necessary, that the scientific knowledge of the native Americans, applied to so many vegetable substances unused in the rest of the world, can still provide the latter with important contributions.

(Lévi-Strauss 1977, p. 338)

Exposing how relative our sense of history is, and how bound to a particular, i.e. non-universal experience (for all of our technology's might), Lévi-Strauss is able to send back the charge of ethnocentrism. To abstraction he prefers the most material agriculture, and so elegantly establishes a primacy for the New World, and an organic integrity, which have been too long resisted academically, for the most blatant ideological reasons. And, beyond this, he exhibits one intellectual accomplishment, the use of zero, whose single force is enough to embarrass a whole cohort of Old World prejudice. Throughout, he takes care to remind us that these developments were not the result of 'Naturall Chance', but of conscious, unvain and persistent human wish. To all this, we may add the millennial time-depth invoked in *Mythologiques* for the cultural communality of the New World. And we may note, too, the bold leaps he makes through space and time in Vol. 3 of that work (1968) where, contrary to his own limitation and possibly in response to Derrida's strictures of the year before (*De la Grammatologie*, 1967), he invokes paradigms that unequivocally exceed the oral and rely on such script-bound modes as astronomy, number theory and calendrics, all of which are given their graphic due in the illustrations. For example, he goes so far as to compare a Mandan disposition of sun, moon and mother with a text carved by a lowland Maya scribe at Tikal in the seventh century AD (Lévi-Strauss 1968, p. 240). In all, we are presented with a phenomenon, the Fourth World of Renaissance cartography, which has clearly not been conceded its place in so-called universal history.

If, on this firm base, we then graft Derridean notions of graphic and scriptual history, in the name of a grammatology of America, we can begin to sense this Fourth World as the great unacknowledged chapter of world literature. Two complementary concepts emerge as essential to this enterprise. The first is geographical focus, which may be derived partly from within Lévi-Strauss's terrestrial corpus; partly from the literary process so far as Derrida has helped us to understand it; and partly from the political predicament of native Americans today, which neither regards to the point of agony. The second is that of the classic text or charter, which defines and is defined by such a focus. Such texts amount in Derrida's terms to alternative Pentateuchs: and in Lévi-Strauss's to what he has rigorously dismembered, in the French abridgements of the New World literature he supplies us with in *Mythologiques*.

Of the possible New World foci which may in these terms be identified as major, the most readily recognizable for us is Middle or Meso America, since the very definition of this region archaeologically depends in part on the manufacture and use there of screenfold books of paper and parchment. And that these books were perceived to have had a function equivalent to ours can be confirmed, on the one side, by the missionaries' bonfires, and on the other by the response, say, of the Aztec priests to the Franciscans who came to convert them in 1524, citing the written authority of the Bible (cf. Lehmann 1949). The Christian claim was met with civilized sarcasm and oblique references to the gods of their own books (the Night, the Wind) (Brotherston 1979a, p. 66).

The images consecrated over millennia in this Mesoamerican tradition continue to operate in therapy and politics today, among the paper-making Otomi of Pahuatlan in northern Puebla, for example (cf. Dyckerhoff 1984); or the Quiche Maya of highland Guatemala, whose soul-rending defence of their land, against constant genocidal attack, is motivated by values grounded in their great classic the *Popul vuh*, transcribed from an iconographic original around AD 1600 and justly known as the 'Bible of America' (cf. Edmonson 1971). Similarly, as heirs to the hieroglyphic variety of Mesoamerican script, the lowland Maya have continued to defend their life through the *Chilam Balam* or Community Books of Yucatan: the question that ends the book from the town Chumayel, with all its literary guile, might have been pondered to advantage by Jack Goody before he chose to pronounce anthropologically on the people of this region: 'Who is the prophet, who is the priest who shall read the word of this book?' (*Mac to ah bovat, mac to ah kin bin tohol cantic u than uooh lae*). In the texts of the lowland Maya, notably those concerning the calendrical Katun Count (*u kahlay katunob*) found alike in the classic hieroglyphic inscriptions and as the core of the alphabetic Community Books – the charter of the so-called 'Caste War' of Yucatan – we have an example of direct literary continuum for almost two millennia.

Underlying and unifying these different political interests within Mesoamerica is the script system itself, in so far as both its iconographic and hieroglyphic varieties rely on exactly the same fund of sign-sets and numbers: and these can be shown to derive from such ancient social practices as shamanism on the one hand (the midwife's Nine Figures of gestation, the augur's Thirteen lunar Birds, both of which were integrated into the 260 units of the tonalamatl or time-book); and, on the other, the levy of labour and commodity tribute (according to the eighteen twenty-day weeks of the agricultural and working year). And this Mesoamerican patrimonium commune, as Eduard Seler once called it, grammatological *par excellence*, formally embodies and extends to the larger philosophy of time and world ages within which local municipal histories are set, as part of this Era with its base-date in the year -3113. While once dismissed with the tell-tale epithets legendary and mythical, this Era framework is now being vindicated archaeologically as an apt measure of Mesoamerica's demographic and political reality: and it is notable that this is a New World time-depth, both articulated and material, the very notion of which has been constantly suppressed or reviled by western orthodoxies and ideologies of all kinds, Marxist included.[2]

Once established and understood in its own terms, this Mesoamerican focus may serve as an invaluable term of reference for the rest of North America. In the liturgy and sand-paintings of the 'Anasazi' Southwest for example, we find astonishingly close parallels with pages from Mesoamerica's screenfold books, tokens of a common formulation which persist as far as the great watershed of the Midewiwin, between the Great Lakes, the Mississippi and Hudson Bay. So clear is this latter focus that it has been defended against modern attempts to change it physically by altering the surrounding river systems; for it stands as the deep historical goal in the migration scrolls of the Mide scribes, and is even highlighted (though on less scriptural grounds) by Lévi-Strauss in his literary map of native North America (*Mythologiques* 3, Fig. 25). The Mide pictographic system along with its intricate time-shift mechanisms (reminiscent of those of Mesoamerica), has likewise functioned southwards towards the Ohio, as the medium for the Lenape classic the *Walam Olum*, so often ignored or rumoured to be fraudulent (as by Brinton), precisely because it so firmly exposes as fallacious the official US history of that area; and the script as such further relates to the histories and Winter Counts of the Plains, grossly neglected still a hundred years on from Wounded Knee. At the time of the first European invasions, the significance of this Mide and northern Algonkin tradition was typified by those Algonkin shamans who discussed scripture with Roger Williams, just as their Aztec counterparts did with Franciscans in Mexico, in both cases the imported authority of the Bible being matched against pre-existing ideas and experience of the written.

Mesoamerica also stands as an invaluable term of comparison for South America, both the Inca or Andean Tahuantinsuyu and the vast lowlands which extend beyond its eastern frontier. With Tahuantinsuyu, the principle of comparison is mathematics, rather than shamanism. For the system used to record and process all official information within its frontier, the quipu, involves that use of the zero noted by Lévi-Strauss in his encomium of the New World; and this is also the case with Maya hieroglyphics (cf. Luxton 1977). The power of quipu in shaping a model of the state can be seen in the transcription from that source made by Guaman Poma in his *Nueva corónica* (*c.* AD 1600); and it may fairly be said to have contributed to that massive Andean capacity for resistance which extends from Vilcabamba in the sixteenth century, through Tupac Amaru II in the eighteenth, to the Sendero Luminoso today. Crossing the old frontier into the lowlands the Inca in their day described as 'wild', we find the most extensive redoubt to have survived supposed European conquest over 450 years ago, one which includes the Nambikwara and their neighbours and which is of course now terribly threatened. Typical of a host of local centres linked among other things by curare – the curare praised by Lévi-Strauss that 'kills, cures and binds' (to use Françoise Barbira's phrase) – is that found on the most propitious of watersheds, the El Dorado fastness which actually links the Orinoco and the Amazon and which provides the focus of the Carib *Watunna*. The profound analogies between this text and the Quiche-Maya *Popul vuh*, with their common story of human evolution and shifts through levels of time up to the encounter with Europe, further argue for a grammatological reading of the New World and its Bible-charters.

Finally, in this textual survey of mankind from Canada to Peru, we may note the isthmian Cuna with whom we began. Nestling at the west end of the Caribbean, at the hinge between north and south, they have used script as an integral part of their paideuma of eight great ways (ikala), the sustenance in turn of a political identity so strong that in this century it has led to a declaration of national independence (in 1925). This dimension of Cuna experience could not even be suspected from Lévi-Strauss's approach to one of the Ikala, the Mu, as merely 'magico-religious' and above all 'purely oral'.

Throughout this brief New World excursion, the attempt has been made to follow those lines of Lévi-Strauss's and Derrida's thought which support rather than negate each other, within what is openly a political perspective. And it is precisely because this perspective is lacking in both that they can so satisfactorily disagree with one another. Denying the denizens of his New World their material–historical existence, Lévi-Strauss will refer for example to the vast sweep of the Algonkin language family from Massachusetts to the Rockies as if they were still there, as if nothing had happened and, yet more to the point, as if nothing was now happening every year and every day.[3] With his genealogical Old World obsessions, Derrida likewise denies the native Americans their historicity and, by ignoring their master texts, reproduces on an intellectual plane the very hegemony he would claim to be combating. Hence fantasy and fatalism: equals our disease and our guns.

Notes

1 Since its first publication, the Mu Ikala has received widespread attention; besides Lévi-Strauss and the other critics noted below, Jerome Rothenberg offers a commentary in his *Shaking the Pumpkin* (1972, pp. 312–20).
2 In this respect it is highly significant that in his otherwise masterly study of native Mesoamerican texts, *Tlacuilolli*, Nowotny should have chosen to deny at one and the same time the historicity of the longer screenfold annals (e.g. those of Tepexic) *and* the true capacity of the script they are written in (1961, pp. 47–8).
3 This point has been most passionately made by those scholars who have worked the closest not just with native American texts but with the people who have produced and continue to produce them, e.g. José María Arguedas with the Quechua, de Civrieux with the Carib, Maarten Jansen with the Mixtec, and so on. Rowe (1984) has exposed the use made of structuralism within Latin American societies reluctant to admit the fact of their native history and present.

11

Orientalism reconsidered

EDWARD W. SAID

There are two sets of problems that I should like to take up, each of them deriving from the general issues addressed in *Orientalism*, of which the most important are: the representation of other cultures, societies, histories; the relationship between power and knowledge; the role of the intellectual; the methodological questions that have to do with the relationships between different kinds of texts, between text and context, between text and history.

I should make two things clear at the outset. First of all, I shall be using the word 'Orientalism' less to refer to my book than to the problems to which my book is related; moreover, I shall be dealing, as will be evident, with the intellectual and political territory covered by *Orientalism* (Said 1978) as well as the work I have done since. This imposes no obligation on my audience to have read me since *Orientalism*; I mention it only as an index of the fact that since writing *Orientalism* I have thought of myself as continuing to look at the problems that first interested me in that book but which are still far from resolved. Second, I would not want it to be thought the license afforded me by the present occasion is an attempt to answer my critics. Fortunately, *Orientalism* elicited a great deal of comment, much of it positive and instructive, yet a fair amount of it hostile and in some cases (understandably) abusive. But the fact is that I have not digested and understood everything that was either written or said. Instead, I have grasped some of the problems and answers proposed by some of my critics, and because they strike me as useful in focusing an argument, these are the ones I shall be taking into account in the comments that follow. Others – like my exclusion of German Orientalism, which no one has given any reason for me to have *included* – have frankly struck me as superficial or trivial, and there seems no point in even responding to them. Similarly the claims made by Dennis Porter (1983), among others, that I am ahistorical and inconsistent, would have more interest if the virtues of consistency (whatever may be intended by the term) were subjected to rigorous analysis; as for my ahistoricity that too is a charge more weighty in assertion than it is in proof.

Now let me quickly sketch the two sets of problems I would like to deal with here. As a department of thought and expertise Orientalism, of course, refers to several overlapping domains: first, the changing historical and cultural relationship between Europe and Asia, a relationship with a 4000-year-old history; second, the scientific discipline in the west according to which, beginning in the early nineteenth century, one specialized in the study of various Oriental cultures and traditions; and, third, the ideological suppositions, images and fantasies about a currently important and politically urgent region of the world called the Orient. The relatively common denominator between these three aspects of Orientalism is the line separating Occident from Orient and this, I have argued, is less a fact of nature than it is a fact of human production, which I have called imaginative geography. This is, however, neither to say that the division between Orient and Occident is unchanging nor is it to say that it is simply fictional. It is to say – emphatically – that as with aspects of what Vico calls the world of nations, the Orient and the Occident are facts produced by human beings, and as such must be studied as components of the social, and not the divine or natural, world. And because the social world includes the person or subject doing the studying as well as the object or realm being studied, it is imperative to include them both in any consideration of Orientalism for, obviously enough, there could be no Orientalism without, on the one hand, the Orientalists, and on the other, the Orientals.

Far from being a crudely political apprehension of what has

been called the problem of Orientalism, this is in reality a fact basic to any thoery of interpretation, or hermeneutics, Yet, and this is the first set of problems I want to consider, there is still a remarkable unwillingness to discuss the problem of Orientalism in the political or ethical or even epistemological contexts proper to it. This is as true of professional literary critics who have written about my book, as it is of course of the Orientalists themselves. Since it seems to me patently impossible to dismiss the truth of Orientalism's political origin and its continuing political actuality, we are obliged on intellectual as well as political grounds to investigate the resistance to the politics of Orientalism, a resistance that is richly symptomatic of precisely what is denied.

If the first set of problems is concerned with Orientalism reconsidered from the standpoint of local issues like who writes or studies the Orient, in what institutional or discursive setting, for what audience, and with what ends in mind, the second set of problems takes us to wider issues. These are the issues raised initially by methodology and then considerably sharpened by questions as to how the production of knowledge best serves communal, as opposed to factional, ends, how knowledge that is non-dominative and non-coercive can be produced in a setting that is deeply inscribed with the politics, the considerations, the positions and the strategies of power. In these methodological and moral reconsiderations of Orientalism I shall quite con-sciously be alluding to similar issues raised by the experiences of feminism or women's studies, black or ethnic studies, socialist and anti-imperialist studies, all of which take for their point of departure the right of formerly un- or misrepresented human groups to speak for and represent themselves in domains de-fined, politically and intellectually, as normally excluding them, usurping their signifying and representing functions, over-riding their historical reality. In short, Orientalism recon-sidered in this wider and libertarian optic entails nothing less than the creation of new objects for a new kind of knowledge.

But let me now return to the local problems I referred to first. The hindsight of authors not only stimulates in them a sense of regret at what they could or ought to have done but did not; it also gives them a wider perspective in which to comprehend what they did. In my own case I have been helped to achieve this broader understanding by nearly everyone who wrote about my book, and who saw it – for better or worse – as being part of current debates, conflicts and contested interpretations in the Arab-Islamic world, as that world interacts with the United States and Europe. Certainly there can be no doubt that – in my own rather limited case – the consciousness of being an Oriental goes back to my youth in colonial Palestine and Egypt, although the impulse to resist its accompanying impingements was nurtured in the heady atmosphere of the post-Second World War period of independence when Arab nationalism, Nasserism, the 1967 War, the rise of the Palestine national movement, the 1973 War, the Lebanese Civil War, the Iranian Revolution and its horrific aftermath, produced that extra-ordinary series of highs and lows which has neither ended nor allowed us a full understanding of its remarkable revolutionary impact.

The interesting point here is how difficult it is to try to understand a region of the world whose principal features seem to be, first, that it is in perpetual flux, and second, that no one trying to grasp it can by an act of pure will or of sovereign understanding stand at some Archimedean point outside the flux. That is, the very reason for understanding the Orient generally, and the Arab world in particular, was first that it prevailed upon one, beseeched one's attention urgently, whether for economic, political, cultural, or religious reasons, and second, that it defied neutral, disinterested or stable definition.

Similar problems are commonplace in the interpretation of literary texts. Each age, for instance, reinterprets Shakespeare, not because Shakespeare changes, but because, despite the existence of numerous and reliable editions of Shakespeare, there is no such fixed and non-trivial object as Shakespeare independent of his editors, the actors who played his roles, the translators who put him in other languages, the hundreds of millions of readers who have read him or watched performances of his plays since the late sixteenth century. On the other hand, it is too much to say that Shakespeare has no independent existence at all, and that he is completely reconstituted every time someone reads, acts or writes about him. In fact, Shakespeare leads an institutional or cultural life that among other things has guaranteed his eminence as a great poet, his authorship of thirty-odd plays, his extraordinary canonical powers in the west. The point I am making here is a rudimentary one: that even so relatively inert an object as a literary text is commonly supposed to gain some of its identity from its historical moment interacting with the attentions, judgements, scholarship and performance of its readers. But, I discovered, this privilege was rarely allowed the Orient, the Arabs, or Islam, which separately or together were supposed by mainstream academic thought to be confined to the fixed status of an object frozen once and for all in time by the gaze of western percipients.

Far from being a defence of the Arabs or of Islam – as my book was taken by many to be – my argument was that neither existed except as 'communities of interpretation' which gave them existence, and that, like the Orient itself, each designation represented interests, claims, projects, ambitions and rhetorics that were not only in violent disagreement, but were in a situation of open warfare. So saturated with meanings, so overdetermined by history, religion and politics are labels like 'Arab' or 'Muslim' as subdivisions of 'the Orient' that no one today can use them without some attention to the formidable polemical mediations that screen the objects, if they exist at all, that the labels designate.

I do not think that it is too much to say that the more these observations have been made by one party, the more routinely they are denied by the other; this is true whether it is Arabs or Muslims discussing the meaning of Arabism or Islam, or whether an Arab or Muslim disputes these designations with a western scholar. Anyone who tries to suggest that nothing, not even a simple descriptive label, is beyond or outside the realm of interpretation, is almost certain to find an opponent saying that science and learning are designed to transcend the vagaries of interpretation, and that objective truth is in fact attainable. This claim was more than a little political when used against Orientals who disputed the authority and objectivity of an Orientalism intimately allied with the great mass of European settlements in the Orient. At bottom, what I said in *Orientalism* had been said before me by A.L. Tibawi (1961, 1966), by Abdullah Laroui (1976, 1977), by Anwar Abdel Malek (1963,

1969), by Talal Asad (1979), by S.H. Alatas (1977a, 1977b), by Fanon (1969, 1970) and Césaire (1972), by Panikkar (1959), and Romila Thapar (1975, 1978), all of whom had suffered the ravages of imperialism and colonialism, and who in challenging the authority, provenance and institutions of the science that represented them to Europe, were also understanding themselves as something more than what this science said they were.

Nor was this all. The challenge to Orientalism, and the colonial era of which it is so organically a part, was a challenge to the muteness imposed upon the Orient as object. In so far as it was a science of incorporation and inclusion by virtue of which the Orient was constituted and then introduced into Europe, Orientalism was a scientific movement whose analogue in the world of empirical politics was the Orient's colonial accumulation and acquisition by Europe. The Orient was therefore not Europe's interlocutor, but its silent Other. From roughly the end of the eighteenth century, when in its age, distance and richness the Orient was rediscovered by Europe, its history had been a paradigm of antiquity and originality, functions that drew Europe's interests in acts of recognition or acknowledgement but *from* which Europe moved as its own industrial, economic and cultural development seemed to leave the Orient far behind. Oriental history – for Hegel, for Marx, later for Burkhardt, Nietzsche, Spengler and other major philosophers of history – was useful in portraying a region of great age, and what had to be left behind. Literary historians have further noted in all sorts of aesthetic writing and plastic portrayals that a trajectory of 'westering', found for example in Keats and Hölderlin, customarily saw the Orient as ceding its historical pre-eminence and importance to the world spirit moving westwards away from Asia and towards Europe.

As primitivity, as the age-old antetype of Europe, as a fecund night out of which European rationality developed, the Orient's actuality receded inexorably into a kind of paradigmatic fossilization. The origins of European anthropology and ethnography were constituted out of this radical difference and, to my knowledge, as a discipline anthropology has not yet dealt with this inherent political limitation upon its supposedly disinterested universality. This, by the way, is one reason Johannes Fabian's book, *Time and The Other: How Anthropology Makes Its*

Object (1983), is both so unique and so important; compared, say, with the standard disciplinary rationalizations and self-congratulatory clichés about hermeneutic circles offered by Clifford Geertz, Fabian's serious effort to redirect anthropologists' attention back to the discrepancies in time, power and development between the ethnographer and his/her constituted object is all the more remarkable. In any event, what for the most part got left out of Orientalism was precisely the history that resisted its ideological as well as political encroachments, and that repressed or resistant history has returned in the various critiques and attacks upon Orientalism, which has uniformly and polemically been represented by these critiques as a science of imperialism.

The divergences between the numerous critiques made of Orientalism as ideology and praxis, at least so far as their aims are concerned, are very wide none the less. Some attack Orientalism as a prelude to assertions about the virtues of one or another native culture: these are the nativists. Others criticize Orientalism as a defence against attacks on one or another political creed: these are the nationalists. Still others criticize Orientalism for falsifying the nature of Islam: these are, *grosso modo*, the fundamentalists. I will not adjudicate between these claims, except to say that I have explicitly avoided taking stands on such matters as the real, true or authentic Islamic or Arabic world, except as issues relating to conflicts involving partisanship, solidarity or sympathy, although I have always tried never to forsake a critical sense or reflective detachment. But in common with all the recent critics of Orientalism I think that two things are especially important – one, a rigorous methodological vigilance that construes Orientalism less as a positive than as a critical discipline and therefore makes it subject to intense scrutiny, and two, a determination not to allow the segregation and confinement of the Orient to go on without challenge. My own understanding of this second point has led me to the extreme position of entirely refusing designations like 'Orient' and 'Occident'; but this is something that I shall return to a little later.

Depending on how they construed their roles as Orientalists, critics of the critics of Orientalism have either reinforced the affirmations of positive power lodged within Orientalism's discourse, or, much less frequently alas, they have engaged Orientalism's critics in a genuine intellectual exchange. The reasons for this split are self-evident: some have to do with power and age, as well as institutional or guild defensiveness; others have to do with religious or ideological convictions. All, irrespective of whether the fact is acknowledged or not, are political – something that not everyone has found easy to acknowledge. If I may make use of my own example, when some of my critics in particular agreed with the main premises of my argument they tended to fall back on encomia to the achievements of what one of their most distinguished individuals, Maxime Rodinson, called '*la science orientaliste*'. This view lent itself to attacks on an alleged Lysenkism lurking inside the polemics of Muslims or Arabs who lodged a protest with 'western' Orientalism, despite the fact that all the recent critics of Orientalism have been quite explicit about using such 'western' critiques as Marxism or structuralism in an effort to over-ride invidious distinctions between east and west, between Arab and western truth, and the like.

Sensitized to the outrageous attacks upon an august and formerly invulnerable science, many accredited members of the certified professional cadre whose division of study is the Arabs and Islam have disclaimed any politics at all, while pressing a rigorous, but for the most part intellectually empty and ideologically intended counter-attack. Although I said I would not respond to critics here, I need to mention a few of the more typical imputations made against me so that you can see Orientalism extending its nineteenth-century arguments to cover a whole incommensurate set of late twentieth-century eventualities, all of them deriving from what, to the nineteenth-century mind, is the preposterous situation of an Oriental responding to Orientalism's asseverations. For sheer heedless anti-intellectualism unrestrained or unencumbered by the slightest trace of critical self-consciousness no one, in my experience, has achieved the sublime confidence of Bernard Lewis, whose almost purely political exploits require more time to mention than they are worth. In a series of articles and one particularly weak book (1982), Lewis has been busy responding to my argument, insisting that the western quest for knowledge about other societies is unique, that it is motivated by pure curiosity, and that in contrast Muslims neither were able nor interested in acquiring knowledge about Europe, as if knowledge about Europe was the only acceptable criterion for true knowledge. Lewis's arguments are presented as emanating exclusively from the scholar's apolitical impartiality whereas, at the same time, he has become an authority drawn on for anti-Islamic, anti-Arab, Zionist and Cold War crusades, all of them underwritten by a zealotry covered with a veneer of urbanity that has very little in common with the 'science' and learning Lewis purports to be upholding.

Not quite as hypocritical, but no less uncritical, are younger ideologues and Orientalists like Daniel Pipes whose expertise as demonstrated in his book *In the Path of God: Islam and Political Power* (1983) is wholly at the service not of knowledge but of an aggressive and interventionary state – the US – whose interests Pipes helps to define. Even if we leave aside the scandalous generalizing that allows Pipes to speak of Islam's anomie, its sense of inferiority, its defensiveness, as if Islam were one simple thing, and as if the quality of his either absent or impressionistic evidence were not of the most secondary importance, Pipes's book testifies to Orientalism's unique resilience, its insulation from intellectual developments everywhere else in the culture, and its antediluvian imperiousness as it makes its assertions and affirmations with little regard for logic and argument. I doubt that any expert anywhere in the world would speak today of Judaism or Christianity with quite that combination of force and freedom that Pipes allows himself about Islam, although one would have thought that a book about Islamic revival would allude to parallel and related developments in styles of religious resurgence in, for example, Lebanon, Israel and the US. For Pipes, Islam is a volatile and dangerous business, a political movement intervening in and disrupting the west, stirring up insurrection and fanaticism everywhere else.

The core of Pipes's book is not simply its highly expedient sense of its own political relevance to Reagan's America, where terrorism and communism fade imperceptibly into the media's image of Muslim gunners, fanatics and rebels, but its thesis that Muslims themselves are the worst source for their own history. The pages of *In the Path of God* are dotted with references to Islam's incapacity for self-representation, self-understanding, self-consciousness, and with praise for witnesses like V.S. Naipaul who are so much more useful and clever in understanding Islam. Here, of course, is perhaps the most familiar of Orientalism's themes – they cannot represent themselves, they must therefore be represented by others who know more about Islam than Islam knows about itself. Now it is often the case that you can be known by others in different ways than you know yourself, and that valuable insights might be generated accordingly. But that is quite a different thing from pronouncing it as immutable law that outsiders *ipso facto* have a better sense of you as an insider than you do of yourself. Note that there is no question of an *exchange* between Islam's views and an outsider's: no dialogue, no discussion, no mutual recognition. There is a flat assertion of quality, which the western policy-maker or his faithful servant possesses by virtue of his being western, white, non-Muslim.

Now this, I submit, is neither science, knowledge, or understanding: it is a statement of power and a claim for relatively absolute authority. It is constituted out of racism, and it is made comparatively acceptable to an audience prepared in advance to listen to its muscular truths. Pipes speaks to and for a large clientèle for whom Islam is not a culture, but a nuisance; most of Pipes's readers will, in their minds, associate what he says about Islam with the other nuisances of the 1960s and 1970s – blacks, women, post-colonial Third World nations that have tipped the balance against the US in such places as UNESCO and the UN, and for their pains have drawn forth the rebuke of Senator Moynihan and Mrs Kirkpatrick. In addition, Pipes – and the rows of like-minded Orientalists and experts he represents as their common denominator – stands for programmatic ignorance. Far from trying to understand Islam in the context of imperialism and the revenge of an abused, but internally very diverse, segment of humanity, far from availing himself of the impressive recent work on Islam in different histories and societies, far from paying some attention to the immense advances in critical theory, in social science and humanistic research, in the philosophy of interpretation, far from making some slight effort to acquaint himself with the vast imaginative literature produced in the Islamic world, Pipes obdurately and explicitly aligns himself with colonial Orientalists like Snouck

Hurgronje and shamelessly pre-colonial renegades like V.S. Naipaul, so that from the eyrie of the State Department and the National Security Council he might survey and judge Islam at will.

I have spent this much time talking about Pipes only because he usefully serves to make some points about Orientalism's large political setting, which is routinely denied and suppressed in the sort of claim proposed by its main spokesman, Bernard Lewis, who has the effrontery to dissociate Orientalism from its two-hundred-year-old partnership with European imperialism and associate it instead with modern classical philology and the study of ancient Greek and Roman culture. Perhaps it is also worth mentioning about this larger setting that it comprises two other elements, about which I should like to speak very briefly, namely the recent (but at present uncertain) prominence of the Palestinian movement, and second, the demonstrated resistance of Arabs in the United States and elsewhere against their portrayal in the public realm.

As for the Palestinian issue, between them the question of Palestine and its fateful encounter with Zionism on the one hand, and the guild of Orientalism, its professional caste-consciousness as a corporation of experts protecting their terrain and their credentials from outside scrutiny on the other hand, these two account for much of the animus against my critique of Orientalism. The ironies here are rich, and I shall restrict myself to enumerating a small handful. Consider the case of one Orientalist who publicly attacked my book, he told me in a private letter, not because he disagreed with it – on the contrary, he felt that what I said was just – but because he had to defend the honour of his profession! Or, take the connection – explicitly made by two of the authors I cite in *Orientalism*, Renan and Proust – between Islamophobia and anti-Semitism. Here, one would have expected many scholars and critics to have seen the conjuncture, that hostility to Islam in the modern Christian west has historically gone hand in hand with, has stemmed from the same source, has been nourished at the same stream as anti-Semitism, and that a critique of the orthodoxies, dogmas and disciplinary procedures of Orientalism contribute to an enlargement of our understanding of the cultural mechanisms of anti-Semitism. No such connection has ever been made by critics, who have seen in the critique of Orientalism an opportunity for them to defend Zionism, support Israel and launch attacks on Palestinian nationalism. The reasons for this confirm the history of Orientalism for, as the Israeli commentator Dani Rubenstein has remarked, the Israeli occupation of the West Bank and Gaza, the destruction of Palestinian society and the sustained Zionist assault upon Palestinian nationalism have quite literally been led and staffed by Orientalists. Whereas in the past it was European Christian Orientalists who supplied European culture with arguments for colonizing and suppressing Islam, as well as for despising Jews, it is now the Jewish national movement that produces a cadre of colonial officials whose ideological theses about the Islamic or Arabic mind are implemented in the administration of the Palestinian Arabs, an oppressed minority within the white European democracy that is Israel. Rubenstein notes with some sorrow that the Hebrew University's Islamic studies department has produced every one of the colonial officials and Arabs experts who run the Occupied Territories.

One further irony should be mentioned in this regard: just as some Zionists have construed it as their duty to defend Orientalism against its critics, there has been a comic effort by some Arab nationalists to see the Orientalist controversy as an imperialist plot to enhance American control over the Arab world. According to this seriously argued but extraordinarily implausible scenario, we are informed that critics of Orientalism turn out not to be anti-imperialist at all, but covert agents of imperialism. The next step from this is to suggest that the best way to attack imperialism is either to become an Orientalist or not to say anything critical about it. At this stage, however, I concede that we have left the world of reality for a world of such illogic and derangement that I cannot pretend to understand its structure or sense.

Underlying much of the discussion of Orientalism is a disquieting realization that the relationship between cultures is both uneven and irremediably secular. This brings us to the point I alluded to a moment ago, about recent Arab and Islamic efforts, well-intentioned for the most part, but sometimes motivated by unpopular regimes, who in attracting attention to the shoddiness of the western media in representing the Arabs or

Islam divert scrutiny from the abuses of their rule and therefore make efforts to improve the so-called image of Islam and the Arabs. Parallel developments have been occurring, as no one needs to be told, in UNESCO where the controversy surrounding the world information order – and proposals for its reform by various Third World and socialist governments – has taken on the dimensions of a major international issue. Most of these disputes testify, first of all, to the fact that the production of knowledge, or information, of media images, is unevenly distributed: the centres of its greatest force are located in what, on both sides of the divide, has been polemically called the metropolitan west. Second, this unhappy realization on the part of weaker parties and cultures has reinforced their grasp of the fact that although there are many divisions within it, there is only one secular and historical world, and that neither nativism, nor divine intervention, nor regionalism, nor ideological smokescreens can hide societies, cultures and peoples from each other, especially not from those with the force and will to penetrate others for political as well as economic ends. But, third, many of these disadvantaged post-colonial states and their loyalist intellectuals have, in my opinion, drawn the wrong set of conclusions, which in practice is that one must either attempt to impose control upon the production of knowledge at the source or, in the worldwide media economy, attempt to improve, enhance, ameliorate the images currently in circulation without doing anything to change the political situation from which they emanate and on which, to a certain extent, they are based.

The failings of these approaches strike me as obvious, and here I do not want to go into such matters as the squandering of immense amounts of petro-dollars for various short-lived public relations scams, or the increasing repression, human rights abuses and outright gangsterism that have taken place in many formerly colonial countries, all of them occurring in the name of national security and fighting neo-imperialism. What I do want to talk about is the much larger question of what, in the context provided by such relatively small efforts as the critique of Orientalism, is to be done, and on the level of politics and criticism how we can speak of intellectual work that is not merely reactive or negative.

I come now finally to the second and, in my opinion, the more challenging and interesting set of problems that derive from the reconsideration of Orientalism. One of the legacies of Orientalism, and indeed one of its epistemological foundations, is historicism, that is, the view pronounced by Vico, Hegel, Marx, Ranke, Dilthey and others, that if humankind has a history it is produced by men and women, and can be understood historically as, at each given period, epoch or moment, possessing a complex, but coherent unity. So far as Orientalism in particular and the European knowledge of other societies in general have been concerned, historicism meant that the one human history uniting humanity either culminated in or was observed from the vantage point of Europe, or the west. What was neither observed by Europe nor documented by it was, therefore, 'lost' until, at some later date, it too could be incorporated by the new sciences of anthropology, political economics and linguistics. It is out of this later recuperation of what Eric Wolf (1982) has called people without history, that a still later disciplinary step was taken, the founding of the science of world history whose major practitioners include Braudel (1972–3, 1981–4), Wallerstein (1974–80), Perry Anderson (1974) and Wolf himself.

But along with the greater capacity for dealing with – in Ernst Bloch's phrase – the non-synchronous experiences of Europe's Other, has gone a fairly uniform avoidance of the relationship between European imperialism and these variously constituted, variously formed and articulated knowledges. What, in other words, has never taken place is an epistemological critique at the most fundamental level of the connection between the development of a historicism which has expanded and developed enough to include antithetical attitutes such as ideologies of western imperialism and critiques of imperialism on the one hand and, on the other, the actual practice of imperialism by which the accumulation of territories and population, the control of economies, and the incorporation and homogenization of histories are maintained. If we keep this in mind we will remark, for example, that in the methodological assumptions and practice of world history – which is ideologically anti-imperialist – little or no attention is given to those cultural practices like Orientalism or ethnography affiliated with imperialism, which in genealogical fact fathered world history itself; hence the emphasis in world history as a discipline has been on economic and political practices, defined by the processes of world historical writing, as in a sense separate and different from, as well as unaffected by, the knowledge of them which world history produces. The curious result is that the theories of accumulation on a world scale, or the capitalist world state, or lineages of absolutism depend (a) on the same displaced percipient and historicist observer who had been an Orientalist or colonial traveller three generations ago; (b) they depend also on a homogenizing and incorporating world historical scheme that assimilated non-synchronous developments, histories, cultures and peoples to it; and (c) they block and keep down latent epistemological critiques of the institutional, cultural and disciplinary instruments linking the incorporative practice of world history with partial knowledges like Orientalism on the one hand and, on the other, with continued 'western' hegemony of the non-European, peripheral world.

In fine, the problem is once again historicism and the universalizing and self-validating that has been endemic to it. Bryan Turner's exceptionally important little book *Marx and the End of Orientalism* (1978) went a very great part of the distance towards fragmenting, dissociating, dislocating and decentring the experiential terrain covered at present by universalizing historicism; what he suggests in discussing the epistemological dilemma is the need to go beyond the polarities and binary oppositions of Marxist-historicist thought (voluntarism *v.* determinism, Asiatic *v.* western society, change *v.* stasis) in order to create a new type of analysis of plural, as opposed to single objects. Similarly, in a whole series of studies produced in a number of both interrelated and frequently unrelated fields, there has been a general advance in the process of, as it were, breaking up, dissolving and methodologically as well as critically reconceiving the unitary field ruled hitherto by Orientalism, historicism and what could be called essentialist universalism.

I shall be giving examples of this dissolving and decentring process in a moment. What needs to be said about it immediately is that it is neither purely methodological nor purely reactive in intent. You do not respond, for example, to the tyrannical conjuncture of colonial power with scholarly Orientalism simply by proposing an alliance between nativist sentiment buttressed by some variety of native ideology to combat them. This, it seems to me, has been the trap into which many Third World and anti-imperialist activists fell in supporting the Iranian and Palestinian struggles, and who found themselves either with nothing to say about the abominations of Khomeini's regime or resorting, in the Palestine case, to the time-worn clichés of revolutionism and, if I might coin a deliberately barbaric phrase, rejectionary armed-strugglism after the Lebanese débâcle. Nor can it be a matter simply of recycling the old Marxist or world-historical rhetoric, which only accomplishes the dubiously valuable task of re-establishing intellectual and theoretical ascendancy of the old, by now impertinent and genealogically flawed conceptual models. No: we must, I believe, think both in political and above all theoretical terms, locating the main problems in what Frankfurt theory identified as domination and division of labour and, along with those, the problem of the absence of a theoretical and utopian as well as libertarian dimension in analysis. We cannot proceed unless therefore we dissipate and redispose the material of historicism into radically different objects and pursuits of knowledge, and we cannot do that until we are aware clearly that no new projects of knowledge can be constituted unless they fight to remain free of the dominance and professionalized particularism that comes with historicist systems and reductive, pragmatic or functionalist theories.

These goals are less grand and difficult than my description sounds. For the reconsideration of Orientalism has been intimately connected with many other activities of the sort I referred to earlier, and which it now becomes imperative to articulate in more detail. Thus, for example, we can now see that Orientalism is a praxis of the same sort, albeit in different territories, as male gender dominance, or patriarchy, in metropolitan societies: the Orient was routinely described as feminine, its riches as fertile, its main symbols the sensual woman, the harem, and the despotic – but curiously attractive – ruler. Moreover Orientals, like Victorian housewives, were confined to silence and to unlimited enriching production. Now much of this material is manifestly connected to the configurations of sexual, racial and political asymmetry underlying mainstream modern western culture, as adumbrated and illuminated respectively by feminists, by black studies critics and by antiimperialist activists. To read, for example, Sandra Gilbert's recent and extraordinarily brilliant study of Rider Haggard's *She* (1983) is to perceive the narrow correspondence between suppressed Victorian sexuality at home, its fantasies abroad and the tightening hold of imperialist ideology on the male late-nineteenth-century imagination. Similarly, a work like Abdul JanMohamed's *Manichean Aesthetics* (1983) investigates the parallel but unremittingly separate artistic worlds of white and black fictions of the same place, Africa, suggesting that even in imaginative literature a rigid ideological system operates beneath a freer surface. Or in a study like Peter Gran's *The Islamic Roots of Capitalism* (1979), which is written out of a polemically although meticulously researched and scrupulously concrete anti-imperialist and anti-Orientalist historical stance, one can begin to sense what a vast invisible terrain of human effort and ingenuity lurks beneath the frozen Orientalist surface formerly carpeted by the discourse of Islamic or Oriental economic history.

There are many more examples that one could give of analyses and theoretical projects undertaken out of similar impulses as those fuelling the anti-Orientalist critique. All of them are interventionary in nature, that is, they self-consciously situate themselves at vulnerable conjunctural nodes of ongoing disciplinary discourses where each of them posits nothing less than new objects of knowledge, new praxes of humanist (in the broad sense of the word) activity, new theoretical models that upset or at the very least radically alter the prevailing paradigmatic norms. One might list here such disparate efforts as Linda Nochlin's explorations of nineteenth-century Orientalist ideology as working within major art historical contexts (1983); Hanna Batatu's immense restructuring of the terrain of the modern Arab state's political behaviour (1984); Raymond Williams's sustained examination of structures of feeling, communities of knowledge, emergent or alternative cultures, patterns of geographical thought, as in his remarkable *The Country and the City* (1973); Talal Asad's account of anthropological self-capture in the work of major theorists (1979,

1983), and along with that his own studies in the field; Eric Hobsbawm's new formulation of 'the invention of tradition' or invented practices studied by historians as a crucial index both of the historian's craft and, more importantly, of the invention of new emergent nations (1983); the work produced in re-examination of Japanese, Indian and Chinese culture by scholars like Masao Miyoshi (1969), Eqbal Ahmad, Tariq Ali, Romila Thapar (1975, 1978), the group around Ranajit Guha (*Subaltern Studies*), Gayatri Spivak (1982, 1985), and younger scholars like Homi Bhabha (1984, 1985) and Partha Mitter (1977); the freshly imaginative reconsideration by Arab literary critics – the *Fusoul* and *Mawakif* groups, Elias Khouri, Kamal Abu Deeb, Mohammad Banis, and others – seeking to redefine and invigorate the reified classical structures of Arabic literary performance, and as a parallel to that, the imaginative works of Juan Goytisolo (1976, 1980) and Salman Rushdie (1979, 1983) whose fictions and criticisms are self-consciously written against the cultural stereotypes and representations commanding the field.

It is worth mentioning here, too, the pioneering efforts of the *Bulletin of Concerned Asian Scholars*, and the fact that twice recently, in their presidential addresses, an American Sinologist (Benjamin Schwartz) and Indologist (Ainslee Embree) have reflected seriously upon what the critique of Orientalism means for their fields, a public reflection as yet denied Middle Eastern scholars; perennially, there is the work carried out by Noam Chomsky in political and historical fields, an example of independent radicalism and uncompromising severity unequalled by anyone else today (1969, 1983); or in literary theory, the powerful theoretical articulations of a social, in the widest and deepest sense, model for narrative put forward by Fredric Jameson (1981), Richard Ohmann's empirically arrived-at definitions of canon privilege and institution in his recent work (1976), his revisionary Emersonian perspectives formulated in the critique of contemporary technological and imaginative, as well as cultural ideologies by Richard Poirier (1971), and the decentring, redistributive ratios of intensity and drive studies by Leo Bersani (1978).

One could go on mentioning many more, but I certainly do not wish to suggest that by excluding particular examples I have thought them less eminent or less worth attention. What I want to do in conclusion is to try to draw them together into a common endeavour which, it has seemed to me, can inform the larger enterprise of which the critique of Orientalism is a part. First, we note a plurality of audiences and constituencies; none of the works and workers I have cited claims to be working on behalf of one audience which is the only one that counts, or for one supervening, overcoming truth, a truth allied to western (or for that matter eastern) reason, objectivity, science. On the contrary, we note here a plurality of terrains, multiple experiences and different constituencies, each with its admitted (as opposed to denied) interest, political desiderata, disciplinary goals. All these efforts work out of what might be called a decentred consciousness, not less reflective and critical for being decentred, for the most part non- and in some cases anti-totalizing and anti-systematic. The result is that instead of seeking common unity by appeals to a centre of sovereign authority, methodological consistency, canonicity and science, they offer the possibility of common grounds of assembly between them. They are therefore planes of activity and praxis, rather than one topography commanded by a geographical and historical vision locatable in a known centre of metropolitan power. Second, these activities and praxes are consciously secular, marginal and oppositional with reference to the mainstream, generally authoritarian systems from which they emanate, and against which they now agitate. Third, they are political and practical in as much as they intend – without necessarily succeeding in implementing – the end of dominating, coercive systems of knowledge. I do not think it too much to say that the political meaning of analysis, as carried out in all these fields, is uniformly and programmatically libertarian by virtue of the fact that, unlike Orientalism, it is not based on the finality and closure of antiquarian or curatorial knowledge, but on investigative open models of analysis, even though it might seem that analyses of this sort – frequently difficult and abstruse – are in the final account paradoxically quietistic. I think we must remember the lesson provided by Adorno's negative dialectics and regard analysis as in the fullest sense being *against* the grain, deconstructive, utopian.

But there remains the one problem haunting all intense,

self-convicted and local intellectual work, the problem of the division of labour, which is a necessary consequence of that reification and commodification first and most powerfully analysed in this century by George Lukács. This is the problem sensitively and intelligently put by Myra Jehlen for women's studies (1981), whether in identifying and working through anti-dominant critiques, subaltern groups – women, blacks, and so on – can resolve the dilemma of autonomous fields of experience and knowledge that are created as a consequence. A double kind of possessive exclusivism could set in: the sense of being an excluding insider by virtue of experience (only women can write for and about women, and only literature that treats women or Orientals well is good literature), and second, being an excluding insider by virtue of method (only Marxists, anti-Orientalists, feminists can write about economics, Orientalism, women's literature).

This is where we are now, at the threshold of fragmentation and specialization, which impose their own parochial dominations and fussy defensiveness, or on the verge of some grand synthesis which I for one believe could very easily wipe out both the gains and the oppositional consciousness provided by these counter-knowledges hitherto. Several possibilities impose themselves, and I shall conclude simply by listing them. A need for greater crossing of boundaries, for greater interventionism in cross-disciplinary activity, a concentrated awareness of the situation – political, methodological, social, historical – in which intellectual and cultural work is carried out. A clarified political and methodological commitment to the dismantling of systems of domination which since they are collectively maintained must, to adopt and transform some of Gramsci's phrases, be collectively fought, by mutual siege, war of manoeuvre *and* war of position. Lastly, a much sharpened sense of the intellectual's role both in the defining of a context and in changing it, for without that, I believe, the critique of Orientalism is simply an ephemeral pastime.

Bibliography

Abbott, Paul (1979) 'On authority', *Screen*, XX(2), 11–64.

Abdel Malek, Anwar (1963) 'Orientalism in crisis', *Diogenes*, 441, 102ff.

—— (1969) *Ideologie et renaissance nationale*, Paris.

Abraham, Karl (1978) 'Transformations of Scopophilia', in his *Selected Papers in Psychoanalysis*, London, 169–234.

Abrahamian, Ervand (1980) 'The guerrilla movement in Iran, 1963–77', *MERIP Reports*, no. 86.

Adorno, Theodor (1967) *Prisms: Cultural Criticism and Society*, trans. Samuel and Shirley Weber, London.

Alatas, S.H. (1977a) *Intellectuals in Developing Societies*, London.

—— (1977b) *The Myth of the Lazy Native*, London.

Althusser, Louis (1971) *Lenin and Philosophy and Other Essays*, trans. Ben Brewster, London.

Anderson, Perry (1974) *Lineages of the Absolutist State*, London.

Arnold, Matthew (1973) 'Wordsworth', in *The Complete Prose Works of Matthew Arnold*, IX, Ann Arbor, 36–55.

Asad, Talal (1979) 'Anthropology and the analysis of ideology', *Man*, n.s. XIV(4), 607–27.

—— (1983) 'Anthropological conceptions of religion: reflections on Geertz', *Man*, n.s. XVIII(2), 237–59.

—— (ed.) (1979), *Anthropology and the Colonial Encounter*, London.

Ascher, Marcia and Robert (1981) *Code of the Quipu. A Study in Media, Mathematics, and Culture*, Ann Arbor.

Bakhtin, Mikhail (1973) *Problems of Dostoevsky's Poetics*, trans. R.W. Rotsel, Ann Arbor.

—— (1981) *The Dialogic Imagination*, transl. Caryl Emerson and Michael Holquist, Austin.

Balibar, Etienne and Macherey, Pierre (1981) 'On literature as an ideological form', in Young, Robert (ed.) *Untying the Text: A Post-Structuralist Reader*, London, 79–100.

Balibar, Renée (1974) (with G. Merlin and G. Tret) *Les français fictifs: le rapport des styles littéraires au français national*, Paris.

—— (1985a), 'L'Ecole de 1880. Le français national: republicain, scolaire, grammatical, primaire', in Antoine, G. (ed.) *Histoire de la langue française*, 14, Paris.

—— (1985b), *L'Institution du français: Essai sur le colinguisme, des Carolingiens à la République*, Paris.

—— and Laporte, Dominique (1974) *Le Français national: politique et practique de la langue national sous la Revolution*, Paris.

Barker, Francis (1977) *Solzhenitsyn: Politics and Form*, London.

—— (1984) *The Tremulous Private Body: Essays on Subjection*, London.

—— *et al.* (eds) (1977) *Literature, Society and the Sociology of Literature*, Colchester.

—— *et al.* (eds) (1978) *1848: The Sociology of Literature*, Colchester.

—— *et al.* (eds) (1979a) *1936: The Politics of Modernism*, Colchester.

—— *et al.* (eds) (1979b) *1936: Practices of Literature and Politics*, Colchester.

—— *et al.* (eds) (1981) *1642: Literature and Power in the Seventeenth Century*, Colchester.

—— *et al.* (eds) (1982) *1789: Reading Writing Revolution*, Colchester.

—— *et al.* (eds) (1983) *The Politics of Theory*, Colchester.

—— *et al.* (eds) (1984) *Confronting the Crisis: War, Politics and Culture in the Eighties*, Colchester.

—— *et al.* (eds) (1985) *Europe and Its Others*, 2 vols, Colchester.

Barrera Vasquez, A. and Rendón, S. (1984) *El libro de los libros de Chilam Balam*, Mexico.

Barthes, Roland (1972) *Mythologies*, trans. Annette Lavers, London.

Batatu, Hanna (1984) *The Egyptian, Syrian and Iraqui Revolutions: Some Observations on their Underlying Causes and Social Character*, Washington.

Batsleer, Janet, Davis, Tony, O'Rourke, Rebecca, and Weedon, Chris, (1985) *Rewriting English: Cultural Politics of Gender and Class*, London.

Baudelaire, Charles (1968) 'Salon de 1845', *Oeuvres complètes*, Paris.

Belsey, Catherine (1980) *Critical Practice*, London.

—— (1981) 'Tragedy, justice and the subject', in Barker, F. *et al.* (eds) *1642: Literature and Power in the Seventeenth Century*, Colchester, 166–86.

—— (1985) *The Subject of Tragedy: Identity and Difference in Renaissance Drama*, London.

Benjamin, Walter (1968) *Illuminations*, trans. Harry Zohn, New York.
—— (1973) *Charles Baudelaire: A Lyric Poet in the Era of High Capitalism*, trans. Harry Zohn, London.
Bennett, Tony (1979) *Formalism and Marxism*, London.
Benveniste, Emile (1971) *Problems in General Linguistics*, trans. Mary E. Meek, Miami.
Bersani, Leo (1978) *A Future for Astyanax: Character and Desire in Literature*, Cambridge.
Bhabha, Homi (1984) 'Of mimicry and men: the ambivalence of colonial discourse', *October*, 28, 125–33.
—— (1985) 'Signs taken for wonders: questions of ambivalence and authority under a tree outside Delhi, May 1817', in Barker, F. *et al.* (eds) *Europe and Its Others*, II, Colchester, 89–106.
Bloch, Marc (1968) *La Société féodale*, Paris.
Bouché, C. (1981) 'Materialist literary theory in France, 1965–75', *Praxis*, 5, 3–20.
Braudel, Fernand (1972–3) *The Mediterranean and the Mediterranean World in the Age of Philip II*, trans. Sîan Reynolds, 2 vols, New York.
—— (1981–4), *Civilization and Capitalism*, trans. Sîan Reynolds, 3 vols, London.
Brecht, Bertolt (1964) *Brecht on Theatre*, trans. John Willett, New York.
Brinton, D. G. (1882–90) *The Library of Aboriginal American Literature*, 8 vols, Philadelphia.
Brotherston, Gordon (1977) *The Emergence of the Latin American Novel*, Cambridge.
—— (1979a), *Image of the New World. The American Continent portrayed in Native Texts*, London.
—— (1979b) 'Artaud, Mexican ritual, and D.H. Lawrence', in Barker, F. *et al.* (eds) *1936: The Politics of Modernism*, Colchester, 133–45.
—— (1981), 'A controversial guide to the language of America', in Barker, F. *et al.* (eds) *1642: Literature and Power in the Seventeenth Century*, Colchester, 84–100.
Brunot, F. (ed.) (1968) *Histoire de la langue française*, 1–13, revised edn, Paris (continued with G. Antoine (ed.) 1985–).
Buci-Glucksmann, Christine (1974) *Gramsci et l'état*, Paris.
Burke, Edmund (n.d.) *Writings and Speeches*, vol. IX, London.
—— (1968) *Reflections on the Revolution in France*, Harmondsworth.
Butor, Michel (1969) *Histoire extraordinaire*, trans. Richard Howard, London.
Cardenal, Ernesto (1973) *Homage to the American Indians*, Baltimore.
Carlin, Norah (1980) 'Marxism and the English Civil War', *International Socialism* II(10), 106–28.

Césaire, Aimé (1972) *Discourse on Colonialism*, trans. J. Pinkham, New York.

Chomsky, Noam (1969) *American Power and the New Mandarins*, New York.

—— (1983) *The Fateful Triangle: Israel, the United States and the Palestinians*, New York.

Civrieux, Marc de (1980) *Watunna. An Orinoco Creation Cycle*, trans. D.M. Guss, San Francisco.

Clark, Katerina and Holquist, Michael (1984) *Mikhail Bakhtin*, Cambridge, Mass.

Clark, T. J. (1973a) *The Absolute Bourgeois: Artists and Politics in France 1848–1851*, London.

—— (1973b) *Image of the People: Gustave Courbet and the 1848 Revolution*, London.

Cohn, Norman (1970) *The Pursuit of the Millenium*, New York.

Cone, C.B. (1964) *Burke and the Nature of Politics: The Age of the French Revolution*, Lexington.

Cousins, Mark (1978) 'The logic of deconstruction', *The Oxford Literary Review*, III(2), 70–8.

Delfau, G. and Roche, A. (1977) *Historie Littérature. Histoire et interpretation du fait littéraire*, Paris.

Derrida, Jacques (1976) *Of Grammatology*, trans. Gayatri Chakravorty Spivak, Baltimore.

—— (1978) *Writing and Difference*, trans. Alan Bass, Chicago.

—— (1981a) *Positions*, trans. Alan Bass, London.

—— (1981b) *Dissemination*, trans. Barbara Johnson, London.

Dewdney, Selwyn (1975) *The Sacred Scrolls of the Southern Ojibway*, Toronto.

Diringer, David (1968) *The Alphabet*, 2 vols, London.

Dollimore, Jonathan (1984) *Radical Tragedy: Religion, Ideology and Power in the Drama of Shakespeare and his Contemporaries*, Brighton.

—— and Sinfield, Alan (eds) (1985) *Political Shakespeare: New Essays in Cultural Materialism*, Manchester.

Drakakis, John (ed.) (1985) *Alternative Shakespeares*, London.

Duchet, C. (ed.) (1979) *Sociocritique*, Paris.

Du Garde Peach, L. (1958) *The Story of the First Queen Elizabeth*, London.

Dyckerhoff, Ursula (1984) 'La historia de curación antigua de San Pablito, Pahuatlán', *Indiana* (Berlin), 9, 69–86.

Eagleton, Terry (1976a) *Criticism and Ideology*, London.

—— (1976b) *Marxism and Literary Theory*, London.

—— (1985) 'Literature and history', *Critical Quarterly*, XXVII(4), 23–6.

Easthope, Antony (1983) 'The trajectory of *Screen*, 1971–9', in Barker, F. *et al.* (eds) *The Politics of Theory*, Colchester, 121–33.

Edmonson, Munro (1971) *The Book of Counsel: The Popol Vuh of the Quiche Maya of Guatemala*, New Orleans.

Edwardes, Michael (1976) *Warren Hastings, King of the Nabobs*, London.

Eikhenbaum, Boris (1971) 'The theory of the formal method', in Matejka, L. and Pomorska, K. (eds) *Readings in Russian Poetics*, Cambridge, Mass., 3–37.

—— (1974) 'How Gogol's "overcoat" is made', in Maguire, R.A. (ed.) *Gogol from the Twentieth Century*, Princeton, 267–91.

—— (1975) 'Leskov and contemporary prose', *Russian Literature Tri-Quarterly*, XI, 211–29.

Eliot, T.S. (1966) 'A note on the verse of John Milton', in Martz, Louis (ed.) *Milton*, Englewood Cliffs, New Jersey.

Fabian Johannes (1983) *Time and the Other: How Anthropology Makes its Object*, New York.

Fanon, Frantz (1969) *The Wretched of the Earth*, trans. Constance Farrington, Harmondsworth.

—— (1970) *Black Skin White Masks*, trans. Charles Lam Markmann, London.

Faye, Jean-Pierre (1972) *Théorie du récit*, Paris.

—— (1973) *La Critique de langage et son économie*, Paris.

Fayolle, R. (1978) *La Critique*, Paris.

Feuchtwang, Stephan (1980) 'Socialist, feminist and anti-racist struggles', *m/f*, 4, 41–56.

Fokkema, D.W. (1976) 'Continuity and change in Russian Formalism, Czech structuralism and Soviet semiotics', *PTL*, 1, 153–96.

Foucault, Michel (1977) *Discipline and Punish: The Birth of the Prison*, trans. Alan Sheridan, London.

—— (1979) *The History of Sexuality. Volume One: An Introduction*, trans. Robert Hurley, London.

—— (1980a) *Power/Knowledge: Selected Interviews and Other Writings*, 1972–1977, ed. Colin Gordon, Brighton.

—— (1980b) *Herculine Barbin*, trans. Richard McDougall, Brighton.

Freud, Sigmund (1953–73) *The Standard Edition of the Complete Psychological Works*, trans. James Strachey, 24 vols, London.

—— (1981) 'Fetishism' [1927], in his *On Sexuality* (Pelican Freud Library, vol. 7), Harmondsworth, 345–58.

Frow, John (1980) 'System and history: a critique of Russian Formalism', *The Oxford Literary Review*, IV (2), 56–71.

Gallop, Jane (1983) 'The mother tongue', in Barker, F. *et al.* (eds) *The Politics of Theory*, Colchester, 49–56.

Gates, Henry Louis (ed.) (1984) *Black Literature and Literary Theory*, New York.

Gelb, I.J. (1963) *A Study of Writing*, Chicago.

Gilbert, Sandra (1983) 'Rider Haggard's heart of darkness', *Partisan Review*, 50, 444–53.

Glass, J.B. and Gibson, C. (1975) 'Census of Middle American . . . manuscripts', *Handbook of Middle American Indians*, vols 14–15, Austin.

Goldmann, Lucien (1967) 'The sociology of literature: status and problems of method', *International Social Science Journal*, XIX(4), 493–516.

Goody, Jack (1968) *Literacy in Traditional Societies*, Chicago.

Goytisolo, Juan (1976) *Revindicación del conde Julián*, Barcelona.

—— (1980) *Señas de identidad*, Barcelona.

Gramsci, Antonio (1973) *Prison Notebooks*, ed. and trans. Q. Hoare and G. Nowell Smith, London.

—— (1985) *Selections from Cultural Writings*, ed. and trans. D. Forgacs and G. Nowell Smith, London.

Gran, Peter (1979) *The Islamic Roots of Capitalism: Egypt 1760–1840*, Austin.

Guaman Poma de Ayala, Felipe (1936) *Nueva corónica y buen gobierno*, Paris, facsimile edition.

Guha, Ranajit (1963) *A Rule of Property for Bengal: An Essay on the Idea of Permanent Settlement*, New Delhi.

Hall, Stuart (1977) 'A critical survey of the theoretical and practical achievements of the last ten years', in Barker, F. *et al.* (eds) *Literature, Society and the Sociology of Literature*, Colchester, 1–7.

Halliday, Fred (1979) 'Theses on the Iranian Revolution', *Race and Class*, XXI(1), 81–90.

Hastings, Warren (1948) 'Benares Diary', ed. C. Collins Davies, *Camden Miscellany*, XVIII.

Heath, Stephen (1975) 'Film and system, terms of analysis', *Screen*, XVI(1 and 2), 7–77, 91–113.

—— (1978) 'Difference', *Screen*, XIX(3), 51–112.

Helbig, J.W. (1984) 'Einige Bemerkungen zum muu ikala, einem Medizingesang der Cuna Panamas', *Indiana* (Berlin), 10, 71–88.

Hill, Christopher (1975) *The World Turned Upside Down*, Harmondsworth.

Hirschkop, Ken (1985) 'A response to the forum on Mikhail Bhaktin', *Critical Inquiry*, XI, 672–8.

Hobsbawm, Eric and Ranger, Terence (eds) (1983) *The Invention of Tradition*, Cambridge.

Holmer, N.M. and Wassen, S.H. (1947) *Mu-Igala, or the Way of Muu, a Medicine Song from the Cunas of Panama*, Göteborg.

Howard, J.H. (1979) *The British Museum Winter Count*, Occasional Paper of the British Museum no. 4, London.

Humm, Peter, Stigant, Paul and Widdowson, Peter (eds) (1986) *Popular Fictions: Essays in Literature and History*, London.

Jakobson, R. and Tynyanov, J. (1977) 'Problems of research in literature and language', *Russian Poetics in Translation*, IV, 49–51.

Jameson, Fredric (1971) *Marxism and Form*, Princeton.

—— (1972) *The Prison-House of Language*, Princeton.

—— (1981) *The Political Unconscious: Narrative as a Socially Symbolic Act*, London.

JanMohamed, Abdul (1983) *Manichean Aesthetics: The Politics of Literature in Colonial Africa*, Amherst.

Jehlen, Myra (1981) 'Archimedes and the paradox of feminist criticism', *Signs*, VI(4), 575–601.

Kramer, F.W. (1970) *Literature among the Cuna Indians*, Göteborg.

Kristeva, Julia (1971) *Le Texte du roman*, Paris.

—— (1980) *Desire in Language: A Semiotic Approach to Literature and Art*, trans. Thomas Gora, Alice Jardine and Leon S. Roudiez, London.

Lacan, Jacques (1977) *Ecrits*, trans. Alan Sheridan, London.

—— (1979) *The Four Fundamental Concepts of Psychoanalysis*, trans. Alan Sheridan, Harmondsworth.

Laplanche, J. and Pontalis, J.B. (1980) 'Phantasy (or fantasy)', *The Language of Psychoanalysis*, London, 314–19.

Laroui, Abdullah (1976) *The Crisis of the Arab Intellectuals*, trans. Diarmid Cammell, Berkeley.

—— (1977) *The History of the Maghrib*, trans. Ralph Manheim, Princeton.

Le Goff, Jacques (1977) *Pour un autre Moyen-Age*, Paris.

Lehmann, Walter (1949) *Sterbende Gotter und Christliche Heilsbotschaft*, Stuttgart.

Lemon, L.T. and Reis, M.J. (eds) (1965) *Russian Formalist Criticism: Four Essays*, Lincoln, Nebraska.

Lévi-Strauss, Claude (1955) *Tristes Tropiques*, Paris.

—— (1964–71) *Mythologiques*, 4 vols, Paris.

—— (1975–9) *La Voie des masques*, 2 vols, Paris.

—— (1977) *Structural Anthropology*, trans. Claire Jacobson and Brooke Grundfest Schoepf, Harmondsworth.

—— (1978) *Structural Anthropology*, vol. II, trans. M. Layton, Harmondsworth.

Lewis, Bernard (1982) *The Muslim Discovery of Europe*, New York.

Lewis, M.G. (1973), *The Monk*, ed. Howard Anderson, London.

Longhurst, Derek (1982) '"Not for all time, but for an age": an approach to Shakespeare studies', in Widdowson, Peter (ed.) *Re-Reading English*, London, 150–63.

Lo Piparo, Franco (1979) *Lingua, Intellettuali, Egemonia in Gramsci*, Bari.

Lovell, Terry (1983) 'Writing like a woman: a question of politics', in Barker, F. *et al.* (eds) *The Politics of Theory*, Colchester, 15–26.

Luxton, R.N. (with Pablo Canche) (1977) *The Hidden Continent of the Maya and the Quechua*, Ph.D. dissertation, University of Essex.

Macaulay, T.B. (1850) 'Warren Hastings', in his *Critical and Historical Essays*, IV, Leipzig, 213–349.

MacCabe, Colin (1976) 'Theory and film: principles of realism and pleasure', *Screen*, XVII(3), 7–27.

—— (1978) *James Joyce and the Revolution of the Word*, London.

—— (ed.) (1981) *The Talking Cure: Essays in Psychoanalysis and Language*, London.

Macherey, Pierre (1978) *A Theory of Literary Production*, trans. Geoffrey Wall, London.

Marshall, P.J. (1965) *The Impeachment of Warren Hastings*, Oxford.

—— (1970) *The British Discovery of Hinduism in the Eighteenth Century*, Cambridge.

Marx, Karl and Engels, Friedrich (1973) *Selected Works*, 3 vols, Moscow.

Matejka, L. and Pomorska, K. (eds) (1971) *Readings in Russian Poetics*, Cambridge, Mass.

Medvedev, P.N. and M.M. Bakhtin (1978) *The Formal Method in Literary Scholarship: A Critical Introduction to Sociological Poetics*, trans. Albert J. Wehrle, Baltimore.

Mercer, Colin (1979) 'Gramsci and grammar', in Barker, F. *et al.* (eds) *1936: The Politics of Modernism*, Colchester, 72–88.

Metz, Christian (1982), 'The imaginary signifier', trans. Ben Brewster, in his *Psychoanalysis and Cinema*, London, 1–87.

Miller, Perry (1968) *The New England Mind*, Boston.

Milton, John (1957) *Complete Poems and Major Prose*, ed. M.Y. Hughes, Indianapolis.

Mitter, Partha (1977) *Much Maligned Monsters: History of Europe's Reaction to India*, Oxford.

Miyoshi, Masao (1969) *The Divided Self: A Perspective on the Literature of the Victorians*, New York.

Moi, Toril (1983) 'Sexual/textual politics', in Barker, F. *et al.* (eds) *The Politics of Theory*, Colchester, 1–14.

—— (1985) *Sexual/Textual Politics: Feminist Literary Theory*, London.

Mukařovský, Jan (1976) *On Poetic Language*, trans. John Burbank and Peter Steiner, Lisse.

Mukherjee, Ramkrishna (1974) *The Rise and Fall of the East India Company*, New York.

Neale, Steve (1979/80) 'The same old story: stereotypes and differences', *Screen Education*, 32–3, 33–7.

Needham, Rodney (1972) *Belief, Language and Experience*, Chicago.

Nochlin, Linda (1983) 'The Imaginary Orient', *Art in America*, 5, 118–31, 187–91.

Nordenskiöld, Erland (1925) *The Secret of the Peruvian Quipus*, trans. G.E. Fuhrken, 2 vols, Göteborg.

—— (with Pérez Kantule, Rubén) (1938) *An Historical and Ethnographical Survey of the Cuna Indians*, trans. Mary Frodi, Göteborg.

Norris, Christopher (1982) *Deconstruction: Theory and Practice*, London.

Nowotny, Karl Anton (1961) *Tlacuilolli. Die mexicanischen Bilderhandschriften*, Berlin.

Oakley, John, Bromley, Roger and Harper, Sue (1983) 'The boundaries of hegemony', in Barker, F. *et al.* (eds) *The Politics of Theory*, Colchester, 148–78.

O'Brien, Conor Cruise (1968) 'Introduction' to Edmund Burke, *Reflections on the Revolution in France*, Harmondsworth, 9–76.

Ohmann, Richard (1976) *English in America: A Radical View of the Profession*, Oxford.

Panikkar, K.M. (1959) *Asia and Western Dominance: A Survey of the Vasco da Gama Epoch of Asian History, 1498–1945*, London.

Pechey, Graham (1980) 'Formalism and Marxism', *The Oxford Literary Review*, IV(2), 72–81.

Pipes, Daniel (1983) *In the Path of God*, New York.

Plumb, J.H. (1950) *England in the Eighteenth Century*, Harmondsworth.

Poirier, Richard (1971) *Performing Self: Composition and Decomposition in the Language of Contemporary Life*, Oxford.

Porter, Dennis (1983) '*Orientalism* and its problems', in Barker, F. *et al.* (eds) *The Politics of Theory*, Colchester, 179–93.

Preuss, Konrad Theodor (1921) *Die Religion und Mythologie der Uitoto*, Gottingen-Leipzig.

'Race, "writing" and difference' (1985) *Critical Inquiry*, XII(1).

Reeve, Clara (1967) *The Old English Baron*, ed. James Trainer, London.

Rodgers, Betsy (1958) *Georgian Chronicle: Mrs Barbauld and her Family*, London.

Rose, Jacqueline (1981) 'The Imaginary', in MacCabe, Colin (ed.) *The Talking Cure: Essays in Psychoanalysis and Language*, London, 132–61.

Rothenberg, Jerome (1972) *Shaking the Pumpkin. Traditional Poetry of the North American Indians*, Garden City, NY.

Rowe, William (1984) 'Paz, Fuentes and Lévi-Strauss: the creation of a structuralist orthodoxy', *Bulletin of Latin American Research*, III(2), 77–82.

Rudé, George (1964) *The Crowd in History, 1730–1848*, New York.

Rule, Margaret (1983) *The Mary Rose: The Excavation and Raising of Henry VIII's Flagship*, London.

Rushdie, Salman (1979) *Midnight's Children*, London.

—— (1983) *Shame*, London.

Russo, Mary (1983) 'Notes on "post-feminism"', in Barker, F. *et al.* (eds) *The Politics of Theory*, Colchester, 27–37.

Said, Edward (1978) *Orientalism*, London.
—— (1980) *The Question of Palestine*, London.
—— (1981) *Covering Islam: How the Media and the Experts Determine How We See the Rest of the World*, London.
Saussure, Ferdinand de (1959) *Course in General Linguistics*, trans. Wade Baskin, New York.
Shklovsky, Victor (1965) 'Art as technique', in Lemon. L.T. and Reis, M.J. (eds) *Russian Formalist Criticism*, Nebraska, 3–24.
Shukman, Ann and O'Toole, L.M. (1977) 'A contextual glossary of formalist terminology', *Russian Poetics in Translation*, IV, 13–48.
Spivak, Gayatri Chakravorty (1982) ' "Draupaudi" by Mahasveta Devi', in Abel, Elizabeth (ed.) *Writing and Sexual Difference*, Chicago, 261–82.
—— (1985) 'The Rani of Sirmur', in Barker, F. *et al.* (eds) *Europe and Its Others*, I, Colchester, 128–51.
Stone, Jennifer (1983) 'The horrors of power: a critique of Kristeva', in Barker, F. *et al.* (eds) *The Politics of Theory*, Colchester, 38–48.
Subaltern Studies: Writings on south-east Asian history and society (1982) ed. Ranajit Guha, vol. 1, Oxford.
Temple, Charles (1971) 'The native races and their rulers', excerpted in P.D. Curtin, *Imperialism*, London, 93–104.
Thapar, Romila (1975) *Ancient India: A Textbook of History for Middle Schools*, New Delhi.
—— (1978) *Medieval India: A Textbook of History for Middle Schools*, New Delhi.
The History of the Times (1935) London.
The History of the Trial of Warren Hastings (1796) London.
Tibawi, A.L. (1961) *British Interests in Palestine, 1800–1901*, London.
—— (1966) *American Interests in Syria, 1800–1901*, Oxford.
Todorov, Tzvetan (1982) *La Conquête de l'Amérique. La question de l'autre*, Paris.
—— (1985) *Mikhail Bakhtin: The Dialogical Principle*, trans. Wlad Godzich, Manchester.
—— (ed. and trans.) (1965) *Théorie de la littérature*, Paris.
Turner, Bryan (1978) *Marx and the End of Orientalism*, London.
Tute, Warren (1983) *The True Glory*, London.
Tynyanov, Juri (1971) 'On literary evolution', in Matejka, L. and Pomorska, K. (eds) *Poetics*, Cambridge, Mass., 66–78.
—— (1982) 'The fundamentals of cinema', in Taylor, R. (ed.) *The Poetics of Cinema*, Oxford, 32–54.
Vinogradov, Victor (1975) 'The problem of *skaz* in stylistics', *Russian Literature Tri-Quarterly*, XII, 237–50.
Voloshinov, V.N. (1973) *Marxism and the Philosophy of Language*, trans. L. Matejka and I.R. Titunik, New York.

—— (1976), 'Discourse in life and discourse in art', in his *Freudianism: A Marxist Critique*, trans. I.R. Titunik, New York, 93–116.

Wallerstein, Immanuel (1974–80) *The Modern World System*, 2 vols, New York.

Walpole, Horace (1964) *The Castle of Otranto*, ed. W. S. Lewis, London.

Weitzman, S. (1929) *Warren Hastings and Philip Francis*, Manchester.

Wellek, René (1968) 'Romanticism re-examined', in Frye, Northrop (ed.) *Romanticism Reconsidered*, New York, 107–33.

White, Allon (1984) 'Bakhtin, sociolinguistics and deconstruction', in Gloversmith, F. (ed.) *The Theory of Reading*, Brighton, 123–46.

Willemen, Paul (1980) 'Letter to John', *Screen*, XXI(2), 53–65.

Williams, Raymond (1958) *Culture and Society 1780–1950*, London.

—— (1973) *The Country and the City*, London.

—— (1977) *Marxism and Literature*, Oxford.

Wolf, Eric (1982) *Europe and the People without History*, Berkeley.

Woolf, C. and Moorcroft Wilson, J. (eds) (1982) *Authors Take Sides on the Falklands*, London.

Wordsworth, William (1952) *The Poetical Works*, ed. E. de Selincourt, Oxford.

—— (1959) *The Prelude*, ed. E. de Selincourt, rev. Helen Darbishire, Oxford.

Wright, Patrick (1985) *On Living in an Old Country*, London.

List of papers given at the Essex Conference 1976–84

Literature, Society and the Sociology of Literature

Proceedings of the 1976 Essex Conference

edited by

Francis Barker
John Coombes
Peter Hulme
David Musselwhite
Richard Osborne

A critical survey of the theoretical and practical achievements of the last ten years
Stuart Hall
Towards a political aesthetics
David Musselwhite
The boundaries of hegemony: Pater
John Oakley
The boundaries of hegemony: Thomas Hardy and *The Mayor of Casterbridge*
Roger Bromley
Problems of reflection
Pierre Macherey
Ecriture and eighteenth-century fiction
Terry Eagleton
Theory and film: principles of realism and pleasure
Colin MacCabe

Evolution and revolution: politics and form in *Felix Holt* and *The Revolution in Tanner's Lane*
Charles Swann
Russian Formalism and Marxism: an unconcluded dialogue
Ray Selden
Little magazines: notes towards a methodology
Alan Wall
Jane Austen and gentry society
Terry Lovell
Problems of radical drama: the plays and productions of Trevor Griffiths
Janet Wolff, Steve Ryan, Jim McGuigan, Derek McKiernan
Wuthering Heights: the unacceptable text
David Musselwhite
Browning and Arnold as cultural critics
Susan Harper and Brendan Kenny
Some problems in Trotsky's literary criticism
Francis Barker

1848: The Sociology of Literature

Proceedings of the 1977 Essex Conference

edited by

Francis Barker
John Coombes
Peter Hulme
Colin Mercer
David Musselwhite

Marx's concept of class in 'The 18th Brumaire of Louis Bonaparte'
Lawrence Wilde
The political aesthetics of 'The 18th Brumaire of Louis Bonaparte'
John Coombes
'The 18th Brumaire' and the construction of a Marxist aesthetics
Stanley Mitchell
An example of literary work in France: George Sand's *La Mare au Diable / The Devil's Pool* of 1846
Renée Balibar
Young Ireland: literature and nationalism
Maurice Colgan
Zola and 1848
Ian Birchall
Portrait of the artist as a young German: Karl Gutzkow's political attitudes and 1848
R.J. Kavanagh

The Brontes and death: alternatives to revolution
Patsy Stoneman
Tennyson: Politics and sexuality in *The Princess* and *In Memoriam*
Terry Eagleton
J. Sheridan le Fanu's *Richard Marston* (1848): the history of an
Anglo-Irish text
W.J. McCormack
The 'time' of 1848: Lukács on Flaubert's *Sentimental Education*
Jay Bernstein
Nestroy and politics
Michael Rogers
The boundaries of hegemony: Lytton
John Oakley
Women's writing: *Jane Eyre, Shirley, Villette, Aurora Leigh*
Marxist-Feminist Literature Collective
The novel as narcotic
David Musselwhite
Baudelaire and the city: 1848 and the inscription of hegemony
Colin Mercer
Carlyle and *Mary Barton*: problems of utterance
Gillian Beer
Notes on fathers and sons from *Dombey and Son*
Michael Green
Edgar Quinet and messianic nationalism in the years
preceding 1848
Ceri Crossley
Forms of English fiction in 1848
Raymond Williams

1936: The Sociology of Literature
Volume I – The Politics of Modernism

Proceedings of the 1978 Essex Conference

edited by

Francis Barker
Jay Bernstein
John Coombes
Peter Hulme
David Musselwhite
Jennifer Stone

Aesthetics and politics symposium: introductory notes
Ernst Bloch
R.S. Livingstone

A note on Brecht and realism
Terry Eagleton
On the presentation of Adorno in *Aesthetics and Politics*
Gillian Rose
The dispute over modernism
Gillian Rose
Mirror image/collage: reality, representation and revolution
in Pirandello
Jennifer Stone
Gramsci and grammar
Colin Mercer
Surrealism and the Popular Front
Robert Short
Georges Bataille (1897–1962): *Jouissance* and revolution
John Hoyles
Artaud, Mexican ritual and D.H. Lawrence
Gordon Brotherston
Céline and the débâcle of idealism
Leslie Davis
San Camilo 36: a retrospective view of the Spanish Civil War
Patricia MacDermott
Modernism, revaluation and commitment
Alan Wall
Floating the pound: the circulation of the subject of the *Cantos*
Maud Ellmann
Towards a definition of negative discourse
Victoria Maubrey-Rose
Virginia Woolf's *The Waves*: a materialist reading of an almost
disembodied voice
Anna Coombes
Modernism in the 1930s: Dorothy Richardson and Virginia Woolf
Michele Barrett and Jean Radford
The boundaries of commitment: God, lover, comrade – Malcolm
Lowry's *Under the Volcano* as a reading of the 1930s
Roger Bromley

1936: The Sociology of Literature
Volume II – Practices of Literature and Politics

Proceedings of the 1978 Essex Conference

edited by

Francis Barker
Jay Bernstein

John Coombes
Peter Hulme
David Musselwhite
Jennifer Stone

Thinking the thirties
English Studies Group, CCCS, Birmingham
Dilemmas of radical culture: forms of expression and relations
of production
Graham Murdock
Socialism in Britain and France: the general elections of 1935
and 1936
David Rubinstein
NS literary policies
Jorg Thunecke
The Popular Front in the south of France: memory and oral
transmission
Ann Roche
Lewis Grassic Gibbon
Brian Scobie
Socialist novels of 1936
H. Gustav Klaus
The novel and the party
Ian H. Birchall
Edward Upward and the novel of politics
Anthony Arblaster
Statement for the Essex Conference
Edward Upward
John Middleton Murry and *Adelphi* Socialism, 1932–8
Jim Philip
Orwell: Political criticism and fictional vision
Roger Hartley
A new dissection of Orwell's *Elephant*
John Coombes
Drieu la Rochelle and the Popular Front
Geraldi Leroy
From unreliable writer to reliable writing
Leo Hickey
Karl Kraus and the language of the thirties
M.A. Rogers
Traditional metre and the poetry of the thirties
Antony Easthope
Scars and emblems: 1936 and the crisis of the subject
Stan Smith

Mortmere and Guernica: poets exploding like bombs
Bernard Benstock

1642: Literature and Power in the Seventeenth Century

Proceedings of the 1980 Essex Conference

edited by

Francis Barker
Jay Bernstein
John Coombes
Peter Hulme
Jennifer Stone
Jon Stratton

The tremulous private body
Francis Barker
Seventeenth-century women's autobiography
Sandra Findley and Elaine Hobby
Spiritual whoredom: an essay on female prophets in the seventeenth century
Christine Berg and Philippa Berry
Hurricanes in the Caribbees: the constitution of the discourse of English colonialism
Peter Hulme
A controversial guide to the language of America, 1643
Gordon Brotherston
The appropriation of Pascal
Ian Birchall
Merit and destiny: ideology and narrative in French classicism
Jerry Palmer
The articulation of social, ideological and literary practices in France: the historical moment of 1641–3
Jean Rohou
Tragedy, justice and the subject
Catherine Belsey
Anglicans, Puritans and plain style
Roger Pooley
Psychoanalysis, the Kabbala and the seventeenth century
Terry Eagleton
The significance of allegory in the *Ursprung des Deutschen Trauerspiels*
Howard Caygill
Revolution, the Levellers and C.B. Macpherson
Anthony Arblaster

Beyond the sex-economy of mysticism: some observations on the
communism of the imagination with reference to Winstanley
and Traherne
John Hoyles
Law and the ideology of order: the problem of knowledge in
Th. Hobbes' *Leviathan*
Jon Stratton
Law and consciousness in early seventeenth-century England
Michael Lane
Historical process, individual and communities in Milton's
early prose
David Aers and Gunther Kress
Towards the autonomous subject in poetry: *Milton on his Blindness*
Antony Easthope
Religion and ideology
Fredric Jameson

1789: Reading Writing Revolution

Proceedings of the 1981 Essex Conference

edited by

Francis Barker
Jay Bernstein
Peter Hulme
Margaret Iversen
Jennifer Stone

The republican calendar: a diagnostic of the French Revolution
Gordon Brotherston
Guarding the body politic: Volney's catechism of 1793
L.J. Jordanova
Volney's rationalist apocalypse: *Les Ruines ou méditations sur les
révolutions des empires*
Brian Rigby
Fiction and woman in *La Nouvelle Hélöise* and the heritage of '1789'
John Lechte
1789 and after: mutations of 'Romantic' discourse
Graham Pechey
The Romantic construction of the unconscious
Catherine Belsey
Strategies for representing revolution
*UEA English Studies Group (David Punter, David Aers, Robert Clark,
Jonathan Cook, Thomas Elsasser)*

A description of Blake: ideology, form, influence
Edward Larrissy
The revolutionary poetics of William Blake – part I: the critical tradition
Peter Middleton
Novelty and continuity in English Romanticism: A 'Lucy' poem
Antony Easthope
William Godwin's *Caleb Williams*: truth and 'things as they are'
Kelvin Everest and Gavin Edwards
The critics' choice
Samuel Weber
The 'natural' economy: a note on some rhetorical strategies in political economy – Adam Smith and Malthus
S. Copley
1789/1859: revolution, ideology and entrepreneurship
Norman Feltes
Aesthetics and politics in the age of the French Revolution
Stanley Mitchell
Friedrich Hölderlin and Jacobinism
R.J. Kavanagh
From theory to practice: Georg Forster and the French Revolution
Udo Kürten
Family and politics in the drama of *Sturm und Drang*
Helga Geyer-Ryan
The trial of Warren Hastings
D.E. Musselwhite
The American Indian in 1789
Helen Carr
The destinies of empire
Jacqueline Kaye
Insurrection and repression: Bligh's 1790 *Narrative of the Mutiny on board H.M. Ship Bounty*
Jocelyn Dunphy
The genesis of protestant ascendancy
W.J. McCormack

The Politics of Theory

Proceedings of the 1982 Essex Conference

edited by

Francis Barker
Peter Hulme
Margaret Iversen
Diana Loxley

Sexual/textual politics
Toril Moi
Writing like a woman: a question of politics
Terry Lovell
Notes on 'post-feminism'
Mary Russo
The horrors of power: a critique of 'Kristeva'
Jennifer Stone
The mother tongue
Jane Gallop
Kleinian psychoanalysis and the theory of culture
Michael Rustin
A reply to Michael Rustin: Kleinian psychoanalysis and the theory
of culture
Graham Seymour
Politics, pedagogy, work: reflections on the 'project' of the last
six years
David Punter
The freedom of the critic and the history of the text
L.A. Jackson

In defence of reductionism
Ian H. Birchall
The trajectory of *Screen*, 1971–9
Antony Easthope
National language, education, literature
Renée Balibar
The boundaries of hegemony
John Oakley, Roger Bromley and Sue Harper
Orientalism and its problems
Dennis Porter
Difference, discrimination and the discourse of colonialism
Homi K. Bhabha
The new art history
Margaret Iversen
Annus mirabilis: synchrony and diachrony
John Frow
Bakhtin, Marxism and post-structuralism
Graham Pechey
Capitalizing history: notes on *The Political Unconscious*
Samuel Weber

Confronting the Crisis: War, Politics and Culture in the Eighties

Proceedings of the 1983 Essex Conference

edited by

Francis Barker
Peter Hulme
Margaret Iversen
Diana Loxley

Right approaches: sources of the New Conservatism
Boyd Tonkin
Images of the sixteenth and seventeenth centuries
as a history of the present
Simon Barker
The politics of meaning
Catherine Belsey
On nuclear terms in the UK
Gordon Brotherston
The fall and rise of Labourism
Ian H. Birchall
The Falklands/Malvinas War – 1982: a perspective from the
Republic of Ireland
John Arden
Some notes on media coverage of the Falklands
Or: 'The Soviet Union could teach us a few lessons'
Anthony Barnett
The Falklands War: triumph of an ideology
Christopher Hampton
The government and information in time of war: the Falklands and
the media
David Morrison and Howard Tumber
Television news and the labour movement
Antony Easthope
The verbal arsenal of black women writers in America
Melissa Walker
Literature and society in crisis: the case of Israel
Nurith Gertz
Crisis, institutions and the unconscious
David Punter
'Why I wrote a book on the Yorkshire Ripper'
Nicole Ward Jouve

Europe and its Others
Volume 1

Proceedings of the 1984 Essex Conference

edited by

Francis Barker
Peter Hulme
Margaret Iversen
Diana Loxley

Representation, the despot and the harem: some questions around an academic Orientalist painting by Lecomte-du-Nouÿ (1885)
Olivier Richon
Orientalism reconsidered
Edward W. Said
Ideological voyages: concerning a Flaubertian dis-orient-ation
Richard Terdiman
Yellow peril in the promised land; the representation of the Oriental and the question of American identity
R. Valerie Lucas
Islamic imperialism and the question of some ideas of 'Europe'
Jacqueline Kaye
Early travels to Europe: some remarks on the magic of writing
Michael Harbsmeier
Signs taken for wonders: questions of ambivalence and authority under a tree outside Delhi, May 1817
Homi K. Bhabha
The production of an official discourse on Sati in early nineteenth-century Bengal
Lata Mani
The Rani of Sirmur
Gayatri Chakravorty Spivak
Making strange: race, science and ethnopsychiatric discourse
N. Chabani Manganyi
Translating Europe's others
Talal Asad and John Dixon
Australia 1984: a moment in the archaeology of multiculturalism
Sneja Gunew

**Europe and its Others
Volume 2**

Proceedings of the 1984 Essex Conference

edited by

*Francis Barker
Peter Hulme
Margaret Iversen
Diana Loxley*

Allegories of the atlas
José Rabasa
Polytropic man: tropes of sexuality and mobility in early
colonial discourse
Peter Hulme
National romances and populist rhetoric in Spanish America
Doris Sommer
Woman/Indian: 'The American' and his others
Helen Carr
Towards a grammatology of America: Lévi-Strauss, Derrida, and the
native New World text
Gordon Brotherston
Writing and speech after Derrida: application and criticism
John Peacock
Ireland and natural man in 1649
Norah Carlin
Prefigurative racism in Goethe's *Iphigenie Auf Tauris*
Helga Geyer-Ryan
A trope of desire: geographical implications of voice
Ewa Slawek and Tadeusz Slawek
Lukács and his others
Ian Fairley
The management of Scott's novels
Elaine Jordan
Imperialism and class: the French War in Algeria
Ian H. Birchall
A black public: practicalities of policing in British cities
Stephan Feuchtwang
Racist social fantasy and paranoia
Tim Rackett

Index